M000189590

THE LITURGY OF THE CHURCH

ȚHE LIȚURGY
of the Church
According to the Roman Rite

DOM VIRGIL MICHEL, OSB

Foreword by Dom Alcuin Reid

AROUCA
PRESS

Originally published by The Macmillan Company in 1937
Reprinted by Arouca Press 2022
Foreword © Alcuin Reid 2022

ISBN: 978-1-990685-33-0 (pbk)
ISBN: 978-1-990685-34-7 (hc)

Arouca Press
PO Box 55003
Bridgeport PO
Waterloo, ON N2J3G0
Canada
www.aroucapress.com
Send inquiries to info@aroucapress.com

Imprimi Potest
✠ ALCUINUS DEUTSCH, O. S. B.
Abbot of St. John's

Nihil obstat
ARTHUR J. SCANLAN, S. T. D.
Censor Librorum

Imprimatur
✠ PATRICK CARDINAL HAYES
Archbishop, New York

New York, April 26, 1937

CONTENTS

CONTENTS

FOREWORD

DOM Virgil Michel OSB (1890–1938) is a largely unknown figure of the early twentieth century liturgical movement and yet he is responsible for much of its momentum in the English-speaking world. From the 1920s onward through the organisation of liturgical days, his foundation of the Liturgical Press, the journal *Orate Fratres* (1926; now *Worship*)[1] and the widespread promotion of the liturgical apostolate and renewal of which it quickly became an important herald, Dom Virgil was one on the liturgical movement's most zealous pioneers.

Dom Virgil had himself imbibed the liturgical spirit during his studies in Europe following the first world war and quickly came to see its importance—nay, its absolute centrality—for Christian life. It was truly Providential that he, with the blessing of his Abbot and the support of his brethren, was able to dedicate all his energies, and more, to its propagation in the United States and beyond.

---

1 A study of the first years of *Orate Fratres* is instructive in respect of the nature of the twentieth century liturgical movement in general and of Dom Virgil Michel's contribution to it in particular. The first issue (November 1926) reads as a charter for the journal, if not the movement. For those with stronger stomachs a study of the later years of *Orate Fratres*, and then of *Worship*, clearly demonstrates its change in emphasis from facilitating liturgical participation in the Sacred Liturgy of the Church through formation in it, to changing the Church's liturgy in the hope of facilitating participation more easily.

Almost a century later the twentieth century liturgical movement has 'mixed reviews', as it were, depending on one's stance in respect of the waves—and then the tsunami—of liturgical reform which washed over the Roman rite from the middle of the twentieth century onward. But Dom Virgil's early death at the age of only 48 meant that he neither agitated for, rode in triumph on, or danced in the aftermath of these waves. His was a more serious and sober task: to place before every Catholic that which they have a full right to know and understand: the liturgy of the Church, the rightful heritage of all the faithful.[2]

That is not to say that he himself did not hope for some moderate liturgical reform, principally in the extension of the use of the vernacular and in the possibility of celebrating Holy Mass in the evening where this would assist modern populations to attend it.[3] But for Dom Virgil these reforms were a means to an end, not an end in themselves. The end of all the baptised participating fully, consciously and actively in the liturgy *of* the Church was what was paramount, not remodelling the liturgy in the image and likeness of modern man (however that creature is defined by whomsoever at any given time).

It is precisely here that we encounter the value of this book—then, and especially now—for it is not in any sense a polemic, nor is it riddled with a reformist agenda. Rather, it is a presentation of and an introduction to the Sacred Liturgy of the Roman rite of the Catholic Church as it has been received in Tradition, aimed at increasing the lifegiving participation in the liturgical rites that is so necessary for each of us if

2   See: Preface, p. xv.
3   See: Alcuin Reid, *The Organic Development of the Liturgy*, 2nd. edn. Ignatius Press, San Francisco, 2005, pp. 97–100.

we are indeed truly to be Christian. It is important to underline these two elements.

The first is that liturgy is received by us in Tradition as something sacred, to be reverenced and to be handed on intact. Certainly, history shows us that the Sacred Liturgy develops organically, proportionately, in response to particular influences, but the liturgy is never the positivistic or political play-thing of popes or other prelates: "Even the supreme authority in the Church may not change the liturgy arbitrarily, but only in the obedience of faith and with religious respect for the mystery of the liturgy."[4]

The second element is that truly to live the Christian life we must participate in the Sacred Liturgy. This may sound eccentric to generations whose concept of Christianity is the observance of (at least elements of) a certain moral code, but that is simply because we have forgotten the first commandment of both the Decalogue and of Our Lord Jesus Christ Himself. The love and worship of Almighty God is our first duty from which right belief and moral behaviour flows. If we do good but do not worship Almighty God, the good that we

4 *Catechism of the Catholic Church*, n. 1125. In the light of this reality, the exuberance of a newly created cardinal in asserting (in respect of the Sacred Liturgy) that "it's the church that makes the tradition" is astonishing in the extremely dangerous positivism it promotes as well as its—at best—naïve understanding of the nature of Tradition. As the *Catechism* teaches, authority is at the humble service of (liturgical) Tradition and is neither its author nor its editor. The cardinal's words form part of a response to a question about the scandal caused by the Holy See's recent ideological attempts to restrict the celebration of the *usus antiquior* of the Roman rite. This context makes the reply even more concerning: the exercise of power in order to achieve a political end is a long way from being a humble and faithful steward of the Tradition "in the obedience of faith and with religious respect for the mystery of the liturgy." See: Elise Ann Allen, "Vatican's liturgy czar says Church makes tradition, not 'people in lobbies'", *Crux*, 29 August 2022.

do lacks its proper foundation—it is not rooted in the love and adoration of Christ—and may simply become an expedient political or even an egotistical exercise. If, however, I participate fully in the worship of Christ as God in the sacred rites of His Church, that worship needs must overflow into the moral conversion of my life and the service of Christ in my neighbour.

This is a reality upon which Dom Virgil insisted again and again,[5] and it is an imperative which so many young people who encounter the unedited riches of the Church's liturgical Tradition experience today. Dom Virgil's *The Liturgy of the Church* is, then, a fundamental textbook for Christian life today, not because it teaches us an updated moral code, but because it introduces us to Christ living and working in the Church today through the *usus antiquior*—the older and fuller forms of the Sacred Liturgy of His Church.

This intrinsically pastoral nature of the *usus antiquior* is not widely understood beyond the communities and individuals who celebrate it and live from it. Indeed, its devotees are sometimes loudly decried as nostalgic, backward-looking, deniers of progress who pick and choose their spiritual practices *à la carte*. Such condemnations say more about those who pronounce them than they do about the reality to hand—which is that the liturgy of the Church known, loved and promoted by Dom Virgil as the basis of Christian life, serves as exactly that still regardless of (or possible even more so because of)

5 The memorial issue of *Orate Fratres* (vol. XIII n. 3; January 1939) is an eloquent testament to Dom Virgil's multi-faceted apostolate, all thoroughly grounded in the necessity of participation in the Church's liturgy. Several chapters in Paul B. Marx's *Virgil Michel and the Liturgical Movement*, Liturgical Press, Collegeville, MN, 1957 study this in more detail.

the reforms that the Church imposed on the Roman rite in the middle of the twentieth century and which, for some, have become an ideological end in themselves.

That the older liturgy lives and gives life in our times is, perhaps, an anomaly of liturgical history, but it is a fact—even a sign of the times. And that *The Liturgy of the Church* will assist those who encounter these rites to immerse themselves in them—in the reality of Christ Himself living and acting in and through the sacred rites of His Church—is something for which we must give thanks. Dom Virgil could never have imagined such a scenario, but we can be sure that he and his contemporaries would approve, for they knew that this or that particular liturgical reform was, ultimately, not essential. They knew only too well that what is truly essential is that all of Christ's faithful participate consciously in the Church's liturgical rites, of which there is and has always been a rich and legitimate plurality.

Thus, despite his relative obscurity, through *The Liturgy of the Church* Dom Virgil Michel has much to offer the Church of the twenty-first century, and beyond—as does a good deal of the literature of the early twentieth century liturgical movement. Arouca Press is, then, to be congratulated on allowing us to hear the voice of this "apostle of liturgical life"[6] once again.

DOM ALCUIN REID
Prior
Monastère Saint-Benoît, Brignoles, France

13 November 2022

---

6 See: William Busch, "An Apostle of Liturgical Life" in: *Orate Fratres* (vol. XIII n. 3; January 1939) pp. 102–106.

PREFACE

THE following chapters have arisen out of a series of lectures delivered at the Pius X School of Liturgical Music, New York City, in the summer of 1936. They are therefore popular in presentation and content, and are in no way the product of expert liturgical knowledge, of which I am quite innocent. They are written in the spirit of the liturgical revival which is now happily spreading into every aspect of our Catholic life. There is nothing in these pages except what every priest and seminarian should know and what every Catholic layman has a full right to know, since the liturgy of the Church is the rightful heritage of all the faithful.

In the capitalization I have followed the text of the Douay bible, which is also followed in the best English versions of liturgical texts. Hence capitals are not used for pronouns referring to the Deity.

It is impossible to make a complete acknowledgment of all the persons and sources from which I have received inspiration. The list of books appended gives only such as have been quoted in the text. Besides the general literature of the liturgical movement and personal contacts with many of its apostles in various countries, I owe much to my own confreres at St. John's Abbey and to the associate editors of *Orate Fratres*. To these in particular I am happy to express my appreciation for the considerable encouragement and inspiration I have received from them at all times.

I wish to express my sincere thanks to those authors and publishers who have for years extended to me and my confreres a generous permission to quote at any time from their liturgical works, likewise to the American and British publishing houses who have so willingly granted me the particular permissions requested for the more extensive quotations I have made from their books.

I am happy to express my special gratitude to my confrere, Dom Aidan Germain, O.S.B., Ph.D., Assistant Professor of History in the Graduate School of Fordham University, who kindly consented to read the manuscript of the present book, and whose suggestions have helped greatly to improve it.

VIRGIL MICHEL, O.S.B.

THE LITURGY OF THE CHURCH

CHAPTER I

WHAT IS THE LITURGY?

I. Liturgy as Worship

The word *liturgy* according to its etymology means a
public work or service. The original Greek word comes
from *leitos*, public or belonging to the people, and from
the root of the word *ergon*, work. It was used to designate
any work or service done especially by a public-minded
citizen for the benefit of the people or the public. Even
in the Old Testament it meant the temple service which
was conducted by the official priests in the name of the
people, and from there it was taken into the New Testament to designate the Christian development or counterpart of this service.

Taking this meaning in its most general scope, one might
define liturgy today as "the totality of all the acts of divine
service of a religious fellowship." [1] The Christian liturgy,
understood in this sense, took over some elements from
the Old Testament service, added elements peculiar to
the Christian revelation, and then gradually developed
the humble beginnings of the early days into a thing of
great complexity as well as beauty. The Protestant breakoff from the progressive Christian tradition of many centuries was in great part also a rejection of much of the

[1] *Der Grosse Herder.*

1

Christian liturgy. In our own day there are few Protestant denominations with religious church services that one could rightly designate as liturgical. The Protestant rejection of a mediating priesthood of human beings logically meant the rejection of the exercise of such mediatorship by means of liturgical action. An additional, extrinsic reason why the term *liturgy* has not been applied to the Protestant services to any extent may be the fact that it came into more general use only since the sixteeenth century. Before that the customary word was *cultus* or worship. On the other hand the Greek rite, which has not seen the same development in the course of time as the Roman, used the word to designate the sacrifice of the altar or the Eucharist. The latter is simply "The Liturgy."

Here we are concerned with the general Christian tradition as maintained in the Catholic Church under the guidance of Peter, and specifically as developed in the Roman rite of the Church. A general definition of this Catholic liturgy is given as follows by Dom Festugière: "The liturgy is the exterior worship which the Church renders to God" or more briefly "the exterior worship of the Church." Here the genus or general class to which the liturgy belongs is "exterior worship" and the specific difference which distinguishes the liturgy from exterior worship in general is given by the added phrase "of the Church" (*Qu 'est-ce que la liturgie?*, p. 28).[2]

[2] One may well be inclined at first blush to object to the definition given by Dom Festugière. The word *exterior* is referred in the dictionary to *external* and one of the meanings of the latter is given as "that which makes a show rather than that which is intrinsic." Taken in that sense, the definition would express exactly what many non-Catholics accuse the Church's liturgy of being, and what—we may as well be frank—the Church's liturgy actually is for many Catholics, at least in practice if not in theory. However, taken in that sense, there is also inner contradiction in their very juxtaposition of the two words in one and the same phrase, "exterior worship."

True worship, or worship of God, is an exercise of the virtue of religion. This virtue consists in an acknowledgement of the supreme excellence of God as our Creator and Father and of our total dependence on him in every respect. In our lives, then, the virtue of religion should direct our actions so that they give full expression to this relation of ourselves to God. For this reason have we been endowed with understanding and will, that we may freely turn to God, direct our actions in accordance with his divine will, and gladly acknowledge his infinite goodness. As by God's creative act all things came from him, so by practicing the virtue of religion men return freely to more intimate union with him. All the actions of life by which men thus conform themselves to the will of God, recognize his supremacy, and pay him due honor come under the virtue of religion and constitute acts of divine worship. Man therefore worships God more strictly by directing thoughts and words of honor and homage to him, and in a wider sense also by his entire life in thought, word, or deed. Worship by means of directing thoughts or words of homage to God, *i.e.*, of praise, adoration, thanksgiving, petition, is the worship of prayer.

Worship is thus always a rendering of due homage to God by intelligent beings. There can be no worship without intelligence, without the quality of mind or of consciousness. Any actions of man that are devoid of the quality of mind are in so far merely actions of his body, and not actions of man as such, *i.e.*, of man as a rational animal. Yet it is only as a rational animal that man can perform acts of homage to God or acts of worship. From this it is evident in what way the definition of liturgy as exterior worship must be understood and alone can have meaning, and in what way the phrase could contain a contradiction.

Worship is sometimes divided into external and internal worship. But this division is not one that separates into two exclusive kinds of worship in the sense that one kind is external and not internal, and the other internal and not external. Such mutual exclusiveness should follow according to the ordinary custom of logical divisions. It is not necessary to labor the point that all worship, since it is possible only through our abilities of expression, intellect and will, must necessarily always be mental or interior. Without that interior quality, worship ceases to be worship and becomes mere external formality if not mockery. All worship is therefore interior. However, this interior worship may in turn be expressed in external words and signs or it may remain purely mental. In the former case it is properly termed exterior worship. It is then not the external make-believe of worship, but the exteriorizing of real interior worship.

Such a type of worship is natural to man since he is constituted of both soul and body. And insofar as the composition of soul and body in man is not merely a sort of accidental putting together of the two according to Christian tradition, but is an essential union, it becomes essential to man that he exercise the virtue of religion also by means of exterior worship. Without the latter he is not doing his full religious duty to his Father in heaven.

There is a twofold object attained in all true worship. First of all it is directed to God and gives him due homage and honor. But God in turn extends his divine love more fully to the creature that turns to him in prayer, so that all true worship brings perfection to man and the help of God's grace for living true to the sentiments expressed in prayer. Furthermore, true prayer will with the help of this grace of God also produce fruits in daily life. The prayer of a person who makes no efforts to honor God also in the daily actions of his life can hardly be called sincere. It is deserving of the severe censure passed by Christ on the Pharisees: "Hypocrites, well hath Isaias prophesied of you, saying: This people honoreth me with their lips; but their heart is far from me."[3] True worship or prayer, then, not only honors God but also sanctifies man.

II. Worship of the Church

The liturgy is the exterior worship of the Church, that is, of the Church as such. It is therefore the official worship of the Church, initiated and prescribed and enacted by her in her capacity as the Church of Christ. Only worship that conforms to these conditions is truly liturgical.

Worship may be individual and private or social and public. The former is initiated by single persons according to their own inspiration; the latter is performed by groups in some co-operative manner and is therefore also public. The official worship of the Church here on earth is always both exterior and social because the Church is a visible society or fellowship of souls. Just as man is by nature both soul and body, so also is he social by nature. Since his worship of God must be an expression of his whole self, the virtue of religion also obliges man to social worship, without which he cannot pay full homage to God as he should. This social worship is rendered easily possible

[3] Matt. 15:7–8.

by him through the Church's liturgy, which is the official
social exercise of the virtue of religion by the Church in
the name of her children, and in which all her children
can and should join.

As the Church is one, holy, catholic, and apostolic, so
is also her official worship, which is her essential life. The
liturgy of the Church is one, since it centers everywhere
in one and the same sacrifice of the altar and the seven
sacraments, despite the great variety of languages and
rites in which these essential actions of worship are enacted. The liturgy is holy in its very nature as worship
that renders homage to God and sanctifies man; and it is
catholic since it is essentially the same everywhere.
Finally, it is apostolic, since it comes down to us through
the ages from Christ himself and his apostles. There
have been many developments in it in the course of time,
but all these are built up around the central core of the
Eucharist and the sacraments as these were given to the
Church by her divine Founder.

In the Old Testament the official worship was directed
and prescribed in detail by God himself. In the New
Testament the nucleus of the official worship, the sacrifice
and the matter and form of the sacraments, has come from
Christ, but the further developments, the rites and ceremonies in which these are enacted, have been amplifica-
tions under the direction of the Church acting with the
powers received from her divine Founder. Besides the
Mass and the sacraments there are the many sacramentals,
the divine office and numerous rites of processions and
blessings. All of these will receive ample treatment later
on. Among the prayers recited publicly in our churches
there are also many devotions and customs that are not

really part of the liturgy, as, *e.g.*, the *tre ore* of Good Friday, although they take place with the permission of the proper ecclesiastical authorities.

In the earlier days there was much liberty left to bishops and priests in the detailed development of the liturgical services. But as the Church grew in numbers and spread over distant places, this liberty ran the danger of destroying all unity and uniformity of worship in the one Church. Hence, after centuries of tradition, the liturgical texts, forms, rites, seasons and the like, were definitely fixed by laws and regulations. They are no longer subject to arbitrary change by individuals. Yet new customs still arise even now that in the long run affect the liturgical worship itself. After all, the latter is something living, and not the least of the hopes among many modern liturgical apostles is for various changes in the present liturgical forms or customs. As real liturgical changes, of course, they must be official, that is, sanctioned and set down by the Church herself.

To be the official worship of the Church the liturgy must be enacted by legitimately appointed ministers and must be performed in the manner prescribed by her. Preconditions for personal participation in the liturgical worship are, on the one hand, membership in Christ and his Church through the sacrament of Baptism, without which no one can have any share, active or passive, in the sacramental or liturgical life of the Church. On the other hand, there is needed the sacrament of Holy Orders, through which certain members are officially empowered to enact the liturgy in the name of the Church and as the official representatives of the people. As to the manner prescribed by the Church, the circumstances of place and time, the kind of action, words, etc.,—these have varied greatly in the course of centuries but are laid down definitely for us in the official liturgical books of the Church. After saying a word on the elements that enter into the liturgical worship, we shall describe in brief these liturgical books.

III. Liturgical Elements

Since the liturgy is exterior worship, or exteriorized interior worship, it should follow that it makes full use of the external means of expressing the inner sentiments of man, and that there is no element of the externals of the liturgical worship that is without meaning or without its definite relation to the entire action. All the perceptible elements of expressing one's sentiments come into play in the liturgy. In enumerating these briefly, I shall follow the excellent treatment in Vacant, *Dictionnaire de Théologie Catholique*, article "Liturgy," in the section entitled: "Liturgical attitudes and gestures, signs, formulas, actions and rites."

(1) *Liturgical Attitudes and Gestures.* The expressiveness of postures in worship hardly needs more than a mere mention. In religious worship at all times special attitudes were employed as significant of the inner act of homage. Kneeling and prostrations are attitudes of petition and humility. Not even the sitting posture is liturgically neutral, much less that of standing. The latter is in fact the one attitude that receives mention in the very text of the Mass (*"circumstantes"*—those standing about the altar).

There are liturgical gestures that are of earliest Christian origin, such as the sign of the cross, which recurs endlessly in all parts of the liturgy, while others are of relatively recent origin, like the elevation of the consecrated Host and Chalice. In the sacramental rites anointings occur frequently, and blessings with the sign of the cross abound, as also the sprinkling with holy water. These are but the most common of the liturgical gestures.

(2) *Sensible Signs or Elements.* In imitation of Christ himself and in accordance with his institution of the sacraments, the liturgy makes frequent use of material things for the better expression of the Church's sentiments of honor and homage to God and sanctification of man. We need but mention here such things as bread, wine, oil, ashes, water, fire, salt, and the like. These are used not merely in a general and undifferentiated way as signs of inner homage to God or of God's grace to man; but the different elements have a specific meaning in accordance with their natural functioning, as is abundantly shown in the liturgical prayer-texts that accompany their use.

(3) *Liturgical Forms or Formulas.* Without these prayer-texts or formulas the gestures and actions would lose much of their significance for us. The most natural mode of human expression is by word of mouth, and the other external means are generally used only to accompany and to lend emphasis and color to the verbal expression. The liturgical formulas range over the entire field of human sentiments of worship. They embrace chiefly the following:

(*a*) Acclamations. These are emphatic exclamations of joy, acclaim, consent, etc. Among the most common are the Hebrew terms, *Alleluia, Hosanna, Amen,* and the Latin *Deo Gratias.*

(*b*) Litanies. Prayers in litany form held a favorite place among the early Christians. In general, long series of intentions were announced and after each one a petition was repeated. They were especially used in connection with liturgical processions. Only a few of the older litanies are now in use, the most common being the Litany of All Saints. One of the most ancient forms is the Major Litany of the Good Friday service. The *Kyrie eleison* of the Mass is a relic of a litany of former times.

(*c*) Collect Prayers. This is a most frequent form of collective prayer, notably in the Mass (collect, secret, postcommunion), in which the officiant prays in a special way in the name of all the people. Hence the form is preceded by the exhortation of the people, *"Oremus— Let Us Pray,"* and is followed by their "Amen—So be it." The collect prayers of the various Mass texts of the entire year make up a most rich treasury of the best religious sentiments of the Christian mind and tradition.

(*d*) Benedictions. These are prayers in which persons, objects or places are dedicated to God, purified for the greater sanctification of man. There is a great number of these in the liturgy, some occurring in the Mass and in the rites of the sacraments, but the majority in the ritual of sacramental blessings. The latter continue to grow in number and adapt themselves to the changing developments of material progress.

(*e*) The Eucharistic Prayer. This is the prayer text of the Mass containing the words of consecration. It is the most ancient of all Christian liturgical prayers, taking its very form in part from the action and words of Christ himself at the Last Supper. It was quite definite in form by the third century, much earlier than other liturgical formulas, although it has had minor developments since, especially in the Roman rite. It is the most august and venerable prayer of the liturgy. It begins with the dialog of the preface and enacts the essential offering of the sacrifice of Christ in the holy Eucharist.

Eucharistic formularies of the preface type occur also in other liturgical rites, *e.g.*, the conferring of Major Orders, blessing of the baptismal font, of the palms on Palm Sunday, etc. A most notable one outside of the Mass is the *Exultet* of Holy Saturday.

(*f*) Exorcisms. Prayers for the expulsion of the devil or of the powers of evil are very ancient. In fact they go back to the example of Christ himself. Besides the specific rite for the expulsion of the devil from possessed persons, which can be employed only with express permission of the bishop for each occasion, there are exorcisms in some of the sacramental rites, as for instance in baptism, in the blessing of salt for holy water or in milder form in the blessing of the ashes and palms.

(*g*) Symbol or Creed. Various forms of the symbol, or the official summary and profession of faith, go back to the earliest times. The chief liturgical forms are the Apostles' Creed, used, *e.g.*, for the profession of faith in baptism, the Nicene Creed of the Mass, and the Athanasian Creed which is recited on certain Sundays, but especially on Trinity Sunday because of its notable expression of the doctrine of the three persons in God.

(*h*) Doxologies. These are short formulas of praise of God in the Blessed Trinity. The most common form in the liturgy is the Glory be to the Father, etc. A frequent form in varying phraseology is that of the ending of liturgical hymns. The most notable large form is the *Gloria in excelsis,* while the most notable short form is the minor doxology at the end of the Canon of the Mass.

(*i*) Admonitions. This is a liturgical form less rich in religious sentiments and less important because of its occasional character. It occurs chiefly in the general exhortations given to the candidates for the minor and major orders. In the sacramental rites it occurs in the votive Mass for a wedding, and in baptism immediately after the first questions. Semi-liturgical instances occur in the vernacular, according to rubrical advice, before the sacrament of marriage takes place and after sacramental confession before the penance and absolution.

(*j*) Chants and Psalmody. By these terms are meant certain formulas, such as antiphons, responsories, versicles, and the like, which are specially suited for rendition in chanted form, although the chant is by no means confined officially to them. They are usually exhortations to a special elevation of mind to God, expressions of deep-felt prayer-sentiments or meditative aspirations. In the Mass these occur especially in the gradual and in the introit, offertory, and communion verses.

(*k*) Readings. In the Mass the readings are of the inspired word of God, in gospel and epistle. In the divine office, the readings include also homilies of the Fathers and Doctors of the Church, and lives of saints. The purpose of all these is instructional. In the mind of the liturgy religious sentiments must always be grounded firmly in truths of faith and in their maximum understanding by man.

(*l*) Hymns and Sequences. A final element in the liturgical texts are the hymns and sequences, the former chiefly in the divine office and the latter in the Masses.

After the ninth century both hymns and sequences were introduced in great numbers into different services. Today there are five sequences in universal use and about one hundred and fifty hymns. The hymns and sequences differ greatly in theological content and in literary quality. Thus the sequences and hymns of St. Thomas for the feast of Corpus Christi are models of theological expression; while the sequence of Easter is dramatic, and has given inspiration to many a mystery play of old.

In mentioning the various forms in which the liturgical text is expressed, the chant has received no special treatment. But the chant is not so much a separate element as a mode of more complete or intensified expression of the liturgical worship. If one examines more closely the various elements just enumerated one will be struck by the degree to which the chant actually has a part in many of them as well as by the universally social character of the liturgy as evinced in its language and mode of expression.

(4) *Rites or Ceremonies.* The term rite is sometimes used to designate the totality of prayers and ceremonies of the liturgy according to some definite custom and language. Thus we speak of the Roman rite, the Eastern rite, the Byzantine rite, and so forth. Often the word *liturgy* is used in the same way, *e.g.,* Roman or Byzantine liturgy. But the term *rite* is also used in a narrower sense to mean any complete liturgical ceremony having a particular purpose within the larger scope of the liturgy. Thus we speak of the rite of baptism, of the blessing of a house, etc. The chief rites, in this sense, are those of the administration of the sacraments, and of the blessings of the sacramentals. Any such rite is usually made up of

several elements or types of formula enumerated in the preceding section.

All the official rites of the Church are described in detail as to text and action in the various liturgical books of the Church. The prescriptions for action, *e.g.*, are called rubrics (from the red color in which they are printed), and it is a telling confirmation of our general loss of liturgical sense that many persons think the liturgy is nothing but these rubrical prescriptions.

IV. LITURGICAL BOOKS

The official liturgical books of the Church, in which alone her liturgy is committed to writing, are the following:

(1) *The Missal.* Fortunately the liturgical movement is bringing large numbers of the faithful back to what was for most of them the forgotten book of the centuries. It contains the prayers common to all Masses as well as the prayers that are proper to the different Masses of the seasonal feasts or of the saints as well as optional or votive Masses for special occasions or devotional purposes.

(2) *The Breviary.* This contains all the prayers of the divine office for the different seasons and feasts of the year; that is, for the various hours of the day, the different days of the week, and the seasons of the year. At one time the breviary prayers or excerpts from them were the only generally accepted forms of prayer for the faithful apart from the Mass itself. The breviary, too, has suffered a marked neglect among Catholics; and only in our day are we witnessing the first steps towards its rehabilitation as a book of daily prayer for the layfolk.

(3) *The Pontifical.* This book describes the liturgical functions reserved to bishops. Chief among them are the administration of confirmation, the conferring of tonsure and the different holy orders; consecrations of churches, altars, chalices; excommunications and absolutions therefrom, and degradation from orders; solemn reception of a bishop, and the like.

(4) *The Ritual.* In this book are contained all the ordinary services performed by priests, and not contained in the missal and the breviary. It is the book to be used for all the ordinary sacramental ministrations and for the general blessings for all kinds of occasions and conditions.

(5) *The Ceremonial of Bishops.* This book contains some matters for others than bishops, contrary to its title, but in the main it gives general directions, ceremonial and otherwise, for special episcopal functions and activities, some of which are liturgical while others are not (*e.g.,* formal visit of a bishop to the civil ruler of a province).

(6) *The Martyrology.* This book gives in brief, for each day of the year, the names and main biographical facts of all the saints that are honored in different parts of the Catholic world.

Besides the above books there is a *Memorial of Rites,* the "small ritual." It contains some of the liturgical rites as these may be performed in a simpler manner in small places without the aid of ministers (deacon and subdeacon).

V. LITURGY AND THEOLOGY

The liturgical books of the Church could by no stretch of the imagination be termed scientific treatises on the Christian truths. Yet they may rightly be called "handbooks of the dogma and moral" for the faithful at large. They contain the fundamental truths of Christ's revelation and redemption as the basis of their worship of God. And the conscientious and intelligent use of them by the faithful will serve also for their ever better instruction in the truths of the Christian faith. No one has said this more emphatically than Pius XI. Had some person of little prominence made the pope's statement, a storm of protest might have arisen from men who feel secure in their own righteousness and mistake their own views for those of the universal Church. In the encyclical *Quas primas* "on instituting the feast of Christ the King," Pius XI says:

"The annual celebrations of the sacred mysteries are far more efficacious for the instructing the people in matters of faith and thereby leading them to the inner joys of life than any, even the most weighty, pronouncements of the teaching Church. For the latter reach mainly the few more erudite men, while the former attain and teach all the faithful; the latter speak, so to say, once, the former daily and continuously; the latter have a salutary effect chiefly on the mind, the former on both mind and soul, *i.e.*, on the entire man. Indeed, since man is constituted of soul and body, he must be so moved and inspired by the exterior solemnities of the feast days that he learns the divine teachings more abundantly through the variety and the beauty of the sacred rites, and that, having absorbed them into his flesh and blood, he may have them serve unto progress in the spiritual life."

This is eminently true because the liturgy is essentially the Christian faith prayed; it is dogma set to prayer in the official worship of the Church of Christ under the unerring guidance of the Holy Ghost, the Spirit of Truth. It is not surprising, then, that changes in the formulas of the liturgy were brought about by the need of stressing truths that had been questioned or that had received more definite formulation in the course of time. "As soon as dogma became more precise in doctrinal teaching," writes Dom Lambert Beauduin, "the liturgical formula took on the same character. Arianism had used the formula of prayer address to the Father, *per Christum Dominum nostrum:* through Christ our Lord, as a pretext for denying the divinity of Christ. Immediately a second part of the conclusion came into liturgical use, *qui tecum vivit et regnat:* who liveth and reigneth with thee. The Pelagian errors led to a continuous appeal to divine assistance; and the use of the versicle, *Deus in adjutorium:* O Lord, come unto my assistance, was multiplied." [4]

What better historical evidence can there be for the beliefs of earlier Christians than the very liturgical prayers in which they gave living expression to these beliefs? The liturgy is one of the chief theological sources, as they are called, one of the chief sources for evidence of the theological truths consciously held by traditional Christianity. That this had been denied in our day, or at least lost sight of to some extent, will surprise none who is aware of the great loss of liturgical sense that Catholics as a whole have been suffering from. Regarding the liturgy as a theological source, the *Dictionnaire de Théologie Catholique* (article "Liturgie") has the following to say:

"In last analysis the theological sources can be reduced to Scripture and tradition. The liturgy is one of the ways

[4] Beauduin, *Liturgy the Life of the Church,* p. 105

in which this tradition expresses itself, we would say the principal way. Some have at times considered Bossuet's opinion as exaggerated: 'The principal instrument of the tradition of the Church is contained in her prayers. . . .' But this phrase seems rigorously exact to us. The liturgy must come immediately after the Scriptures, and before the Fathers, for its testimony, whether considered from the standpoint of antiquity, of universality or of dignity, surpasses all the others."

It is because of this eminent Christian character of the liturgy that Pius X could make the statement that has become the watchword of the liturgical movement: "Our most ardent desire being that the true Christian spirit flourish again in every way and maintain itself among the faithful, it is necessary to provide above all for the sanctity of the temple of God, where the faithful unite precisely for the purpose of there finding this spirit at its primary and indispensable source, which is the active participation in the public and solemn prayer of the Church." [5]

That we are now far from this norm of Christian spriitual life, the very words of the pope indicate. This "true Christian spirit" has not been alive among us, but must be made "to flourish again." What a difference it would make in the lives of Christians, in the spiritual influence of Catholics and of the Church if they could again open their hearts fully to the lessons taught by the liturgical celebrations of the sacred feasts according to the purpose for which these were instituted! The *Catechism of Pius X* says in this regard: "If the faithful were well instructed in this purpose desired by the Church in instituting them,

[5] *Motu proprio*, November 22, 1903

and celebrated the feasts with this spirit, there would be a notable renewal and increase of faith, of piety, and in consequence the interior life of the Christians would become much stronger and better." [6]

The realization of this purpose is the chief aim of the liturgical revival of our day. It is in the spirit of this revival that the present book was written. Hence much of the following exposition will be in direct reference to the liturgical texts themselves.

But before entering upon that part of our task it will be necessary to go deeper into an understanding of the true nature of the liturgy of the Church. So far we have described it almost exclusively from the human standpoint, so to say. The liturgy as the life of the Church must have also a divine element even as the Church herself has. It is from this angle that the following definition of the liturgy was written: "Catholic liturgy in its proper sense is the divine service or worship which the Church celebrates as the mystical body of Christ in union with the head Christ and in his name and at his behest, and that, as a continuing representation and making present of the mystery of the redemption." [7]

Our next efforts will be concerned with this divine element in the liturgy according to the teachings of our faith as handed down from Christ and the apostles.

[6] Quoted in Caronti, *The Spirit of the Liturgy*, p. 14
[7] *Der Grosse Herder*, art. "Liturgie"

CHAPTER II

DIVINE CHARACTER OF THE LITURGY

I. MISSION OF THE CHURCH

IT has already been noted in the previous chapter that
not a few persons are wont to consider the liturgy merely
in terms of the externals connected with the performance
of the Church's official acts of worship. In this sense, the
liturgy would be merely an external garb that achieves
all its aim, all its beauty and truth of its own accord, regardless of what the garment conceals within, or rather
without any thought given to whether there is any more
substantial kernel within the shell or not. It is not at all
surprising that many non-Catholics should hold this view,
since they have been reared in the idea that the Church
is nothing but a human society which is held together by
rigidly formal regulations and requirements. But that
Catholics should think of the liturgy, which has rightly
been called the very life of the Church, as something
merely formalistic and external, however beautiful, is
almost too sad for words.

Being the life of the Church, the liturgy must have a
soul, an inner heart and mind, it must be instinct with
spirit, even as the Church herself. In previous pages we
accepted the definition by Dom Festugiére of the liturgy
as the exterior worship which the Church renders to God,

and we called attention to the necessary interior character of all worship. What this character is in reality depends entirely on what the Church herself is. And the question of the inner nature of the liturgy leads back to that of the true nature of the Church. Since the liturgy is inseparably connected with the Church, we can have no true conception of it without an adequate notion of what the Church actually is. It is in turn impossible to understand properly what the Church is without immediate reference to Christ, her divine Founder. If the liturgy is of the Church, the Church herself is of Christ. Our quest for a proper understanding of the liturgy, therefore, leads us back to a brief investigation of the true nature of the Church and of Christ. The Church was founded by Christ for the express purpose of continuing his divine mission among men, for completing his work throughout time. It is through the Church that Christ is to grow to full maturity. St. Paul tells us that God subjected all things to Christ, and made "him head over all the Church, which is his body, and the fulness of him who is filled all in all." [1] If the Church is the fulfillment of Christ, as the apostle tells us, then we can have no right conception of the Church apart from Christ and apart from a right conception of the person and the mission of Christ.

The two, Christ and the Church, are inseparable. Hence, "the Church cannot be considered apart from her union with him, for she receives from him all that she is and all her substance." [2] The Church is thus essentially something more than a human society useful to the souls of men in some ways, or adapted to some passing moments of human history, just as Christ was more than a man

---

[1] Eph. 1:22–23   [2] Grea, *L'Eglise*, I, p. 56

ministering to men in a human way, and is "Jesus Christ, yesterday, and today; and the same for ever." [3]

The Church embodies an inner mystery that is of Christ himself. "The Church is Christ himself. The Church is the plenitude, the accomplishment of Christ, his body and his real and mystical development—is Christ in his totality and plenitude. Thus among the works of God the Church occupies the very place of Christ; the Church and Christ—they are the same work of God." [4] It is one and the same thing to say that God, in Jesus Christ, the second person of the divine Trinity, issued from his eternity into time in order to fulfill the mission of Christ, and to say that this was done in order to establish his Church, for it is through the Church and the Church alone that he fulfills his mission. It is the mission therefore of the Church both to continue and to consummate the mission of Christ, to lead it to its plenitude of perfection.

What then is the mission of Christ? As Christ told us, his mission was to do the work of his Father. But the work of God can be no other than that of procuring his own greater glory and of communicating his own goodness. This was the purpose of all creation, that God might unite himself with his creatures in a union of love, that he might impart his own goodness and perfection to them and that they might add external glory to the perfection of God's goodness. This was also the mission of the incarnation; this, in fact, is the sole mission in harmony with and worthy of the supreme dignity of God.

Christ's work on earth was a work done for the Father in heaven, out of love and obedience to him, in fulfillment of his divine will. Throughout his life here on earth

[3] Heb. 13:8   [4] Grea, *op. cit.*, p. 6

Christ referred all things to the Father, love and obedience towards whom were the mainspring of his adoration, his expiation, his intercession. It was to this end that Christ offered his whole self, his human nature united to the divine nature, to the Father as an acceptable oblation in man's stead—in order to unite all men again to their divine Father in heaven, in order to heal the rupture between God and creation that man as the king of creation had wrought by his primal disobedience in the garden of Eden. "God so loved the world as to give his only begotten Son; that whosoever believeth in him may not perish, but may have life everlasting." [5]

This mission of Christ was to endure as long as men lived on earth; and the continuation of this mission was the sole purpose of instituting the Church. The mission and the end of the latter can therefore be none other than that of Christ her Founder. "We speak of the Church, with all due proportion, in the same terms as of her divine Founder. Her immediate and first end is God as the sovereign good and union with this sovereign good, and consequently the good of men and their supernatural happiness in eternity. But to this end is necessarily joined another, namely, the greater glory of God, the extension of his kingdom and the sanctification of humanity." [6] Hence we can speak of Christ and of the Church in the same terms: "From the viewpoint of God, the ends of the incarnation and of the Church are first of all that marvellous effusion of divine goodness which we call the salvation of the human race and the restoration of friendship between man and his Creator, then the resplendent mani-

[5] John 3: 16
[6] Festugière, *Qu'est-ce que la liturgie?* pp. 39–40

festation of the divine attributes and the perfect glorification of the holy Trinity." [7]

II. The Powers of Christ

How was the Church to be made capable of fulfilling the mission of Christ with which she had been entrusted? There is only one possible answer: "Through Christ our Lord." For this purpose Christ vested her with his powers of teaching and sanctifying men, his power of offering the one sacrifice acceptable to God, and of governing the souls of men in all matters pertaining to their sanctification, in a word, with his divine priesthood, with the threefold powers of teacher, sanctifier and ruler, or prophet, priest and king. As Christ was vested with these powers and wrought his mission by exercising them on earth, so is the Church in fulfillment of this same mission to exercise them as long as she endures on earth, and to exercise them ever in the name of Christ. For as it is from him that she has these powers, so it is only through him that she exercises them, and only for him, that is, as his trustee.

To the apostles and their successors unto the end of time Christ gave the commission to teach what he had told them. "Teach ye all nations . . . whatsoever I have commanded you: and behold I am with you all days even to the consummation of the world." [8] The teaching office of the Church is therefore Christ's own; and it has the full authority of the divine power of Christ. Through Christ it has come from the divine Father. "The words which thou gavest me, I have given to them," Christ tells

[7] Festugière, *op. cit.*, p. 38   [8] Matt. 28:18-20

his heavenly Father (John 17:8); and he took it upon himself to pray for all those who should believe in him through the words of his apostles, so that the whole world may believe that Christ was sent of the Father.[9] It is therefore Christ himself who taught by the mouth of his apostles, and who today teaches by the mouth of those in the Church whose power of teaching comes down from these same apostles.

But Christ's teaching office has a further purpose; it was preparatory to his office as sanctifier. "Containing in himself," as Dom Grea so well says, "all the treasures of the divinity which he holds from his Father, he bestows on all those who have received the first gift of his word and who believe in him, the gift of being made children of God,[10] and participators in the divine nature.[11] Thus the work of sanctification follows that of teaching the truth; and the Church, which first of all believes in him, that is, which receives his word, in return for her faith enters into this divine communication of the new life, which is the eternal life, and of the new being, which is a mysterious participation in the divine being."[12]

Again: "Jesus Christ, who appeared on earth as teacher, in continuation of his mystery also appeared there as sanctifier. And as he confided to the Church the treasury of his teachings, he also confides to her the treasury of his sanctifying power in the sacraments which he institutes in her and which are the signs and the channels by which his unique sacrifice is communicated and his power is unfolded among men."[13] From Christ the Church received whatever saving power she has of offering the all-redeem-

[9] *Ibid.*, 17:20–21
[10] John 1:12
[11] 2 Peter 1:4
[12] *Op. cit.*, p. 83
[13] *Op. cit.*, pp. 83–84

ing sacrifice of Christ and of administering the life-giving sacraments to the faithful. Her power of offering and ministering, her power of sanctifying, is the inherited power of Christ himself, whereby she continues down the ages the beneficent sanctifying mission which Christ commenced by his descent upon the earth. It is in the Church, and in the Church alone, that the words of St. Paul, used in the epistle of the Mass for a Pontiff Confessor are true: "But Jesus, for that he continueth for ever, hath an everlasting priesthood: Whereby he is able to save for ever them that come to God by him."

By means of the powers of teaching and sanctifying, Christ and the Church render souls, that is, living human beings, acceptable to God, unite to God the children of his adoption. Here on earth, then, the children of God are under the care of the Church as the Bride of Christ and are also her children, over whom she wields authority in the name of Christ and for the purposes of Christ, *i.e.*, for increasing sanctification unto the glory of the Father. Thence comes the governing power of the Church, legislative and judiciary and executive, over the children of God, which is none other than the power of governing that Christ possesses over the children of his kingdom. "He that heareth you, heareth me; and he that despiseth you, despiseth me; and he that despiseth me, despiseth him that sent me," [14] he had told the apostles very definitely. And the liturgy continues to pray for the flock of the faithful, "that it may be governed by those same rulers whom thou didst set over it as shepherds and as thy vicars" (preface for feasts of the apostles).

The threefold powers of Christ the Redeemer were

[14] Luke 10:16

transmitted by him to his apostles, and by them in turn to their successors, *i.e.*, to the perpetual hierarchy of the Church of Christ. Hence the latter in all her official functions acts not in her own name but in the name of Christ, acts not with her own power but with the power of Christ. It is Christ himself that is living and acting in her, and contact with her in official functions is contact with Christ himself, with God.

In the teaching of the Church, then, we have the teaching of Christ, the very truths of God; and in the action of her priesthood we have the action of Christ, the very divine life of God. Thus "Jesus Christ, Sun of the priesthood, extends his rays over all the degrees of the hierarchy" of the Church. The bishops have in their consecration received the powers by direct descent from the apostles, and the priests have them by ordination and delegation from the bishops. In all of them, in their official actions, it is the living Christ himself who is continuing to perform the redeeming mission he took upon himself in the fulness of time at his holy incarnation. "What a sublime mystery this is!" exclaims Dom Grea. "The Son is in the Father as in his source; the Father is in the Son as in his consubstantial splendor. The Church likewise is in Christ as in her source, and Christ is in the Church as in his plenitude." [15]

Christ was ever most faithful in the exercise of his eternal priesthood, Abbot Caronti reminds us. He ordered his entire life in such a way that it was at all times a continuous glorification of the Father in heaven and likewise a continuous elevation of men towards their God and Creator—and this from the first act of circumcision and

[15] *Op. cit.*, p. 65

offering in the temple to the final oblation on Calvary.
And the same work is continued by the Church, adds the
Abbot: "The Church has the same scope and function as
the Word; namely, that of offering to God the acceptable
and pleasing sacrifice of re-establishing harmony between
the creature and the Creator. . . . Issuing forth from
the bloody nuptials of Calvary, the Church with her doctrine, her hierarchy, her sacraments, her preaching, her
ministry, her prayers, her tears and blood, has no other
end than to give the desired proportions to the sacred
humanity of Jesus Christ, to build up, to expand Jesus
in the souls of men, to build up and expand the souls in
Jesus, by continuing on earth the holy temple where the
Divinity receives a legitimate and pleasing worship, where
the voice of praise and thanksgiving is heard, where the
hymn of the glory of God is sung to the unity and trinity
of God." [16]

III. Exercised in the Liturgy

It was by means of his threefold power that Christ enacted the great events of the Redemption in person during
his sojourn on earth. It is by means of these same powers,
as we have seen, that the Church continues his mission.
She does so by bringing men in the name of Christ into
the adoption of new-born children of God, and of sanctifying and governing them in such a way that they may
ever attain in greater abundance unto the fruits of Christ's
redemption. Now the acts by which she exercises her
power of sanctifying the hearts of men through her sacrifice and sacraments, the acts by which she utilizes the

[16] *The Spirit of the Liturgy*, p. 26

great privilege conferred by the Redemption, namely, the power to offer to God an acceptable sacrifice of praise and glory—these acts constitute what is called her official public service or worship, her LITURGY. Is by means of her liturgy in particular that the Church is indeed the continuation of Christ, of the Savior of mankind.

If the Church is viewed as a perfect society, in which resides full authority over her members, the power of jurisdiction or of governing may seem to be of highest importance. But from the standpoint of supernatural dignity, of the mission that is hers, the priestly power of the Church, her sacrificial and sanctifying power, is of primary importance and is first in rank. It is this power in particular that confers on those vested with it, therefore on the Church, a transcendent participation in the nature and energies of Christ. Hence, as Dom Vismara says "the liturgy is the work of the Church *par excellence:* her proper public and official work, as the very name indicates (*leitourgia*—public service). The liturgy evidently does not absorb nor exhaust the entire scope of the Church's action; but it constitutes her principal and most characteristic work, insofar as the Church is eminently a religious society, continuer of the mission and the work of Christ throughout the centuries." [17]

If we review briefly what was said above about the mission of Christ and connect it up with the principal functions of the liturgy, we shall better understand the intimate, the sublime position of the liturgy in the Church of Christ. It should become evident without any doubt or difficulty, that the liturgy, so much neglected by whole groups of the faithful, is in fact of the essence of the

[17] *La liturgia cristiana i la partecipazione del populo,* p. 146

Church, because it is of the essence of Christ our Redeemer.

Christ, the second person of the most blessed Trinity become man, is primarily the Savior of the human race. He came down upon earth and took upon himself a human nature for the purpose of effecting the salvation of mankind. He wrought the Redemption by his august sacrifice on the cross of Calvary, where he offered himself as the one acceptable victim to his heavenly Father. The exercise of his divine priesthood, he transmitted to the Church in her power to offer the sacrifice of the Mass, the holy Eucharist instituted at the Last Supper in direct relation to his death on the cross.

The Mass is therefore the sublimest function the Church is capable of, for it is the continued oblation of Christ himself to the heavenly Father. But it is not an isolated action of the Church; it is an action, rich in its structural composition, in which the faithful are called to assimilate themselves to the redeeming work of Christ. It is at once the most fundamental exercise of the priesthood of Christ and the basic liturgical function of the Church, performed through her legitimately empowered officials for all the faithful, and for them to share in actively. In it both the sanctifying power of the Redeemer and the Redeemer himself are placed within reach of her children.

Around the Eucharist are grouped the other sacraments, sublime liturgical functions of the Church, which prepare for the reception or the dispensation of its fruits, or which strengthen for the full attainment of its beneficent graces and the full exploitation of its virtues and power. In all of them the priestly power of Christ is active and reaches into the very souls of those who participate in them, thus effecting an intimate contact between the Divine and the human.

In a remoter way this work of sanctification and salvation is continued by the liturgical prayers and blessings known as the sacramentals. In these a sacred character, not that of the sacraments, but a spiritual, supernatural blessing, is imparted to the various material instruments of daily life, our working tools, our dwellings, to various persons under special circumstances and to many little acts of private devotion. Everything in the life of man is thereby aligned with his sacred destiny; through them man receives an environment that ever reminds him of his eternal home, where alone his spirit can find its true domestic peace.

In quite another way is Christ's work of glorifying the Father and sanctifying man continued in the official prayers of homage that the Church renders to God in the liturgy of the divine office. This marvellous prayer of the Church is most closely knit up with the prayers which Christ himself constantly offered to his heavenly Father, and receives all its efficacy from being the official service of the official voice of the Church, rendered by her ordained ministers and by others deputed to offer this service in her name.

In all the liturgy, therefore, do we find Christ acting through his Church, exercising in her his priestly powers of sacrificing, sanctifying, praising God. The liturgy is *par excellence* the mediatorial action of Christ in the Church. It is in this sense that the term *Christo-centric* has been applied to the liturgy, that is, centering in Christ. But the phrase must not be misunderstood. The liturgy focusses on Christ in order to establish contact with God through him as mediator. The powers of Christ which the Church employes in her liturgy are always mediatorial in purpose. Christ is not the ultimate goal of the liturgical worship; he is always and everywhere essentially the Mediator between God and man. Such had been the nature of his mission on earth; and such primarily is the mission he entrusted to the Church and her liturgy. The latter is thus the essential means of God's reaching down to man, the essential means of man's reaching through Christ to God as the source of the triune Godhead, the eternal Father of all.

IV. FROM THE FATHER

We should indeed expect nothing else, if we recall that all that is has come ultimately from the Father. Christ himself never tired of calling attention to his position of representative of and intermediary for the Father. Christ was born of the Father from all eternity and in time was sent by him into the world. His generation and his mission bear the same relation to the Father. "For his mission was not established in a different order from that of his generation. It belonged to the Father to send the Son; and the society of the Father and the Son, without disturbing their eternal relations, reveals itself in this mission. Thus our Highpriest, vested with his sacerdotal character by the Father, is sent and consecrated in time by him who generated him from all eternity." [18] "I am come from him, and he hath sent me," says Christ. [19]

The Father is the source of Christ's priesthood; it is he who said to our Lord: "Thou art a priest forever according to the order of Melchisedech." [20] The Father was

---

[18] Grea, *op. cit.*, p. 41   [19] John 7:29   [20] Ps. 109:4

the inspiration of the sacrifice of Christ; it was he who "spared not even his own Son, but delivered him up for us all." [21] The sacrifice was made at the command of the Father, and from him came the resultant glory of Christ. Christ "humbled himself, becoming obedient unto death, even to the death of the cross. For which cause God also exalted him and hath given him a name which is above all names." [22] Likewise did the Father give his Son the power of judge over all men. "For neither doth the Father judge any man," as Christ tells us, "but hath given all judgment to the Son." [23] Thus the Father was ever with Christ and operating with him: "I am not alone, because the Father is with me." [24] "And if I do judge, my judgment is true: because I am not alone, but I and the Father that sent me." [25]

Now if Christ says, "The words that I speak to you, I speak not of myself. But the Father who abideth in me, he doth the works," [26] this same relation was transmitted to the apostles, to the hierarchy of the Church. "The words which thou gavest me, I have given to them; and they have received them, and have known in very deed that I came out from thee, and they have believed that thou didst send me." [27] It is always the Father's commissions that Christ passes on to the Church, even as the glory he transmits is the Father's: "And the glory which thou hast given me, I have given to them." [28] In the same way the Church is called to share in the judgment that Christ received from the Father: "When the son of man shall sit on the seat of his majesty, you also

[21] Rom. 8:32
[22] Philip 2:8–9
[23] John 5:22
[24] John 16:32
[25] Ibid., 8:16
[26] John 14:10
[27] John 17:8
[28] John 17:22

shall sit on twelve seats judging the twelve tribes of Israel." [29]

All the powers, then, which Christ transmitted to the Church, and which find their expression in the official acts of the hierarchy, especially in the liturgy of the Church, Christ himself refers to his heavenly Father. The same proportion that exists between the Father and the Son, exists analogously between the Son and the Church. It is the power of the Father that the Son displays and the glory of the Father that he achieves; and the Church, exercising this same inherited power and aiming at this same glory, thus has the ultimate efficient source of her actions in the eternal Father, who is likewise the final goal of her homage. The Church's sanctifying power, in other words, the exercise of her liturgy, is in truth the reaching down of the divine power of the Father unto the earth. It is this divine energy of the Father that the apostles received from Christ and transmitted to their successors, that the bishops of the Church have received and transmit to their priests in the sacrament of Holy Orders. Through Christ, the liturgy has its beginning and end in the Father.

All of this we meet with continually in the texts of the liturgy itself. The latter is replete with expressions of the mediatorship of Christ. The phrase "through Jesus Christ our Lord" occurs innumerable times. In the Mass we acknowledge the exercise of God's power through Christ: "Through whom, O Lord, thou dost ever provide, make holy, fill with life, make fruitful of good, and bestow upon all these thy gifts," or again, in the summarizing words of the minor doxology at the end of the Canon:

[29] Matt. 19:28

"Through him, and with him, and in him, is to thee, God the Father almighty, in the unity of the Holy Ghost, all honor and glory."

In the same way is the position of the Father brought out elswhere in the Mass. The entire sacrifice of the altar is offered to him. The Canon, for instance, begins with these words: "And now, most gracious Father, we humbly beg of thee and entreat thee, through Jesus Christ, thy Son, our Lord. . . ." Or the first prayer after the consecration: "Wherefore, O Lord, we thy servants, and likewise thy holy people, calling to mind not only the blessed passion of the same Christ thy Son our Lord. . . ." [30] Of the many hundreds of official prayers (collects, secrets, postcommunions, etc.) contained in the missal only about twenty-seven are addressed to Christ, almost all of these having been adopted after the thirteenth century, when the liturgical sense had begun to decline. Apart from these few, they are all addressed to the Father.

As the source of the Godhead, then, from whom all things are derived through Christ, the Father is also the principal recipient of the homage, the petitions, the praises of the liturgy, which is thus eminently latreutic, i.e., rendering the highest homage to God. So does the liturgy fulfill perfectly the mission of Christ himself. As it comes through Christ from the Father, so in turn it addresses itself and directs its action, like Christ and through Christ, to the Father. Christ, in dwelling in the hierarchy of the Church and acting in its functions, has introduced the Church into the living relation existing between the Father and himself.

---

[30] All quotations from the ordinary text of the Mass are from the excellent translation of the Reverend Richard E. Power in Goeb, *Offeramus*.

V. The Liturgy and the Trinity

We see then how the liturgy is the earthly, the temporal expression of the eternal relation between Father and Son, brought down into the realm of time and of man through the descent upon this earth of the incarnate Son.

Thereby, however, the fullness of the action of the Divinity in the liturgy is not yet exhausted. As a necessary result of this aspect of the liturgy, this participation in the eternal bond uniting Father and Son, we should find in the liturgy also the operation of the Holy Ghost, the third divine person, who proceeds necessarily from the mutual eternal love of the Father and the Son. In fact, the liturgy, being an expression of the extended relation between the Father and the Son, must necessarily contain in its action the presence and operation of the Holy Spirit. "The Holy Spirit could not be absent," says Dom Grea; "and in the mystery of the Church united to her Head, he is given to the Church; he lives in the Church, breathes and speaks in her. And his presence in her is a mysterious necessity of the hierarchy, founded on the eternal necessities of the divine life and of the society that is in God. And as he unites the Son to the Father, so he unites the Church to her Head—the Church, in whom is the name of the Son, to her Head, in whom is the operation and the authority of the Father." [81]

In the constitution of the Church, therefore, we cannot but expect the Holy Ghost to play an important part. It is he who is sent down to complete the fullness of Christ's mission, sent down by both the Father and the Son after the Son's return to the Father. "And because you are

[81] *Op. cit.*, p. 59

sons, God hath sent the Spirit of his Son into your hearts," wrote St. Paul.[32] And Christ said: "But when the Paraclete cometh, whom I will send you from the Father, the Spirit of truth, who proceedeth from the Father, he shall give testimony of me. . . . He will teach you all truth" (John 15:26; 16:13). It is this Spirit who operates in the followers of Christ. In him they are "sealed unto the day of redemption."[33] It is by him that the apostles, the hierarchy of the new Church, acted: "For it is not you that speak, but the Spirit of your Father that speaketh in you," as Christ told them.[34]

Since Christ, as the sole means of all sanctification and salvation, performs his mission through the liturgy of his Church, and since the Holy Ghost gives the efficacy to the powers of Christ, the liturgy must finally receive its efficacy through the operation of the Holy Ghost, of the Spirit of Christ and the Father. The liturgical action of the Church being the fulfillment of Christ's missionary work, and the plenitude of Christ coming through the Holy Spirit, the two must converge. And in truth the liturgy of the Church effects her divine mission through the divine Spirit. The power of keys and of forgiveness is transmitted through the reception of the Holy Ghost: "Receive ye the Holy Ghost. Whose sins you shall forgive, they are forgiven them."[35] Indeed, "no man can say the Lord Jesus, but by the Holy Ghost."[36] The action of Christ in the Church, in her liturgy, is therefore the operation of Christ's holy Spirit. "Thus the Holy Spirit lives in the Church: he enacts in her, with an all-powerful efficacy, the wonders of his intimate activity; he in-

[32] Gal. 4:6
[33] Ephes. 4:30
[34] Matt. 10:20
[35] John 20:22-23
[36] 1 Cor. 12:3

forms and animates all her organs. But if he comes to the Church and if he lives in her, it is because the Son himself is in this Church, beloved of the Father and loving the Father; it is because the Son draws down upon this Church, which is his extension and his plenitude, the love of the Father, and because he animates her with his own love; it is because the mystery of the love of the Father and of the Son embraces and contains her in an ineffable solidarity." [87]

All the official actions of the Church, the actions of Christ in her, the active bonds connecting her with the Father, her whole liturgical life, are consequently penetrated by the Holy Spirit; through him do they receive the full stamp of their divine character. It is he who perfects her liturgical actions, raises them to their full efficacy, cements the union of the Church with the three persons in the one God—in a word, completes her participation in the divine Godhead of the most holy Trinity.

In her liturgy the Church gives frequent expression to this. Our individual prayer may at times neglect the fundamental triune aspect of the Godhead. Not so the liturgy. The sign of the cross occurs again and again in the holy sacrifice and the sacraments, in every possible liturgical rite. The Gloria and the Credo are built up on the structure of the Trinity. The psalms of the divine office end regularly with the "Glory be to the Father, etc."; and most hymns conclude with the same sentiment of praise to the Trinity. And by far most of the prayers of missal and breviary end with a mention of the three persons: "Through Jesus Christ our Lord, who liveth

[87] Grea, *op. cit.*, pp. 74–75

and reigneth with thee, in the unity of the Holy Ghost."
After the oblation of the gifts and just before the "Orate
fratres" of the Mass an important and summary prayer
of offering is addressed to the Trinity, and again a similar
one at the end of the Mass before the final blessing.

Therewith we have attained the full dignity and efficacy of the divine character of the liturgical life of the
Church. This life is the life divine of the full Godhead
operating among men here on earth. This is admirably
stated by an author who has been repeatedly quoted. "It
is the eternal society of the Father and the Son by the
communication which flows from the Father to the Son
and which leads back and gives the Son to the Father,
and, in this society, the substantial procession of the Holy
Spirit which consummates it. Behold, this divine and
ineffable hierarchy has extended beyond itself in the mystery of the Church. In the incarnation the Son, sent by
his Father, has come to seek humanity in order to unite
himself to it and associate himself with it. Thereby this
divine society has been extended unto man, and this
mysterious extension is the Church. The Church is humanity embraced, assumed by the Son in the society of the
Father and the Son, entering through the Son into participation in this society, completely transformed, penetrated, surrounded by it." [88]

Whatever is thus realized in the Church of the divine
life of the Trinity is realized in her official priestly actions,
in her sacrifice, sacraments and general prayer, in her
official public worship—in her liturgy. It is in the latter
that we find in an eminent degree all the different characteristics related to the mission of Christ as developed

[88] Grea, *op. cit.*, pp. 22–23

in the preceding pages. We may well repeat them in summary form:

The liturgy exercises the mediatorship of Christ; it reaches through Christ from God to man, connecting man with God.

The liturgy, through Christ, comes from the Father, the eternal source of the divine life in the Trinity. It in turn addresses itself in a special way to the Father, rendering him the homage and the glory of which it is capable through the power of Christ. The flow of divine life between the eternal Father and the Church is achieved and completed through the operation of the Holy Ghost.

The liturgy, reaching from God to man, and connecting man to the fullness of the Godhead, is the action of the Trinity in the Church. The Church in her liturgy partakes of the life of the divine society of the three persons in God.

CHAPTER III

THE WAY OF SALVATION

I. Christ Our Life

OUR consideration of the liturgy in the last chapter was based on the character of Christ as the Savior of the human race. Christ gave his mission of saving man to his Church for all times to come, and the Church exercises the missionary powers of Christ's priesthood essentially through her liturgy. There, as we have seen, the mediatorship of Christ is exercised with the full efficacy of Christ's own person and energies. It is through the liturgy in particular that the life of God descends down to the reach of man; there is enacted the full bounty of the condescending love and goodness of God unto man.

Now if Christ is on the one hand the Savior of the human race, he is on the other hand by proxy the whole saved human race. "Having 'potentially and provisionally' saved the whole human race, and containing in himself the fullness of grace, Christ is virtually the totality of the just. Even as in the first Adam the entire human race was virtually *persona ingrata et maledicta* (displeasing and accursed) before God, so in the second Adam, all mankind becomes virtually before God a *persona grata et benedicta* (acceptable and blessed of God). Christ, replete with sanctifying grace and with charity not merely as an individual but rather as head of the Church, as universal man in whom the entire race is as it were condensed, achieved an act of perfect love of his Father. As a result of this act he is ever the man universal in whom all mankind is concentrated, the object of the infinite pleasure of his Father. In brief word, this aspect of the existence of Jesus is that of mankind-saved-in-Jesus." [1]

But Christ is only virtually or potentially the whole human race saved. The whole human race has been saved only in this sense, that through Christ's work of redemption it has again become possible for all men of all times to attain salvation, to attain God. The redemption enacted by Christ here on earth as the head of the human race broke the bonds of sin that held man in helpless captivity. It opened up the possibility of salvation and reunion with God for all mankind. But the actual attainment of this salvation by each human individual is another matter. That still depends on the co-operative action of each man's own intelligence and free will, on his own freely determined and willing co-operation. Since God wants only an intelligent homage and service, it remains for each individual to do what is necessary for turning the possibility of his salvation into a reality, for actually having the fruits of Christ's redemption applied to his own person.

We have, therefore, two aspects of the mission of salvation wrought by Christ. One of these is the descent of the saving love of God down to earth and its placement within the reach of all men of good will. This was accomplished primarily in the singular series of events in the life of Christ, from the incarnation to the resurrection and the descent of the Holy Ghost, by which the life

---

[1] Festugière, *Qu'est-ce que la liturgie?* pp. 40–41

eternal was again placed within the ambit of human life here on earth. This aspect of the mission of Christ, opening up again the possibility of salvation for all men, was completely achieved by Christ in person during his sojourn here on earth. It reached its culmination with the founding of his Church and the institution of her liturgy. The latter is so to say the last link or step in the descent of God from heaven to man's earth.

But the wider aspect of the redemptive mission of Christ, the actual realization of this possibility in men of all times, the actual obtaining of redemption by human individuals, far from ending with the institution of the Church and the liturgy, was really only begun thereby. It received its actual existence in the downpour of the divine life of Love on the first Pentecost day, and from then on it was destined to continue throughout time, as long as men lived on earth.

Both of these aspects of the redemption, the creating of the possibility and the gradual increasing realization of it in the lives of men, are but aspects of one and the same mission of one and the same Christ. And both are attainable only through Christ, so that it shall remain true as long as men live, that Christ is their only hope of salvation. In this sense Christ taught incessantly. He never ceased emphasizing that he alone is the Way, the Truth, and the Life, that no one can come to the Father except through the Son. "I am the way, and the truth, and the life. No man cometh to the Father but by me." [2] "Amen, amen I say to you, I am the door of the sheep. All others, as many as have come, are thieves and robbers: and the sheep heard them not. I am the door. By me, if

[2] John 14:6

any man enter in, he shall be saved." [3] "For there is one God," says St. Paul, "and one mediator of God and men, the man Christ Jesus, who gave himself a redemption for all." [4] "He that believeth in the Son of God hath the testimony of God in himself. . . . And this is the testimony, that God hath given to us eternal life. And this life is in his Son." [5]

II. THROUGH THE LITURGY

The question that logically follows, where can men today find the Christ through whom alone salvation is to be had, has already found its answer in terms of our last chapter. Christ continues to live here on earth in his Church, and he continues the exercise of his salutary mission in the official actions of this Church, in her liturgy. This was stated succinctly by Pius X who, after pointing out that mankind can come to God only through Christ, added: "But by what way the journey to Christ lies open to us is evident; namely, through the Church." [6] The very church building is called in the liturgy "the house of God and the gate of heaven; and it shall be called the court of God" (introit, feast of the Dedication of a Church); and in the *Vidi aquam* we sing: "I saw water flowing from the right side of the temple, alleluia; and all to whom that water came were saved, and they shall say: Alleluia, alleluia."

In what the saving power of the Church officially consists, we have seen in the last chapter. Since it is in the

[3] John 10:7-9
[4] 1 Tim. 2:5-6
[5] 1 John 5:10-11
[6] Encyclical *E supremi*, October 4, 1903

liturgy of the Church that the sacrifice of Christ is repeated day by day and that the fruitful activity of the Redeemer is perpetuated, it is by association with the liturgical action of the Church's sacrifice that the individual can find Christ. Hence by virtue of her liturgy "the Church has herself become, in a subordinate sense, our way, our truth, and our life, for she conducts us to Christ, for in her teaching she dispenses unto us the word of Christ, for in her sacraments and sacramentals she communicates to us the divine sap of Christ." [7] "All the efforts of the liturgy," writes Dom Festugière, "tend to develop in souls the life of Christ. The liturgy, considered in its effects, both psychological and moral, can be defined as the authentic method instituted by the Church for assimilating souls to Jesus." [8]

From this we can readily see the need, for all those who seek the redemption of Christ, of associating themselves with the liturgy of the Church. "For all alike," writes Dom Beauduin, "wise and ignorant, infants and adults, lay and religious, Christians of the first and Christians of the twentieth century, leaders of an active or of a contemplative life, for *all the faithful of the Church without exception*, the greatest possible active and frequent participation in the priestly life of the visible hierarchy, according to the manner prescribed in the liturgical canons, is the *normal and infallible path* to a solid piety that is sane, abundant, and truly Catholic, that makes them children of their holy mother the Church in the fullest sense of this ancient and truly Christian phrase." [9]

[7] Marmion, *Semaine liturgique de Maredsous*, p. 6
[8] *Op. cit.*, p. 81
[9] *Liturgy the Life of the Church*, pp. 12–13

The liturgy itself prays for the reception of the fruits of Christ's blood through the liturgical worship: "Grant, we beseech thee, that we may so honor by our solemn service this the price of our redemption, and by its virtue be so defended from the evils of our present life on earth, that we may enjoy its fruit in heaven for evermore" (collect, feast of the Precious Blood). The well-known and oft-quoted words of Pius X state explicitly that the primary and indispensable source of the spirit of Christ is "the active participation in the most holy mysteries and in the public and solemn prayer of the Church." It is for this reason that the Church uses her power of command to prescribe for her children a minimum participation in her liturgical functions. Far from being accurate in saying that the need of participation flows from the command of the Church, we must rather say that the Church prescribes the participation because of its indispensability for assimilating the fruits of Christ's redemption.

This then is the sublime function of the liturgy of the Church: to assimilate us unto Christ, to make us partakers of the Christ-life, of the eternal life of God. We attain God through the mediatorship of Christ who lives and acts in his Church. The life of the Church is this continuing life of Christ. Hence we must seek God first of all in this life of the Church, that is, in her liturgy. Without the latter it is impossible to attain union with Christ. To be in the Church, to be a living member of the Church and of Christ, means precisely to be in living union with the divine Godhead of the Trinity. And so the Church, which has been characterized as the continuation of Christ on earth, is constituted not only of those who by special transmission from the apostles exercise the priestly and missionary office of Christ in an official way, but of all those who by participation in the liturgical life of the Church also live the life of Christ.

Thence arises the beautiful idea of the Church as the mystical body of Christ, all the faithful being the members that makes up this body, with Christ as the head; and again the idea of the faithful as the branches of the vine which is Christ. "I am the vine; you the branches: he that abideth in me, and I in him, the same beareth much fruit: for without me you can do nothing." [10] It is the branches that must bring forth the fruit of the spiritual energies of Christ; and without Christ there can be no life and no fruit in the branches. "If there is any difference between the vine and the branches," writes Dom Panfoeder, "it is this, that the vine denotes the whole of which the branches are parts or members. The branches have no existence of themselves; they are dependent on the whole of which they are parts. Nor are they replicas of the vine, or accidental appendages like the candles of a Christmas tree. They are the product of the vine, its realization, essentially necessary for the life of the vine. The vine gives unity to the branches, the branches give expression and efficacy to the living energies of the vine. They are nothing without it; it cannot complete itself without them." [11]

The members of the Church of Christ are all engrafted upon him as the vine. They are not an accidental agglomerate or aggregate, like a heap of stones, no matter how close these may be together, but a unified organism. The Church is thus a common fellowship of souls in Christ, a fellow-

[10] John 15:5
[11] *Die Kirche als liturgische Gemeinschaft*, p. 116

ship that extends to all who have been incorporated in Christ. It therefore embraces also the souls of the blessed in heaven and the suffering souls in purgatory—a doctrine which Christian tradition expresses by the term *communion of saints.*

It should not surprise us therefore to find that the liturgy frequently makes mention of the saints in heaven, glorying in their lot, praising God in them, asking their intercession; and likewise prays for the souls of the departed in every Mass and has a special liturgy for the dead. The saints in heaven and in purgatory are really not separated from the saints on earth. All of them belong together, for they are all united in the same Christ. "For as the body is one, and hath many members; and all the members of the body, whereas they are many, yet are one body, so also is Christ." [12] Christ is "the head over all the church, which is his body, and the fulness of him who is filled all in all." [13]

The life of this fellowship of souls in Christ is the true life of Christ in men, and it is destined to increase throughout the existence of time. For this purpose was the Church instituted. Christ "gave some apostles, and some prophets, and other some evangelists, and other some pastors and doctors, for the perfecting of the saints, for the work of the ministry, for the edifying [*i.e.,* building up] of the body of Christ. Until we all meet into the unity of faith, and of the knowledge of the Son of God, unto a perfect man, unto the measure of the age of the fulness of Christ." [14] The Church thus embraces a hierarchy of many members, but all the members without exception constituting the body of Christ, and together living the life of Christ.

[12] 1 Cor. 12:12   [13] Ephes. 1:22–23   [14] Ephes. 4:11–13

III. SHARERS IN CHRIST

If the Church is a living fellowship of souls all sharing mutually in the fruits of Christ's redemption, in the energies of Christ, and if Christ and his members form one unitary body, there must be a common bond of union between Christ and Christians. This is the Spirit of Christ, the Holy Ghost, who is indeed the soul of the mystical body, informing Head and members alike, flowing from Head to members, and operative alike in all. It is the operation of the Holy Ghost that realizes the common participation of all members in the acts of the liturgy. The latter constitutes men as members of Christ's body precisely because through the liturgical action the Holy Ghost enters into the members. One of the first statements in the text of the baptismal rite, the initiation into membership in the mystical body, reminds the candidate that he is to be a temple of the Holy Ghost. "You are bought with a great price," writes St. Paul to the Christians of his day, "glorify and bear God in your body." [15]

The member of the Church is truly a Christ-bearer, a temple of the Spirit of Christ. He can share in the life of Christ, be "another Christ" solely by reason of the fact that the Holy Ghost lives and operates in him.[16] It is through the operation of the Spirit of Christ as exercised in the liturgy that the divine sap of the Christ-life flows from the Vine to the branches; by it alone do the branches live the life of Christ. "Christ and the Church—that is the content of the liturgy. . . . Christ, the God-man, the Savior, who revealed himself as the way and the goal in

[15] 1 Cor. 6:20
[16] *Cf.* Michel, *Life in Christ*, pp. 31ff.

the words: I am the way, the truth, and the life. The
Church, not the accidental sum of the Christians living
today, but the holy fellowship of all who go to the Father
through Christ, who have in themselves the Holy Ghost
and are by divine grace perfect as the Father in heaven:
a holy body, held together and animated by a holy breath
of life, the Spirit of God; a supernatural edifice, built of
select stones of varying size and beauty, all of which, however, mutually support and carry one another and constitute one work of art." [17]

All this sharing in Christ, this union of souls by means
of the common possession of the Holy Ghost, is effected
through the Church's liturgy. By means of the latter "the
Christian is not an isolated being but a member of the body
of the Church of which Christ is the head. The members
derive their life from the life of the body; they cannot live
apart without becoming sterile and paralyzed; only in an
intimate union with the body do they possess their life-
blood and their true strength." [18] Since the constant flow
of life between Head and body, between member and body,
is the living action that is the liturgy, the latter has for its
end either to incorporate men into the living body of
Christ and make them "other Christs," or else to give
them an ever greater degree of the abundance of this life,
to help them to grow constantly in Christ. For that end do
the sacrifice of the Church, her sacraments, and the divine
praises she offers so incessantly exist.

The holy sacrifice of the Mass, as the central act of the
official worship of the Church, is also the primary exercise
of the priesthood of Christ in the Church. It is therefore

[17] *Die Betende Kirche*, p. 187
[18] Caronti, *The Spirit of the Liturgy*, p. 4

also the primary source of contact between the members of the Church and their Head, the primary means of their sharing in Christ. We shall see later how the sacrifice of Christ in the Mass must also be in a special way the sacrifice of the members; and how the members must in the Mass properly assimilate themselves with Christ and his sacrifice; how the sacramental reception of the Eucharist is but the corollary, the logical consummation of the living union that the Mass enacts between the members and the head Christ. Mass and Communion, the latter a part of the former, are the ordinary exercise of the life of Christ as lived in the members of his body.

The sacraments are a further exercise of the ministerial office of Christ entrusted to the priesthood of the Church and realized in her liturgy. They are therefore also further means by which the children of the Church exercise their active membership in the Church. They are all means of cementing the union between Christ and members. The sacrament of Baptism initiates members into the body of Christ, and renders possible the exchange of divine life between Head and members, by means of an outpouring of the Holy Ghost from Christ into the newly born Christian. Confirmation strengthens the life of the member by a spiritual infusion of the fullness of the Holy Spirit. Other sacraments revive the healthy condition of injured members (especially and ordinarily Penance), empower certain members to be the official channels of the life of Christ to other members (Holy Orders), nourish and increase the vitality of the members after their initiation by an essential exercise of their function as "other Christs" (Eucharist as sacrifice-sacrament), prepare them for the special duties connected with the bringing into this world of new candidates for membership in Christ (Matrimony), or fit them for the last earthly struggle and the final complete incorporation into the glorified body of Christ in heaven (Extreme Unction).

Outside of the sacrifice and the sacraments there are the sacramentals and the daily praises of God sung in the divine office. These are so many ways in which the members of Christ can direct their actions and lives more intimately towards God through Christ. They are the wider pulse-beats of the life of Christ as lived in the members of his mystical body by their faithful sharing in the Christ-life of the Church.

The thoughts we have been developing are summarized in the following words of Dom Grea in his own inimitable style: "Jesus Christ receives the nations as his heritage and the elect as his immortal posterity in the order of priesthood and of sacrifice. And the propagation of the new life, by which the children of God are to be born in him, will be accomplished by means of the priesthood and according to the hierarchical laws by which the sacerdotal action will communicate and distribute itself." [19] That is, therefore, by means of the liturgy. It is through the latter alone that the members of the body of Christ are formed and developed. The liturgy alone is the official, primary means of transforming men into Christians, of putting off the old man and putting on "the new man, who according to God is created in justice and holiness of truth," [20] of following the behest of St. Paul, "Put ye on the Lord Jesus Christ." [21] For this also does the liturgy pray when God is asked that "he [Christ] may destroy the old man in us, and give us the grace of his resurrection" (prayer of Maundy Thurs-

[19] *Op. cit.*, p. 53   [20] Ephes. 4:24   [21] Rom. 13:14

day), or that the reception of his sacrament "may transform us into a new creature" (postcommunion, Easter Wednesday).

It is by means of the liturgy alone that we are united in Christ with holy bonds that ever grow stronger, that we become sharers in Christ, part of the humanity justified in Christ the head. Thus incorporated in Christ by the liturgy, man "no longer lives for a time but for Christ and for the Church, in which he is reborn for an eternity. Thus the old humanity has in itself but a frail and temporary existence; it will however be transformed step by step from Adam into Christ and be transferred from its old order into the Church." [22] The liturgy thus furnishes the leaven of constant growth in the living body of Christ on earth, in the Church, which in this regard has been defined so well as "the kingdom of God thoroughly leavening all mankind in slow but irresistible process, the body of Christ embracing the whole of fallen humanity in a suprapersonal unity." [23] Therein is realized the word of St. John, that "as many as received him, he gave them power to be made the sons of God." [24]

IV. Corporate Life

The liturgy, uniting all members in Christ, is then not the prayer or activity of isolated individuals, but of individuals united by a common bond. The liturgy is above all corporate activity, a fellowship in action. "Accordingly the great Fathers and Doctors of the Church do not conceive the liturgical prayer merely as the prayer of individual

[22] Grea, op. cit., p. 35
[23] Karl Adam, The Spirit of Catholicism, p. 141
[24] John 1:12

human persons, but also as the prayer of mankind and the Church in union with their Head. The prayer of the members is prayer of the Head and the prayer of the Head is prayer of the members. Christ is the mouth of the Church, her singing tongue, while in turn the Church is the tongue of Christ; she praises the Father through Christ and Christ praises the Father through her." [25]

In their personal prayer-life the members of the body of Christ should not separate themselves from the prayer of their Head, they must also pray liturgically. The liturgy in no way condemns private individual prayer. The value of the latter is here not under discussion nor can it be placed in doubt even for a moment. But the liturgy in its very essence implies that there are times when the individual member must enter actively into the corporate prayer and worship of the mystical body of Christ, without which he can hardly be said to be living the life of Christ or to be using the ordinary, officially constituted means of uniting himself with Christ. Union of the faithful into one living organism, the mystical body of Christ, wherein is realized the fuller development of Christ, and the corporate action of the latter, are of the essence of the liturgy as also its primary aim.

Time and again do we find this expressed in the prayers of the Church. The text of the Mass is a collective prayer, not only of all present, but also of the entire Church. All that have been nourished at the eucharistic banquet table of the sacrificial altar should become of one mind: "That as thou hast fed us with the one bread from heaven, so mayest thou, by thy mercy, make us of one mind. Through Christ our Lord . . ." (postcommunion, Friday after Ash Wed-

[25] Panfoeder, *Chrisus unser Liturge*, pp. 52–53

nesday). The unity of minds in the liturgical sacrifice should be at once a guarantee against all that may make us impure and separate us from Christ and should effect a unity that has its source in the unity of all in Christ the sacrificial victim: "May the communion of thy sacrament, we beseech thee, O Lord, be to us the source of purity and unity" (postcommunion, ninth Sunday after Pentecost). When we are thus united in mind and heart in the liturgical worship, the actual realization of the mystical body of Christ is at its highest, the realization of the fullness of Christ at its best, Christ himself is most intimately present in his body. Then "it is Jesus Christ himself who prays for us, prays in us, is prayed to and adored by us. He prays for us as our priest, he prays in us as our head, he is adored by us, petitioned, as our head." [26]

The liturgy is thus *par excellence* the most eminent fulfillment of the word of Christ: "For where there are two or three gathered together in my name, there am I in the midst of them." [27] Through the liturgy he acts in the united brethren, and through him they enter into union with all the members of Christ, the entire communion of saints, nay, with the divine mystery of the society of God in the most holy Trinity. Therein is truly realized that "the Church is mankind embraced, taken up by the Son into the society of the Father and of the Son, entering through the Son into participation in this society, and entirely transformed, penetrated and surrounded by it; 'that our fellowship may be with the Father, and with his Son Jesus Christ' (1 John 1:3)." [28] Through it all the Church is united to God, thus achieving the end of the prayer of

---

[26] Panfoeder, *op. cit.*, p. 55
[27] Matt. 18:20

[28] Grea, *op. cit.*, p. 23

Christ: "And not for them only do I pray, but for them also who through their word shall believe in me; that they also may be one in us: that the world may believe that thou hast sent me. And the glory which thou hast given me, I have given to them; that they may be one, as we also are one: I in them and thou in me; that they may be made perfect in one." [29]

The liturgy thus becomes the intimate life of God in the Church lived by the faithful under leadership of the official priesthood. It is "not merely a filial remembrance of Christ, but a continual participation by visible mysterious signs in Jesus and his redemptive might, a refreshing touching of the hem of his garment, a liberating handling of his sacred wounds. That is the deepest purpose of the liturgy, namely, to make the redeeming grace of Christ present, visible and fruitful as a sacred and potent reality that fills the whole life of the Christian." [30]

It is only by means of the liturgy of the Church truly lived that the prayer of the feast of Christ the King can be fulfilled: "Gloriously grant that all the families of the nations, rent asunder by the wound of sin, may be subject to his most sweet rule"; or the similar petition of the preface of the same feast: "That offering himself on the altar of the cross as an immaculate and peaceful oblation, he may achieve the holy mysteries of human redemption: and having subjected all creatures to his dominion, he may give over to thy majesty an eternal and universal kingdom—a kingdom of truth and life, a kingdom of holiness and grace, a kingdom of justice, of love, and of peace."

The mission of Christ, the mission of the Church, the liturgy of the Church, as we have seen abundantly, demand

[29] John 17:20–23   [30] Adam, *op. cit.*, p. 18

contact of the faithful with the living channels of Christ's action here on earth. Without participation of the faithful in the liturgy, these channels have no meaning, no efficacy. But this contact, this participation, is not merely passive, as the very texts of the liturgy also indicate, which incessantly call for active association of the faithful with the action of Christ. While accentuating the hierarchical character of the worship of the Church, its intimate connection with the officially delegated ministers of the powers of Christ, the Church "has not wished to make of it an activity exclusively ecclesiastic. She has maintained for the faithful an intimate and active participation in the action which the priests perform in the name of all. This contact she secures by the continuous dialogue between the celebrant and those assisting, and thereby she unifies in a perfect way the double character of the liturgy, that of being collective as well as hierarchical." [81]

V. Royal Priesthood

We spoke of Christ before under the aspect of the Savior of humanity, which character is transmitted in a special manner, officially, to the bishops and priests of the Church as the successors of the apostles. We have now also spoken of Christ under the aspect of redeemed or saved humanity. This character of Christ is transmitted through the liturgy, the official action of the hierarchy of the Church, to all the faithful, to all the members of the mystical body of Christ. But since all the faithful must ultimately act with reason and free will in the performance of every good work, since their association with

[81] Beauduin, *Semaine Liturgique de Maredsous*, p. 141

the official action of the liturgy, their participation in it, must also be an active one, not merely a passive submission, they also partake in a general way in the character of Christ as the savior of mankind, *i.e.*, they must all without exception partake in some way in the very priesthood of Christ. This should be expected if the assimilation with Christ is to be complete.

But the order of the two aspects of Christ we have been discussing, one may say, is reversed in his members. Christ in himself is primarily the Savior of mankind; and by assimilation of all human nature with his own in the incarnation and redemption he is also the whole saved humanity. The faithful, on the other hand, enter through baptism first of all into the ranks of saved humanity; and thereby they are then enabled to associate themselves actively with the saving action of Christ, with the whole liturgical worship of the Church. It is by becoming redeemed members of Christ that they share also in the whole and undivided Christ, even to the extent of participation in his very priesthood.

Christ is the unique priest of the New Law and his priesthood is exercised above all in the one and only sacrifice of the New Law. But his entire life also was a sacrifice of praise given to God and a sacrifice of subjection of the human to the Divine. This general sacrifice of his can also be, and must be, imitated by us in the sacrifice of our lives to God. But there must also be more than imitation, there must be participation, and for that we must share in the very priestly powers of Christ. Now Christ's special priestly character is perpetuated in full degree by the sacrament of Holy Orders, the ordained ministers alone being able to initiate and enact the official sacrifice of the

New Law. But some share in the priestly character must be possessed by all the faithful if they are to participate actively in this same sacrifice, as the very text of the Mass tells them to do. If the faithful share in Christ, they also share to some degree in his priestly character. This is precisely one of the effects of their initiation into the fellowship with Christ in baptism. It is this sacrament that makes them not only redeemed human beings in Christ, but also in a general and secondary way priests of Christ. That is the full effect of their union with the hierarchical Church of Christ, the embodiment of Christ. This is the meaning of the words of St. Peter so often quoted: "You are a chosen generation, a kingly priesthood." [82]

"The general priesthood conferred on the faithful in baptism gives them the right and duty to do what is necessary for their life as members of Christ; that is, to join in the official sacrifice celebrated by the ordained priests of the Church, and to receive the sacraments necessary for their state of soul or their state of life. They could do neither of these validly without having a share in the general priesthood of Christ." [83] The liturgy is life' and life means activity. The faithful cannot truly take part in the liturgical worship of the Church without to some extent participating actively in the priestly sacrifice from which all further life flows.

It is from this standpoint that the liturgy has so aptly been defined as "the divine service which the mystical Christ, that is, the Church as a fellowship in union with Christ her head, renders to the heavenly Father. It consists of the celebration and the application of the re-

[82] 1 Peter 2:9   [83] Michel, *Life of Christ*, p. 26

demption, which takes place in the form of mystery-actions by means of the general and of the special priesthood." [34] In similar terms has the liturgical movement or the liturgical apostolate been defined: "By liturgical movement we understand the totality of initiatory activities and of the forces that tend to lead souls to come again under the influence of the priestly power which is the superabundant source of life. Now the priestly power of Christ, exercised by the Catholic hierarchy, reaches the individual faithful in the parish priest, who by delegation of the bishop exercises over all the faithful the triple power of teacher, minister, and ruler. The faithful united to their parish priest are by means of him united to the bishop and to the rest of the diocese and therefore to the whole Church and to the supreme head: thus there is one fold under one shepherd. This is the realization of the prayer of the Savior: that they be one." [35]

In this manner is the liturgy truly the way of salvation and sanctification for all mankind. In it the hierarchy of the Church offers up the official homage and worship of the Church to God, and in it the faithful join by both right and duty, taking active part in this worship of adoration, thanksgiving, expiation, petition, and praise. Thus all are joined in the unity of Christ, of the blessed Trinity, and all join in continuing here on earth the mysterious life of their divine Founder and Head.

As a natural result also the individual life of the members of Christ is wonderfully enriched. Participation in the liturgy naturally produces in us the consciousness of our union with Christ and of our dignity as sharers in

[34] *Die Betende Kirche,* p. 25
[35] *Rivista liturgica,* xii [1925], p. 354

the divine nature. It brings us into contact with the many-sided aspects of the life of Christ, with the rich inexhaustible content of his life, and thus manifests the rich possibilities of our life in him. It elevates our minds above the things of this earth and of self, broadens our spiritual outlook while deepening it, gives us a better sense of the truly beautiful and truly valuable, a better sense of unity with and sympathy for our fellow members of the body of Christ, a human family feeling for all mankind; and, being rooted in the wonderful condescension of God, a firmly founded optimism in regard to all the things that count in life.

But all of this, to repeat, is achieved only by active, intelligent participation in the liturgy, and achieved the more perfectly, the more wholehearted is our participation. Therefore again: "To the Father, the fountain-head of eternal life, through Jesus Christ, the way and the light; to Jesus Christ the head of mankind and first-born amongst many brethren through the Church, Christ's mystic body; to the Church, the extension of Christ, by incorporation through the liturgy of baptism, the new life; continual growth of this new life in the communion of saints by drinking deeply from the primary and indispensible source"—which is the liturgy! [36]

[36] Hellriegel-Jasper, *The True Basis of Christian Solidarity*, pp. 24–25

CHAPTER IV

THE DIVINE IN HUMAN FORM

I. The Liturgical Mystery

So far we have spoken primarily of the interior character or spirit of the liturgy, of its messianic mission, which the liturgy receives from the fact that it is the enactment of the priestly powers of Christ and is the true way of salvation for mankind. In this sense the liturgy is a depository of all the principal truths of our revealed religion, of all the theological mysteries of our faith. It presents these to us in their living reality, not only as sources of religious knowledge on our part, but especially also as sources of religious experience, of religious life. It is our faith lived, as Abbé Croegaert well says: "The Mass, the hymns, the rites, the benedictions, the sacraments, the offices, and the celebration of the seasons—all this vast body of liturgical functions in a word—what is it in reality if not the faith prayed, the faith confessed, the faith chanted in the concrete, palpable, living reality that is the Christian community united to its pastor?" [1]

It is by means of the liturgy that theology, the science of revealed truths, best effects its contact with the life of the Christian soul, that it infuses into mind and heart the effective inspirations for a Christian life of virtue and

[1] *La femme chrétienne et la restauration liturgique*, p. 9

produces the great fruits of Christian piety which should ever be the ultimate object of that queen of sciences. Thus the liturgy raises us to the supremest moments of accomplishing what is asked for in the following prayer: "O God, who by thy venerable intercourse with us in this sacrifice makest us partakers of the one supreme Godhead, grant, we beseech thee, that as we know thy truth, so we may follow it up by a worthy life" (secret, eighteenth Sunday after Pentecost).

It is the purpose of all religion to unite the creatures to their Creator. Conviction of God's existence does not constitute religion; nor does the mere asking of graces and favors. There must be also an acknowledgment of our dependence on him and a willingness to live accordingly, that is, to fulfill his wishes in every way. Religion is thus a service of God, an inner oblation of will to him, by means of which we try in some way to approach him and unite ourselves with him. In all religion we find as an essential note the seeking after contact with the Divine.

This contact, as we have seen, is an essential element of the liturgy. The liturgy is therefore properly the embodiment of a divine mystery, of a holy action, by which man, through the condescension of God, reaches the Godhead. Theological mystery is divinely revealed truth about God and His ways that transcends entirely the power of the natural human intellect to understand fully or to attain. The liturgy itself, however, often uses the word *mystery* or *mysteries* in reference to that which is being celebrated in it, especially in sacrifice and sacrament. The Christian liturgical mystery is a holy action or celebration in which is contained the life-giving work of Christ's redemption, made present under the external forms of the worship, so that those participating in it may share in this holy action of God and thus unite themselves more intimately with him. Without this essential characteristic of the Church's liturgical worship, all else that belongs to the liturgy cannot be understood properly. Without it the external dress in which the worship of God is vested has no meaning. Hence, before treating of the external aspect of the liturgy, it may be well to emphasize once more its true inner character.

The liturgy is an eminent example of following out the divine counsel: Seek ye first the kingdom of God. The liturgy directs the mind first of all to God and not to self. It is a stripping off of self for the better giving of oneself, of both mind and soul and body, to God, as behooves the creature, whose whole being is from God and belongs ever to him. "In the liturgy," says Romano Guardini, "man looks not to himself but to God, to God is his eye directed. In the liturgy man is not to educate himself, but to behold the glory of God. The meaning of the liturgy is this, that the soul is in God's presence, pours out her inner self before him, that the soul lives in his life, in the sacred world of divine realities, truths, mysteries, and signs, and there possesses her proper real life." [2] Hence it is that the liturgy addresses much of its prayer exclusively to the Father as the source of the divine Godhead, that it praises his divine majesty, glorifies him, beseeches him, rests in him; that the liturgy, contrary to much of the piety of individual souls, stresses the fullness of the Godhead, the most holy Trinity.

All religions that have had any ritual worthy of the name have sought by its means to achieve contact with

[2] *Vom Geist der Liturgie*, p. 63

the Divine. In all of them the central objective was the mysterious action by which men were in some way united with their God, in which they in some way attained to the higher life of God. This is pre-eminently the case with the one true religion of Christ. "God has appeared to us in the face of Jesus Christ,[3] in the incarnation of the Divine, in the assumption of the human into the Divinity. That is 'the mystery which hath been hidden from ages and generations, but now is manifested to his saints': a becoming imbued and a living permeation of the human by the Divine. What was first realized in Christ the head continues in the members under the head Christ, in the body of Christ which is the Church.[4] Hence the Church is the *mysterium*, the form of the incarnation of the Divine, which has after the ascension of Christ remained near to us in the present redemptive order. In this sense the Church is Christ continuing to live here on earth."[5]

The embodiment of this phase of the life of the Church is the liturgy; it is only of the liturgy that the following can be said in all truth: "The Christian *mysterium* means a holy celebration, in which Christ himself, and with him all the events of the work of redemption wrought by him, become really present to us by means of a holy symbolical representation, and that, in the celebrating community as the mystical body of Christ. The most perfect expression and the highest realization of this Christian *mysterium* are had whenever the assembled fellowship of the saints celebrates the Eucharist."[6] The liturgy, then, being the ordinary channel through which God reveals and gives himself to the soul, through which the soul reaches God, is

---

[3] 2 Cor. 4:6
[4] Coloss. 1:8 and 24
[5] Herwegen, in *Mysterium*, p. 3
[6] Stricker, in *Mysterium*, p. 65

also the divinely appointed channel of true religious experience. It is the achievement of that for which the souls of old, yearning for divine deliverance, sought in vain.

Even for ordinary souls the religious experience had by means of the liturgy will result in an increased knowledge of the greatness and lovableness of God, and in a consequent peace of mind and joy of heart that cannot but sing out in holy jubilation. It forms the basis of a possession of God to which no limits are set. "In its simple naturalness, the liturgy can become for all the ladder by which they ascend from the simple knowledge of faith to a deeper, more penetrating contemplation and finally to the true wisdom, the wisdom divine." [7]

II. Adapted to Man

In mentioning the liturgy as the basis of true religious experience, it may be well to stress two important differences between it and the religious experiences so often mentioned among our non-Catholic brethren. We have seen that the liturgy is a continuation of the active ministry of Christ in souls. It does not ordinarily effect the sudden conversion, the "getting" of religion in a moment's flight of time that others talk of. Its action is rather a gradual transformation, effected through repeated enactments; it includes a constant call for repetition, and envisages a continuous nearer approach of souls to the Divine. In such terms the liturgy itself prays for the "perpetual joy" derived from the "continued work of our redemption" enacted in the Mass, and asks for "advance day by day in

[7] Hammenstede, *Die Liturgie als Erlebnis*, p. 36

the practice of a heavenly life" (secret, Saturday in Easter Week, and Sunday in the octave of Corpus Christi).

Again the liturgical experience, as we have seen, calls for an active participation by the faithful. It is not the mere passive subjection of oneself to an external influence, that of God, even if "all things were made by him and without him was made nothing that was made" (Last Gospel). In the liturgy there is nothing of quietism. "As action the *mysterium* is far removed from all quietism. It seeks after life, stands and lives in the midst of it, receives the creature, the purely human, the everyday, and lifts it up into its transfigured light. It flees neither the world nor men; it comes from heaven and penetrates deep into all earthly existence. It knows, grasps, animates, and sanctifies reality. Without the *mysterium* no sermon, no book, no organism is Catholic." [8]

Liturgical experience calls for repetition and calls for active participation. In both of these traits we see its admirable adaptation to human nature, we see it as the divinely human thing it is; and in them we touch the key to the true nature and the function of the external garb in which the liturgy appears among men, the external form through which its spirit acts and is revealed.

When the Catholic worship is mentioned, especially under the term "liturgy," many persons think immediately of the external grandeur with which it is enacted. In the dramatic unfolding of the liturgical worship all the devices at the service of man are pressed into the service of God and are employed to increase the splendor and beauty of the worship, to enhance its impressiveness. This is but a further development of the fact that the liturgy is the

[8] Herwegen, *Lumen Christi*, pp. 126–27

expression of Christ's priesthood, is the expression of his divine personality in his mystical body the Church. "All the evil comes from this, that people do not love Jesus enough. Jesus is not loved because he is not known. But Jesus is beautiful, he is true, he is good; and it is necessary, therefore, that the priesthood properly display to the eyes of the people the beauty of Jesus by the splendor of its worship, his truth by the clearness of its teaching, his goodness by the charity of its works. There is the program of all true priestly action." [9]

However, the real basis for this fuller expression in Catholic worship of the different characteristics of Jesus rests in our human nature itself. It is there we find a proper explanation of the external grandeur with which the liturgy of the Church is vested. We have so far stressed the internal spiritual, nay divine, character of the liturgy, and have spoken of the active participation of the people in the liturgical action. This participation must occur primarily by means of a mental understanding of the liturgical actions that are being performed at any time and by a conscious mental accompaniment of this action. Human nature is so constituted that internal acts alone are difficult for man to sustain; they are not the full expression of the man until they find their completion in external action. Man naturally reveals his inner thoughts and wishes by means of external actions. Without the latter the former are ordinarily incomplete, and neither of long duration nor of great vigor. "We must consider," says St. Thomas, "that the wills of men are not manifested without external actions."

[9] Tissier, *Semaine liturgique de Maredsous*, p. 310

Moreover, the liturgy is the corporate expression of the religious service of the members of the Church. It is collective, and for that reason again it needs for its accomplishment the external visible enactment of its sentiments. As it is only through external action, sign or word, that our thoughts are communicated to others, so also it is only by means of the external actions that community of sentiment, co-operative action between many in matters spiritual, can be attained. The external action of the priest, perceptible to all, manifests the progress of the liturgical service to all, just as the external activity of all present should indicate their internal co-operation at this service.

Again, man has been placed at the pinnacle of earthly nature, all lower forms of creation are for his use. Like himself they come from God and are for God, and it is the duty and the high privilege of man to use them primarily in their subordinate relation to their Creator. All creation, in a sense, fell with man and was again redeemed with him unto the glory of God. It is through man, and through him alone here on earth, that the material creation can achieve its proper function of serving unto the glory of its Creator. Therefore does man make use of all creation in his liturgical worship, of all nature, so that nature may join him in the more perfect rendering of his due worship of God.

From all these standpoints the external aspects of the liturgy, the words and actions, the material things used, become properly important in the services of the Church. To neglect them is to give incomplete homage to God. Hence we can understand why the great liturgical pope, in inaugurating the liturgical renewal, spoke of the leading duty of every local church as "without question that of maintaining and promoting the decorum of the house of God." [10]

On the other hand, however, we also see the one-sidedness, in fact the total misconception of the true nature of the liturgy, in those persons—still surprisingly large in number—who speak of the externals as if they constituted the whole of the Church's liturgy. The latter indeed contains many minute rubrical regulations and prescriptions. The Church has wisely legislated in detail regarding the external performance of her service. But no number of rubrical prescriptions and ceremonial rites can of itself constitute a true liturgical service. They are never an end in themselves. Fundamentally, they are not so much of the liturgy because their mode of performance has been prescribed, but rather have they been prescribed because they are the official expression of the sacred universal and internal character of the liturgy. The latter must not be subject to individual whims or inspirations, being a corporate possession of many members united in one faith, in one worship, under one divine Head. It very properly possesses official and legitimate forms of expression of the united sentiments of the members of Christ. The prescription of external details is a consequence of the sacred character of the liturgy, a means of safeguarding a common worship. Without the divine sanctifying character of the liturgical action, the prescription of external details would have no meaning. Given this character, the prescriptions become of supreme value, having the official stamp of the Church of Christ.

[10] *Motu proprio* of November 22, 1903

III. The Divine Model

In thus pressing all of nature into her divine service, the Church but follows the example of her divine Founder. The principle on which the external manifestations of the liturgical worship of the Church must rest is exemplified in Christ himself. Christ, we know, could have redeemed mankind by the merest act of his divine will. The mysterious enactment of the incarnation, his sojourn on earth, the awful tragedy of his passion and death, were in no way absolutely necessary for the merciful redemption of fallen mankind. But Christ, full of mercy for man, stooped to the level of human nature, imitated the ways of this human nature, in order thus to facilitate for us our association and assimilation with him and his redeeming work. Christ in assuming our nature sought to give an external, visible expression to his divine mission. He was to substitute himself for mankind. What was more natural, humanly speaking, than to assume a human nature, and by a hypostatic union to raise human nature in himself to the dignity of acceptableness to the Divinity? What more natural than to walk visibly among men, talk to them in their own way, perform visibly the drama of his suffering and death?

The human nature of Christ is near to us and to our way of knowing and doing. The humanity of Christ we can visualize palpably; we can picture it for ourselves, and thus concretely and sympathetically understand the nearness of Christ to man, the reality of his brotherhood, his adoption of all of us, and his love and sympathy for us, his sufferings and death. Through the humanity of Christ, humanly speaking, we approach Christ's divinity with greater assurance. It is through the humanity of Christ, as St. Thomas emphasizes, that we reach his divinity. The divinity of Christ, Aquinas explains, through the wonderful condescension of which we obtain a glimpse of God's love for us, attracts and overpowers our love. But men arrive at the object of their love as they do at the object of their knowledge, namely through their senses.[11] Through the humanity of Christ therefore we see more strikingly all that Christ did for us in the work of redemption. His adoption of mankind, the re-entering of mankind into the grace and pleasure of the Godhead, is visibly expressed in Christ's own person, in the hypostatic union of his two natures. The great love of God, desiring reunion with his creature man, is symbolized, or rather given actual expression, in the fact that God stepped down to human ways of understanding and enacted in a human, corporeal way this reassumption of human nature into his divine pleasure and love.

Christ, our liturgical Highpriest, is thus the first great liturgical symbol, a symbol like all the liturgical—*i.e.*, sacramental—symbols, that not merely designates or hints at something more than itself, but that is really infinitely more than its external form or appearance, is something immeasurably higher than the external garb in which it first approaches the mind through the senses. Christ is the prototype of the liturgical symbolism, of the external expression of all that the liturgy is, just as he is the source and inspiration of its internal spirit, its Alpha and Omega.

Internally the liturgy is the expression of the divine powers of Christ, externally it is a copy of the visible manner chosen by Christ to reveal and act out his divine powers

[11] *Cf.* Grabmann, *Das Seelenleben des hl. Thomas von Aquin*, pp. 107–108

among men. "We are human," writes Abbot Caronti, "and know that our Lord himself has sought the use of sensible means for our salvation. From human flesh he formed the instrument and the victim of his sacrifice; out of visible and palpable things he made vehicles of grace. Similarly, for unfolding his priesthood, he chose legitimate human representatives, to whom he communicated his power that they might act in his name. As author of the supernatural order he alone could establish the character and the means. If he desired to use human agencies, he could not but continue and extend in some way the mysterious constitution of his own existence, in which humanity acts by divine impulse; he could not but adapt himself to the nature of man, in whom the intellectual and the moral activity draw their elements from the senses, and who finds in the senses a mode of expression and of communication." [12]

The Church, in the development of the external expression of her entrusted powers, in the development of her external liturgy, as in all else, is but following in the footsteps of her Master. "In the supernatural contact of man with his Creator," says Dom Hammenstede, "consists the kernel of Catholic religious life. The liturgical symbolism is a welcome, aye, a necessary means for indicating this contact, for intensifying it and for bringing it about. In the incarnation of his Son and later on in the Church instituted by his Son, God himself called into life symbolical actions, with which definite operations of grace remain for ever associated." [18]

In the development of her liturgical symbolism and

[12] *The Spirit of the Liturgy*, pp. 29–30
[18] *Die Liturgie als Erlebnis*, pp. 30–31

worship the Church has but continued her mission in the best spirit of her holy Founder. "Interpreting the intentions of her divine Founder with a fine sense, and at the same time understanding well the needs of human nature, holy Church has increased the number of these symbols. Just as the bodily Christ and the visible Church belong in the liturgy, so also the external action. Just as our Savior revealed the depths of his inner nature, the riches of his love, his devotion and oblation to the Father, by means of his external actions, so too may we send up our innermost sentiments to the Father by means of the external cultural actions. By means of the visible we wish to be inflamed to a love of the invisible." [14] As the preface of Christmas states it: "So that while we recognize him as God seen by men, we may be drawn by him to the love of things unseen."

IV. LITURGICAL SYMBOLISM

Here we see, then, the high purpose of the symbolism of the liturgy, of all in it that appeals to the mind through the senses, of all its externals. The externals of the liturgy are there to express and reveal the internal, they are the visible embodiment of the divine powers exercised in all liturgical functions, the visible expression of the sentiments uniting the members of the mystical body of Christ among themselves and with their Head. Nor are the symbols merely arbitrary or conventional as is so often thought. Being the expression of the relation of the Author of nature to nature itself, especially to its highest representative, man, the symbolism of the liturgy is funda-

[14] Panfoeder, *Das Persoenliche in der Liturgie*, pp. 80–81

mentally natural, as we shall at different times have occasion to indicate.

Again, being the expression of the Godhead through Christ, of him therefore who is all there is, the externals of the liturgy press into the service of God all that is best in creation, and that in the best manner of which man is capable, according to the tested canons of the best human art. "All the resources of human ingenuity are made to contribute their share to the august concert which the Christian family must render to God: the expression of external action, the solemnity of chant, the majesty of gesture, the harmony of poetry, the eloquence of art." [15] Because of this character of the liturgy, the latter has well been defined as the "splendor of revealed truth." In it art reaches its highest point of achievement and service. "If art is indeed a priesthood, then it is above all in the liturgy that it exercises its ministry." [16]

The symbolism of the liturgy is based primarily on nature, which, coming from God, bears upon itself the stamp of its Creator. In nature the most resplendent, most beautiful object is light, and for us it is the natural light of the sun, which is also the source of the power of growth in life. Hence in the liturgy the sun is the symbol of Christ and of his light-giving mission, just as darkness represents the powers of evil and of sin. Christ appeared on earth as man in the midst of the darkness of night, both literally and figuratively, and around him as around the sun revolves the true life, in particular the life of the Church as expressed in her liturgy. There the sacrifice of Christ is the focal center of the life of the Church, and all else revolves around it, takes its cue from it. The

[15] Caronti, op. cit., p. 16   [16] Dom Beauduin

whole idea of the divine office, too, in its different hours, is permeated by the symbolism of the sun, and even centers about the different stages of advance as marked by the position of the sun in the sky. Christ is "the true light which enlighteneth every man that cometh into this world" (Last Gospel).

The same idea is applied to the shining candles. On Holy Saturday the triple candle lighted from the newly blessed fire is saluted as "The Light of Christ," and the paschal candle in a special way represents the light of the resplendent, risen Savior. At the blessing of candles on the feast of the Purification we have the prayer: "O Lord Jesus Christ, the true Light, who enlighteneth every man coming into the world, pour forth thy blessing upon these candles, and sanctify them with the light of thy grace; and mercifully grant that as these lights enkindled with visible fire dispel nocturnal darkness, so our hearts, illumined by invisible fire, that is, by the brightness of the Holy Spirit, may be free from the blindness of all vice."

Other types of symbolism, in which the liturgy is so rich, are equally expressive and natural. Through the imposition of hands is represented the transfer of power conferred in Holy Orders. Like incense, which represents spiritualization, acceptability to God, our thoughts are to ascend upwards. "May my prayer be directed as incense in thy sight," the priest prays while incensing the altar. Water is blessed and by its use we represent the internal washing away of our moral stains—first of all through baptism. The sign of the cross epitomizes the whole doctrine and efficacy of the redemption wrought in the name of the Blessed Trinity. The extending of the hands in prayer represents the posture of the supplicating Christ on the cross and the complete, open oblation of self to God. The folding of the hands is expressive of the soul shut up within its holy prayer.[17]

With equal effect is the realm of color and sound brought into the services of the Church. White, the color of unrefracted light, is the symbol of God, the father of light, and of Christ the light of the world. The liturgy uses white in all feasts pertaining to God and Christ, with the exception of those emphasizing the Passion. It is the sign of purity, and is therefore used on feasts of the angels, the blessed Virgin, the holy confessors and virgins, and on All Saints. It is a sign of joy, like light, and is used on the feast of Corpus Christi, in processions with the Blessed Sacrament, in the ministering of the sacraments with the exception of Penance and Extreme Unction, in most of the solemn blessings, the nuptial Mass, as also the consecration of a church. Red, the color of fire and blood, is a sign of love. On the feasts of the apostles and martyrs it indicates their bloody immolation for Christ. On the feast of Pentecost it represents the fiery tongues in which the Holy Ghost descended. Green, considered an intermediary between the others, is used on days when no marked characteristic is predominant. It is the color of the sprouting fields, expressive of the hope of life, and is especially in place on the ordinary Sundays of the year, which are commemorations of the great Sunday of the Resurrection, when hope once again returned to the world. Black, the color of mourning, is used on Good Friday, and in services for the dead. Violet is now considered a symbol of mourning and penance, of expiation and re-

<hr />

[17] Cf. *Die Betende Kirche*, pp. 18ff.

nunciation of the world. Hence it occurs in the times of penance: Advent, Lent and the time preparatory to Lent; on the Ember days (except those of the joyous Eastertide) and on the vigils (except that of Epiphany); in penitential and supplicatory processions; in the preparatory rites of Baptism, the sacraments of Penance and Extreme Unction, and on the feast of the Holy Innocents.[18]

As expressive as the colors is the music of the Church in its rich variety of moods, not the least effective being the silence of accompanying instruments in certain times, and, for instance, the silence of the bells in the latter part of Holy Week, or on the other hand the profuse welcome of church bells on great feasts, and the mournful toll when death has snatched a victim.

The language of the liturgy, its phrases and expressions, even apart from being to a great extent the inspired word of God, manifest many characteristics of the liturgy itself. The latter is primarily the official action of the Church, not the private action of the individual, and so the liturgy has an official language for any one general rite. The liturgy unites all the members of the body of Christ in unity of faith and sentiments and expresses this in unity of language and of action. In mood the language of the liturgy expresses the richest variety of spiritual sentiments of which the human heart is capable, but ever with a certain measured moderation, such as is expressive of the ultimate calmness of the heart that is truly confiding in God and is assured of the mediatory ministry of Christ.

The very composition of the liturgy, effected in the slow growth of time, represents the universality, the cath-

[18] *Die Betende Kirche*, pp. 105–107

THE DIVINE IN HUMAN FORM 79

olicity of the Church of Christ. "The liturgy is almost
the language of the apostles; it is the voice of the Christian
ages, the work of the Church in its most indisputable form,
the most direct expression of her spirit. It is the collective
work of the Fathers, the Doctors, the popes and bishops,
without being the personal work of any one of them.
There is in the language of the liturgy neither the teaching of any particular school, nor human opinion, but
solely the thought of the Spouse of Christ, assisted by the
Holy Spirit, the *Opus Dei*, the work of God, as the Benedictine Rule calls it." [19]

V. The Whole Man

Among the earliest Christian heretics were some who
considered everything bodily or material as intrinsically
evil. For them there was no thought of using the human
body as a means of rendering a pleasing service to God.
While the spirit was by nature of the divine, the body
and all things material were thought so essentially evil
that they could not possibly serve any good purposes.
Logically it was also denied that Christ ever had a real
human body. This view is so contrary to the spirit of the
liturgy that its acceptance would spell the death of the
Church's liturgical worship. The liturgy itself prays that
the Victim offered in Mass may "sanctify the bodies and
minds of thy servants for the celebration of this sacrifice"
(secret, third Sunday in Lent); and again that through
the annual observances of the Lenten fasts we may please
God "both in body and mind" (collect, fourth Monday in
Lent). The liturgical worship itself therefore calls for a

[19] Douterlungne, *Semaine liturgique de Maredsous*, p. 215

service rendered to God both in body and soul, not only by the soul, not only an interior service of mind. And the liturgy itself, in the aspects we have just reviewed, exemplifies this spirit to perfection. This characteristic of the Church's liturgy has been pointed to as an indication of the fact that "the Church loves and understands man's nature, his bodily and sensitive structure, as well as his mental powers." [20]

Similarly it has been designated as an element of her inner catholicity, "her comprehensive affirmation of the whole man, of human nature in its completeness, of the body as well as the soul, of the senses as well as the intellect. The mission of the Church is to the entire man." [21] The entire man comes from God and must therefore in due justice return to him. "God has a right to my spirituality," says Dom Panfoeder. "My powers of soul, my supernatural life of faith, my freedom as a child of God, I must devote to the liturgical service. God has a right to my individuality, to the special natural and supernatural graces allotted to me, to my truthfulness, my love, my obedience." And this declaration is prefaced by the words: "God has a sacred right to my entire human nature, to body and soul, to an homage uniting body and soul in harmony." [22]

It is this total service that the liturgy renders to God by means of its external expressions. The external signs and symbols, in the sacraments and sacrifice as well as in the liturgy of praise, address the senses by means of gestures, words and melodies. Through the senses they reach the intellect, where worship and faith become firmly

[20] Adam, *op. cit.*, p. 154
[21] *Ibid.*, p. 153
[22] *Das Persoenliche in der Liturgie*, pp. 18–19

grounded in an understanding of the truths presented, even if these are not fathomed. Appearing in their concrete form these truths excite also the will under the impulse of the emotions. Their very liturgical expression is an acting out of the truths, a striving for God through them. Thus all the faculties of man are harmoniously appealed to and blended in the liturgical worship. The latter actuates the emotions and the will, gives them means of expression, but always on the basis of the truths understood.

Were this not the case, the worship would have to become a pure external formalism or emotional aestheticism, or else an abstract vague inner action unconnected with life. It would cramp, sadden, instead of being the expression of soul. The Catholic liturgy as understood by the mind of the Church does not restrict or suppress in this way. It is a joyful lifting up of the heart, based on an enriching of the understanding through the natural and the revealed truths of God. Liturgical service is therefore whole-souled, whole-hearted, because it is a giving over to God of the whole man.

Men speak of Christianity, especially the Christianity of the Middle Ages, as that of a literal fleeing of the world, that of a complete suppression of the natural in man. Far from being such a repression of nature, Christianity is rather the elevation of the natural into the service of the supernatural, as is exemplified in the dual nature of Christ and in the structure of the liturgical worship of the Church. The various aspects of man's nature are not to be crushed out but rather to be properly subordinated to their higher end, God. The liturgy admirably portrays the proper blending, as we might call it, of the

natural and the supernatural in the life of the ordinary
Christian. It represents all the activities of nature as
properly directed to God. Hence, again, active participation by man is of the nature of liturgical worship. The
sacraments, indeed, have their efficacy in themselves. But
the proper disposition in the adult person is also indispensable. This is merely another way of stating that man's
nature must actively subject itself to the divine influences
operating in the liturgy and must co-operate with its
activity. Thus there is not the death of man as such, but
the death of the independent all-sufficient self, a self
which in creatures is really an absurdity. This proper los-
ing of self, which is from another standpoint the true
finding of self, is effected by means of entering into the
external action of the liturgy under the inspiration of its
inner sentiments and disposition which we have made our
own. In this way is the true supernatural life found.

That is the whole purpose of the liturgy, the transforming of the natural man into the supernatural child of
God, the taking possession again by God of what is truly
his own, and what was rebought by the great price of the
Redemption. To that end the redemptive work itself is
present in the liturgical mysteries, but in an outward garb
through which it may reach man after the manner of his
own nature. The divine enters into external form, so
that through this form it may enter into man and make
of him another Christ. "May the fasts we have devoted
to thy name, O Lord," asks a secret of Lent, "sanctify us
for the offering of this sacrifice: that what we show forth
in our outward observance may effectually operate within"
(Thursday of second week).

Being the means of expressing and enacting the di-

vine mysteries, the externals of the liturgy take on a
supreme importance, yet an importance that is ever in
proper relation to, even as it is derived from, this inner
divine reality. Both the inner and the outer aspects are
thus important in the mind of the liturgical revival, but
especially the inner since that has in our day been left
most out of mind. "It is chiefly with this reality that the
present liturgical movement is concerned," says a notable
pamphlet, whose paragraph we may quote as a summarizing conclusion. "Its aim is the renewal and intensification
of the religious life through the Christian mysteries, the
sacraments, and above all the eucharistic sacrifice; spiritual renaissance, therefore, by means of the liturgy. This
spiritual renaissance can come only through the liturgy,
not indeed by mere outward forms, however sacred and
venerable they may be. Nor yet can it be effected by
dogma or canon law or ethics; for these are never the
actual sources of supernatural life. They exert their influence even before conversion, they prepare the way for
supernatural life and guard it and aid it in its operation
and augmentation. But the liturgy as the celebration and
application of the mysteries of the redemption, actually
imparts supernatural life, restores it, perfects it." [23]

[23] Hellriegel-Jasper, *The True Basis of Christian Solidarity*, p. 24

CHAPTER V

THE LITURGICAL YEAR

I. Centered in Christ

THE daily round of sacrificial worship that the Church offers to God in her liturgy, specifically in the Mass and the divine office, varies in its general atmosphere from day to day in accordance with the succession of feasts that make up the liturgical year. In both missal and breviary there are prayers that recur regularly and are called the *ordinary* prayers of the Mass and the office. Many other prayers in each vary with the succession of feasts and seasons. They are called the proper of the season. It is these proper parts of Mass and office that constitute the characteristic elements of the liturgical year. The divine office is a radiation of the sacrifice of the Mass, so that the two belong together. Still more true is it that the liturgical year is inseparable from Mass and office. The liturgical year is realized precisely in the Church's daily offering of the sacrifice of the altar and of the divine praises to the Father. Without the Mass in particular the liturgical year would have no real liturgical significance. In treating here of the liturgical year we shall confine our attention chiefly to the proper parts that give expression to the varying aspects of the liturgical cycle, but it must always be kept in mind that the essential element in the liturgical year is the daily sacrifice. The variable parts of Mass and office that constitute the proper of the liturgy are as such only the background or stage setting within which the official worship of the Church unfolds itself, as within integral elements of her liturgy.

The liturgical year, beginning with the first Sunday of Advent and ending with the last Sunday after Pentecost, does not everywhere give equal emphasis to all the truths and mysteries of Christ's redemption. The different truths and mysteries of our faith are presented singly and in succession in both missal and breviary. One by one they are marshalled forth, commemorated, lived in the way that is peculiar to the divine liturgy of the Church. But in the ordered succession of these Christ is at all times central.

There is a rhythmic ebb and flow running through the liturgical year as through all else in this world. The universe of the heavens has its changing cycles and periods; the solar system gives us our four seasons and the earth gives us the regular recurrence of night and day, the rhythms of which are copied by the various forms of life here on earth. In life itself there have been the vast cycles of species coming into existence in geological time and again disappearing; the stages of youth, maturity, old age in the individual; the seasonal changes in many forms of life; the daily periods of wakefulness and sleep; and the smaller alternations of the rhythmic pulse-beat of breath and blood. Likewise in the liturgical or church year we have the larger seasonal divisions of Advent, Christmas, Epiphany, Septuagesima, Lent, Passiontide, Eastertide, and Pentecost with its longer aftermath; and again the regularly recurring Day of the Lord, and within each day the recurring rhythm of the different hours of the divine office. In all these cycles there is also a progressive change of sentiments and moods, based on special dogmas and mysteries, a changing series of eternal truths accompanied by a corresponding atmosphere of joy and adoration, admiration and wonder, sympathy and compunction, mortification and repentance. The whole spiritual life in all its wondrous variations thereby comes to view and realizes itself in the members of the mystical body ever in intimate union with their divine head Christ.

The symbolism of the sun as representative of Christ, the eternal Sun of Justice, has been mentioned in the preceding chapter. This symbolism finds realization in the prime fact that the liturgical year centers about Christ, just as do the seasons of the natural year around the celestial sun. "The liturgical year is the revolution of the year round Christ, the reproduction of the principal events of his life," as Dom Cabrol says.[1] It was mentioned before that the liturgy puts us in touch with the wonderful richness of the life of Christ. This is done particularly in the whole liturgical cycle. We there have a panorama of the life of Christ in its historical development from his birth to his resurrection. All the mysteries of the redemption are there placed before us, and in them we see the wonderful dispensation of God's love towards man.

"The first half of the cycle," says Dom Festugière in dividing the year from the standpoint of temporal duration, "that in which the series of mysteries is truly condensed, serves to give us in short, but according to their temporal succession, all the phases of the life of Jesus. In the second half, which commences supposedly after the career

[1] *Liturgical Prayer*, p. 171

of Jesus is ended, and which consequently symbolizes the life of the Church herself, the liturgy by means of the gospels freely composes a vista of sacred events that invite the Christians to contemplate the visage of their divine Model under the most varied aspects, and to imbue themselves with his teachings and examples." [2]

The liturgical year thus gives us a sublime manifestation of Christ's devotion to his Father. Christ permeates the liturgical year, even as he is always present in the liturgy. "Always, therefore, is Christ in the liturgy: Jesus Christ in the beatitude of heaven, Jesus Christ in his temporal abasement, Jesus Christ in the work of the redemption, Jesus Christ living in the Church in the course of the centuries. He is the immortal King of the ages, to whom the liturgy incessantly sings its hymn of honor and glory." [3] This is only to be expected, since the liturgy is the life of the Church, and since it is the mission of the Church by means of her liturgy to bring about an ever increasing fullness of Christ in her children, the members of this same Christ.

II. Living in Christ

The recurring celebration of the various mysteries of the life of Christ in the course of the liturgical cycle can therefore be no mere historical commemoration of the events of his career. Between a memorial celebration of the birth of our Savior on Christmas day and, say, of the birth of Washington as the father of our country, there must be all the difference that exists between the liturgy

[2] *Qu'est-ce que la liturgie?* p. 76
[3] Caronti, *The Spirit of the Liturgy*, pp. 42–43

as something divine-human and the purely earthly events of man. A celebration of the latter kind may also have its wholesome moral and psychological effect in the revitalization of the ideals surrounding the event commemorated, but it can have nothing more than that, nothing of the spiritual supernatural actuality that is of the nature of the Church's liturgy such as was described in the preceding chapter.

The symbolical representation of the historical Christ must have also the deeper purpose that exists in all the liturgical worship of his Church. It must have also the higher purpose of producing in the Church, in the members of the living body of Christ, the living actuality of Christ's mystical presence, and that, in all the richness of the life of the Redeemer and in all its aspects. As Abbot Caronti says so well: "The liturgical year, this drama of marvellous beauty, is undoubtedly the official glorification of God which it is the duty of the Church to enact. It has a great historical and dogmatic value; but in the intention of our mother the Church its purpose is also to produce in souls the moral effects which assimilate them to Christ. That which happens in the course of the liturgical periods must reproduce itself in the soul; and no event is celebrated, no truth is commemorated, no great occurrence is narrated, that is not destined to produce its sanctifying effect in the intimacy of the soul, that is not destined also to effect a living practice of some virtue." [4]

By truly participating in the liturgy, then, and drawing from it not only our prime spiritual inspirations but especially also a real share in the very life of Christ, in the

[4] *Op. cit.*, p. 43

divine life of God, the mysteries of the life of Christ, or of our salvation and redemption, become a living present actuality in our souls. That is the true meaning and true nature of the liturgical mysteries celebrated on the altar with the very powers of Christ himself—the enactment in the mystical body of the *opus redemptionis,* the divine redemptive action of the God-Man. "The epenetic liturgy, joint to the sacrificial liturgy, causes the person of Jesus to reign really and mystically over every one of our days; by means of the cycle of feasts, it reproduces mystically, every year here on earth, the phases of the life of Jesus. In fine, it continues really and mystically the prayer and the teaching of Jesus." [5]

These mysteries we enact in ourselves by means of the liturgy, that is, Christ enacts them in the members who are actively united to him in the celebration of the liturgical mysteries; our lives begin to reflect, to contain more and more in themselves, the very life of Christ; we live Christ. "I live, now not I; but Christ liveth in me." [6] This is at once the best possible response of ours to the saying of our Lord: "I have given you an example, that as I have done to you, so do you also," [7] of which we find an echo in the first letter of St. Peter, [8] quoted in the vespers chapter of the second Sunday after Easter: "Dearly beloved, Christ also suffered for us, leaving us an example that you should follow his steps."

The various phases of the liturgy of the year are therefore so many different attempts to enact the life of Christ in us, of developing more and more the presence of Christ in his mystical body, of entering upon the reality of the

[5] Dom Festugière, *op. cit.,* pp. 73–74   [7] John 13:15
[6] Gal. 2:20   [8] 2:21

divine mystery of which we treated in the preceding chapter—the realization of the Divine in man. "The ecclesiastical year," writes Dom Stricker, "represents the chief events of the work of the redemption in order that we may gratefully commemorate the various redemptive acts which God performed for us through Christ, and which have an eternal significance for us. In the ecclesiastical year we go through a continuous memorial celebration. But as we 'commemorate' these great acts of the Redemption in a holy fellowship, something wonderful transpires: the event that we celebrate becomes again a salutary presence in us. With that I have touched upon the profoundest essence of the ecclesiastical year. It is a continuous celebration of divine mystery." [9]

III. GROWTH IN CHRIST

We have seen before that the realization of the divine mystery in us, of the sacred union of members with Christ through participation in the liturgical mysteries, is something gradual that is destined for continuous growth and greater fulfilment. The gradual development of the mysterious life of Christ as unfolded in the liturgical cycle is thus admirably adapted to our nature insofar as our finite being cannot possess its fulness of the Divine at once. It cannot grasp the Divine in one act, it can never grasp or possess it fully, but it can always attain to a greater possession and realization of it. This realization in us, this union with God that is an increasing possession of God by us and of us by him, takes on a fuller form in the course of the year, as one after the other of the aspects

[9] *Mysterium*, p. 65

of the Divine are allowed to shed their efficacious rays of grace on our souls.

However, our nature ever remains finite, no matter how intimate and abundant is its participation in the divine life. It can never grasp this life adequately or in its totality in the course of any year, not even in the course of a lifetime, even while, just because it is finite, it is capable of ever realizing more than it does at any one time. Hence, again, it is admirably in harmony with our human nature that the liturgical cycle is repeated year after year, just as the divine sacrifice is repeated in the Church day after day. As we are unable to exhaust our capacity for the Divine in a day or a year, the Church of Christ, with the infinite patience and the tender love of her divine Founder, continues to present to us the divine means of living Christ, thereby truly fulfilling her mission of achieving the ever increasing plentitude of the Redeemer.

It is for this reason that the recurring daily and annual cycles of the liturgy never grow old for those who enter into their participation with the understanding and love of their divine Head. Ancient as the hills, the liturgy is still ever new, it has ever a new store of the divine life to hold out to our grasp, and with the recurring years the realization of its meaning grows ever richer. Therein lies the difference between the divine and the human, the inexhaustible and the purely finite. Taking our comparisons from our own life of today, we see just the opposite characteristic, e.g., in the popular cinema of our times. How many films should any thinking man care to see a second time, or a third or fourth? Even in different photoplays there is a certain recurrent sameness, which to the intelli-

gent mind becomes tiresome and deadening, so that the
constantly regular enthusiast or "movie fan" is by many
considered a bit abnormal or subnormal.

Now the eternal mysteries of God cannot really change
fundamentally. To have recourse to them regularly should
therefore be equally tiresome, were it not for the fact of
their inner spiritual vitality, of the divine efficacy in them.
If they realize their purpose one year, their possibilities
have not at all been exhausted; they have in fact been
enhanced, for their inner divine efficacy is infinite, and its
realization grows in proportion to the participation already
entered into wholeheartedly. As they recur the next year,
they will find in us an increased capacity for realizing
them, and will thus year after year produce a continuous
growth in the intimate possession of the Christ-life. They
build up stone upon stone in the human temple of God,
wherever one enters truly into the living spirit of the
annual liturgical celebration of the redemptive mysteries.
The growth which can thus be developed by the help of
the ecclesiastical cycle of the liturgy is endless; it admits
of continuous increase; it is truly a divine light that with
increasing years opens ever new vistas to the spiritual eye
of the soul.

Thus not only the Church at large, but also the individual, comes under the full influence of the divine energy
acting in the liturgy. "This succession of mystic seasons,"
said Dom Guèranger, "imparts to the Christian the elements of that supernatural life, without which every other
life is but a sort of death, more or less disguised." [10] The
individual soul, as well as the Church as an organic unity,
realizes this mystic growth by submitting to the guidance

[10] *The Liturgical Year, Advent,* p. 11

of the liturgical cycle. Both take their cue from it for their mode of developing the successive phases of Christ in the yearly routine. However, here again the submission is not merely passive, but is the same peculiar mixture of reception and active disposition and co-operation that was mentioned before. The liturgical year has been well styled the spiritual itinerary of the member of the mystical Christ. As the member goes on the journey as mapped out by the Church, Christ is indeed his sole support, but, not unlike the child that learns to walk while upheld by its mother's supporting arms, the individual must put forth effort step by step in co-operation with the workings of the Spirit of Christ in him.

In reference to the liturgical year the comparison has been made of the gardener who in the various types of work he must do is guided by the days and seasons of the solar year. "A gardener, who works with nature and her rhythm must indeed dig, sow, trim; but all the rest, and just that which is ultimately the energizing factor, is the work of the sun and of nature living by the sun. Under the influence of the latter the plant develops as of itself, it grows and blossoms and bears fruits, and is of a beauty and perfection that are striven after in vain by human effort and art. It is the gardener's part, that in his labors he be guided not by his own whims but by nature, that he expose his young shoots properly to the sun, which alone and freely gives them their increase. The Church is a gardener in her holy year, and everyone is in regard to his soul like a gardener if he associates himself simply and unaffectedly with the Church. He cannot force his sanctification by his own powers; he becomes holy. His holiness is an organically growing life of which the Lord says:

Which of you by taking thought, can add to his stature one cubit? (Matt. 6: 27)." [11]

IV. PARTS OF THE CHURCH YEAR

To many it may come as a surprise to hear that the church year as we now have it and understand it was perhaps more than any other aspect of the liturgy a matter of very gradual development. In the earliest Christian times even the feast of Christmas was entirely unknown. Yet elements of the church year go back directly to the Old Testament out of which the New was evolved. "The general ground-plan of the Christian church year," writes Dom Haering, "was already laid down in the Old Testament law pertaining to feast days, sabbaths, and the division of the weeks. The celebration of the highest Jewish feasts, Easter and Pentecost, was carried over from the Old Testament. But the idea of a church year was not clearly grasped until towards the end of the sixteenth century. And only after the civil year was made to begin with the first of January, in accordance with the Gregorian calendar, was the idea of a church year more clearly understood and adapted to pastoral needs." [12]

The greatest feast in the liturgical year is that of Easter: "This is the day that the Lord hath made, let us rejoice and be glad therein. Alleluia" (gradual, etc). It is also the first great festival in point of origin. After the first Pentecost the apostles went about preaching the gospel and "breaking bread." The Sabbath of the Old Law gave way to the Sunday because of the occurrence of the

[11] *Die Betende Kirche*, p. 219
[12] Haering, *Living with the Church*, p. xv

mysteries of the resurrection and the pentecostal descent on a Sunday. Each Sunday became a special commemoration of the redemptive mysteries of Christ, all of which were concentrated *in toto* in the eucharistic celebration. Naturally the annual recurrence of the anniversary of the first Easter was celebrated with special solemnity. It was called the Paschal mystery, which at the time included the events of the three days leading up to the resurrection itself. The institution of the Eucharist, the passion and death, and the resurrection—all of these received their anniversary commemoration in a solemn manner on the feast of Easter, even as they did with less solemnity every Sunday of the year.

The extension of the Easter solemnity over the forty days ending with Pentecost was natural in the light of the Gospel narratives. "The date of Easter necessarily determined that of Pentecost, which was kept on the fiftieth day after the resurrection. It was the festival of the descent of the Holy Ghost upon the apostles, who were then assembled in the Cenacle. These fifty days formed, as it were, an uninterrupted festival, a jubilee, a time of rejoicing, during which there was no fasting, all penitential exercises ceased, and even the very attitude of prayer was less humble." [18] In the spirit of Christ and in imitation of his suffering, a period of preparation for the Easter celebration was soon observed as a time of special penance and mortification. The length of this Lenten period varied greatly for a long time.

In the first Christian centuries apparently no celebration of the birth of Christ was held. In the East the feast of Epiphany came into vogue but it emphasized

[18] Cabrol, *Liturgical Prayer*, p. 156

the appearance of the Savior, the manifestations of his divinity as, *e.g.*, at his baptism in the Jordan. Only in the fourth century was the feast of Christmas instituted in the West and celebrated on December 25. Gradually a preceding period was set aside as one of preparation for the advent of the Redeemer on the anniversary of his birth, and the general structure of the Christmas period was modeled on that of the Easter period.

Thus the liturgical cycle of the church year, which leads the member of Christ through the successive phases of Christ's life, divides naturally into two periods, that of Christmas and that of Easter. The one centers in the mystery of the incarnation, Christ's coming onto the earth and his revelation of himself as the light of the world; and the other centers in the mystery of the completed redemption, his passion and death, which attain their glory in his resurrection and ascension, with the completing touch put on the Church by the descent of the Holy Ghost on Pentecost, after which comes the mystical reign of Christ in his Church to the end of time. Each of these two periods may be divided into a preparatory season, Advent and Septuagesima to Holy Week, respectively; a main period of the characteristic feasts, Christmas and Epiphany on the one hand, Easter, Ascension and Pentecost on the other; and the aftermath, the echo of the feasts, the Sundays after Epiphany and after Pentecost respectively.

In the preparatory periods the mood is one of compunction and mental preparation for the great grace and deliverance wrought by the mysteries of the main feasts. Hence they are periods of sorrow and penance and the color of the time is violet. The main feasts are feasts of joy and deliverance, true manifestations of the divine love, and the sentiments are those of joy and jubilation. Here the color of the day is white, with the red of flaming love for Pentecost. During the aftermaths we have a sort of continuing echo of the feasts themselves. There is no emphatic further mystery to celebrate in them, but rather the calm onward march of events in the life of Christ and the Church. Here the color of the time is green, symbolizing at once the absence of outstanding mysteries and the progressive development of the fruits of the previous feasts growing into a rich harvest of the life divine.

The mysteries and feasts thus celebrated in accord with the succession of liturgical seasons are said to make up the temporal cycle of the liturgical year, by all odds its most important part. There is also a so-called sanctoral cycle, in which various feasts of our Lord, less related to the mysteries celebrated in the temporal cycle, and of the blessed Virgin and of innumerable saints are celebrated. These feasts are usually dated in accordance with the secular calendar. In their celebration God is honored in his saints and they make intercession to him in our behalf. As with all the liturgy, their purpose is the glorification of God and the sanctification of man, but with the aid now of those members of Christ who have attained their final crown and resting place in the plenitude of their divine Head.

Even among these feasts there are some whose dates seem aptly chosen in relation to the temporal cycle. Thus the feast of the Immaculate Conception occurs shortly before Christmas and that of the Presentation in the Temple after Epiphany. The feasts of John, the beloved disciple, of the Holy Innocents, and of Stephen the first martyr, seem to fit in well with the celebration of Christ's appearance on earth; and the feasts of Corpus Christi and of the apostles Peter and Paul are well placed shortly after Pentecost, in the time commemorative of the spread and growth of the kingdom of God on earth. In a similar way the feasts of Christ the King, of All Saints and of All Souls come naturally towards the end of the Sundays after Pentecost, the end of the entire liturgical year. While the general placement of feasts in the temporal cycle follows the temporal succession of the events of Christ's life in a very foreshortened manner, there is one peculiar exception in the fixing of the feast of the Annunciation on March 25, nine months before the feast of Christ's birth. To this may be added the feast of the Visitation (July 2) and that of John the Baptist (June 24).

In the following two chapters we shall concern ourselves exclusively with the two great periods of the temporal cycle, making only an occasional reference to feasts that do not fall strictly within these periods.

CHAPTER VI

THE CHRISTMAS PERIOD

I. The Spirit of Advent

ADVENT is the time of preparation for the more fitting celebration of the Christmas mysteries, for the more intimate union of the members of the mystical body with their Head. But like all the liturgy this preparation is itself step by step a greater participation in the life of Christ. Moreover, with the broad vision that is characteristic of the liturgy, the Church on the first Sunday of her year bids us look ahead to the final consummation of all things in Christ. The Gospel of the first Sunday gives us the picture of the final coming of Christ as the judge of the living and the dead, towards which all the endeavors of the member of Christ must ever be directed. The vision of Advent is therefore all-embracing; it commemorates not only the first coming of Christ upon this earth, but looks forward also to his final coming in glory at the end of the world.

While the four weeks of Advent have been set aside by the Church as a period of preparation for the coming celebration of Christmas, the forward-looking eye of the Church has not been in abeyance in the previous period of the preceding cycle. Even while then celebrating the events subsequent to Christmas, while still living out the later mysteries of the liturgical year, the Church, the loving guardian of the continuous growth of Christ in souls, has been directing an occasional eye to the next liturgical coming of Christ, to the next renewal of the Christmas mystery. Thus as early as March 25, we have the Feast of the Annunciation of the blessed Virgin Mary, which is preceded by the feast of the archangel Gabriel. The two feasts come together in the Vespers, the antiphons of which beautifully render the dialogue between Mary and Gabriel. It is indeed the first announcement of the glad tidings of great joy that shall be realized on the next Christmas night. The little chapter of the Vespers foreshadows the great event to come most appropriately in the prophetic words of Isaias, the Advent prophet: "Behold a virgin shall conceive and bear a son, and his name shall be called Emmanuel." The antiphon of the Magnificat quotes from Luke the evangelist of the Christmas happenings, and the address is charming in its simple approach: "The Holy Ghost shall come upon thee, Mary, and the power of the Most High shall overshadow thee," while the commemoration of the feast of St. Gabriel gives us the touching consent of Mary, which marks the moment of her divine conception: "The archangel Gabriel said unto Mary: No word shall be impossible with God. And Mary answered: Behold the handmaid of the Lord, be it done to me according to thy word. And the angel departed from her." Well might he depart for his mission was accomplished. But the Precursor of Christ, John the Baptist, whose voice resounds in the liturgy of Advent, was born half a year before Christ, and so we have on the 24th of June the feast of his birth. The predominant note here is one of joy, "the grace of spiritual joys" (collect), for again we hear the announcement of the glad tidings. God is therefore asked that the "Church be glad at the birth of blessed John the Baptist, through whom she knew the author of her new birth, our Lord Jesus Christ" (postcommunion). Both of these feasts in their note of grateful joy, and in their pointing to the birth of Christ, are a distant foreshadowing of the next Advent. They are distant anticipations of the theme of the Advent to. follow, and in spirit belong to this time.

Joy, however, is not the only note of Advent. There is, indeed, as time goes on an increasing note of rejoicing at the coming of the Redeemer, but there is also the consciousness of the sinful condition of humanity, of our own helpless condition. The Redeemer was made necessary for us because of our sinful natures. Of ourselves we can do nothing deserving of supernatural merit. Left to ourselves we should perish miserably, and we have brought this condition upon ourselves through our own wilful disobedience. There is, however, the great longing and expectation for deliverance, based on the consciousness of our own helpless condition together with the promise of God for our deliverance. Advent thus gives solid food for our faith in the knowledge of the consequences of sin and of the coming of the Redeemer; food for the nourishing of hope in the possibility of redemption and in the knowledge of God's willingness to help us; and food for charity in the inspiration thereby given us to turn our wills towards God, in the willingness to do what is necessary for this deliverance.

"No time perhaps is so rich in life and lyric beauty as Advent. Now the Church is rejoicing like a child, now praying with the longings of a spouse, now gazing won-

deringly with the love of those in eternal union. With
Isaias, the evangelist of the Old Law, who sings the
glory of the coming time of redemption with a profound
emotion and inspiration, she advances toward the great
day. His book furnishes the texts for lessons of the
breviary and for many lessons of the missal." [1] Along
with the venerable figure of Isaias we also have that of
the forerunner, John the Baptist, ever calling to us in the
liturgy. As he sent forth his cry to the people of his time,
so the liturgy exhorts us today in his selfsame words: "Prepare ye the way of the Lord, make straight his paths"
(versicle of Benedictus, et al.). Both Isaias and John are
types of the Church, and in their words the Church herself, our loving mother, is exhorting us. She is the great
prophet who announces Christ anew to all the world;
and she is the divine preacher of penance, of a proper
renunciation of the world, of devotion to Christ. She is
truly preparing his way in the liturgy of Advent in particular, and bearing Christ in her bosom at all times for
our participation. She is likewise the fortunate Bethlehem out of which divine Wisdom will come to visit us
and all men of good will, bringing them abundance of
peace even on this earth.

The season of Advent therefore prepares us for celebrating properly the coming of the Redeemer. But it is
to mean for us not merely a commemorative celebration
of the historical event that transpired two thousand years
ago, as we well know by this time. At the guidance of
the Church we indeed hark back to the circumstances of
the past under which Christ was born unto this earth,
and we rejoice at this great event. But the event means

[1] *Die Betende Kirche*, p. 225

little to us unless Christ is also born in our own souls; and Advent becomes a spiritual reality to us only if it also prepares us for the more intimate coming of Christ into each of our souls, for a special renewal of Christ in the members of his mystical body. For this reason, the liturgy of Advent recalls to us not merely the penitential exhortations once addressed to the chosen people by John, but in reality wishes to exhort us here and now to penance and compunction, by which alone we can come to a new realization of Christ in our hearts.

Again, the whole liturgy is but a preparation for the final coming of Christ at the last judgment day, which for his faithful members will be the most glorious coming of all. This last coming is indeed the culmination towards which the whole mission of Christ tends. The first coming of Christ was only a step towards the last. A threefold parallel thus runs through the liturgy of Advent: the historical coming of Christ to this earth as the redeemer; then the coming of Christ to us, that is, the mystical birth of Christ in our souls, which was made possible by the first coming, of which the first coming is used as a type and inspiration; and the final coming of Christ, the glory of which will accrue to all those in whom the second birth is increasingly realized.

II. The Advent Liturgy

All of these phases of the whole life of Christ are introduced to us at the very threshold of the liturgical year, the first Sunday of Advent. This Sunday's liturgy joins expectation of Christ with a picture of the last things. It directs our minds at once to the Redeemer and what he means to the world, to our own inner hearts, and to the coming of Christ on the final day of judgment. Most fittingly does the gospel give us this picture of the final coming of the Judge, when we "shall see the Son of man coming in a cloud with great power and majesty." Thus at the very beginning we survey the world at large, the whole dispensation of God towards man, and we envision the final event towards which everything in between should converge and aim. It is for this final coming that the first descent occurred, and our celebration each year is both an echo of the first and a foreshadowing of the last.

Every year Christ mystically performs these comings in the bosom of his Church. His present coming is a mystical continuation of the event first enacted two thousand years ago, and it is an anticipation, if not indeed a beginning, of what shall be accomplished at his last coming in glory. Thus on the vigil of Christmas, which as it were sums up in concentrated form all the ardor and spirit of the whole of Advent, the collect of the day reads: "O God, who dost gladden us by the annual expectation of our redemption, grant that we, who now with joy receive thine only-begotten Son as our redeemer, may without fear behold him coming as our judge, our Lord Jesus Christ thy Son."

On the first Sunday of Advent the true member of Christ can look forward calmly to all this. Hence the introit and the offertory address the same words of confidence to God: "To thee have I lifted up my soul: in thee, O my God, I put my trust, let me not be ashamed." In the epistle St. Paul reminds us that "it is now the hour for us to rise from sleep," the sleep of the night of sin and spiritual apathy. "For now our salvation is nearer than when we believed. The night is passed, and the day is at hand." And he exhorts us "to walk honestly as in the day, . . . to cast off the works of darkness and put on the armor of light . . . put ye on the Lord Jesus Christ." The collect sends forth a most touching appeal to Christ himself: "Stir up thy might, we beseech thee, O Lord, and come: that from the threatening dangers of our sins we may be rescued by thy protection, and saved by thy deliverance." Postcommunion and secret pray that through the eucharistic sacrifice we may "prepare with becoming honor for the approaching solemnities of our redemption" and that "these sacred mysteries may cleanse us by their mighty power and make us to approach with greater purity to him who is their source."

Thus we see how on the very first day of Advent the theme of our own interior life is struck. The transformation that Christ caused in the world at large by bridging the span between the Old and the New Covenants, by ushering in his own reign and subduing the kingdom of Satan, is to take place in us through the mystical coming of Christ into our own hearts. It is another phase of the fundamental messianic note of all the liturgy: that we put off the old man and put on the new, a process which is to go on at all times with increasing efficacy and fervor.

As this process cannot go on in us without our consent, since no man is saved without his own co-operation, and as the liturgy essentially calls for active co-operation with the mystical action that it presents to us in the sacred mysteries, we must naturally be made more conscious of our need, of our own helplessness, and thus be brought to seek more actively our only redemption. The lessons of the first nocturn of the Sunday ostensibly narrate the desolate condition of the people of Israel before the coming of the Messiah. But this is also our condition whenever we put our hope in ourselves after the fashion of the people of the world. Of ourselves we, too, are "laden with iniquity, a wicked seed, ungracious children, who have forsaken the Lord" and in our actions "have blasphemed the Holy One of Israel." Hence we too are afflicted with disease: "the whole head is sick, and the whole heart is sad . . . wounds and bruises and swelling sores . . . are not bound up nor dressed nor fomented with oil," as long as we look only to ourselves.

Meditating on this theme for the week and thus become more conscious of our sad condition, our hearts are prepared to seek their salvation more earnestly from the Lord. Touchingly we again beseech him to come: "Come, O Lord, visit us in peace" (first Vespers, second Sunday) . . . "show us, O Lord, thy mercy and grant us thy salvation" (offertory) . . . "whereas we have no merits to plead in our behalf, do thou succor us by thy protection" (secret). Turning with such sentiments to the Lord, we are filled with the joy of anticipation: "Arise, O Jerusalem, and stand on high: and behold the joy that cometh to thee from thy God (communion); behold in the clouds of heaven the Lord will come with great power, alleluia. . . . If he tarry, await him, for he will come and will not delay" (antiphons of Lauds).

With this increasing confidence, we cannot but break out in a jubilant exultation on *Gaudete* (third) Sunday: "Rejoice in the Lord always: again I say, rejoice" (introit), for "the Lord is nigh" (epistle). The gospel assures us on the word of John the Baptist that the Lord is truly coming, and so we turn to our weaker brethren to assure also them: "Say to the faint-hearted: Take courage, and fear not: behold our God will come and save us" (communion). In the consciousness of this certainty and of our own duty we pray to God after celebrating the holy sacrifice and partaking of the sacred mysteries that "these divine helps by atoning for our sins may prepare us for the coming festival" (postcommunion). Most appropriately does the Church turn to Mary, the divinely chosen instrument of the coming of Christ, and our representative in giving human co-operation to the work of redemption: "Blessed art thou, O Mary, who hast believed the Lord: those things shall be wrought in thee which were spoken to thee by the Lord, alleluia" (antiphon of the Magnificat).

In Mary we have a type of the Church herself, who in the liturgy is now bringing forth the Redeemer anew "for us and for our salvation." Hence the increased part that Mary has in the third and fourth Sundays of Advent. They were in fact preceded by the special feast of the Immaculate Conception (December 8), when we paused with the Church from the stricter Advent theme to give glory to God in the queen of his saints. Both vigil and feast are replete with the joy of her union with God, who in her person anticipated our own salvation by her special privilege of freedom from all taint of sin. With her the Bride of Christ sings out: "I will greatly rejoice in the Lord . . . for he hath clothed me with the garments of salvation" (introit of the feast), and in the collect of the day the same Church asks God in behalf of all of us: "that, as by the foreseen death of this thy Son thou didst preserve her from all stain, so too thou wouldst permit us, purified through her intercession, to come unto thee."

The love of Mary for her adopted children and the power of her intercession add greatly to our confidence. But in the midst of this joyful assurance we may never neglect to look properly to our sinful selves so that we may become fit to receive the redeeming grace abundantly. The Ember days come between the third and fourth Sundays. Ember days in general are seasonal pauses for special mortification and fasting with their resultant purification of soul. In Advent they harmonize excellently with the spirit of the season. Being aware of the "approaching solemnity of our redemption," which is to "confer upon us assistance in this present life and bestow the rewards of eternal blessedness" (first collect of Ember Wednesday), we enter upon the salutary fast of these days, praying God that these "fasts may be acceptable to thee, O Lord, and by atoning for us make us worthy of thy grace and bring us to thy eternal promises" (secret, Ember Wednesday). We have learned our lesson, and we know that the deliverance was made necessary by our own sinfulness, we realize "that we are afflicted because of our wickedness," and ask "that we may be consoled" by the visitation of Christ, praying God "that we, who are depressed by our old bondage under the yoke of sin, may be freed by the new birth of thine only begotten son for which we look" (collects, Ember Saturday).

As the time approaches, we grow increasingly confident of the Lord's coming, and joyously we again address Mary: "Hail, Mary, full of grace: the Lord is with thee" (offertory, fourth Sunday). "All flesh shall see the salvation of God," John the Baptist tells us in the gospel, and exultingly we sing forth in the introit: "Let the earth be opened and bud forth a Savior. The heavens show forth the glory of God, and the firmament declareth the work of his hands. Glory be to the Father, etc."

In the meantime we have been crying more earnestly to Christ as the time approaches: 'O Adonai, and leader of the house of Israel . . . come and redeem us; O Root of Jesse . . . come and deliver us; O Key of David . . . come and bring forth the captive from his prison house; O Dawn of the East . . . come and enlighten; O Emmanuel our King . . . come to save us, O Lord our God" (the great O antiphons). On the vigil of the great feast we fully "anticipate the adorable birthday" (secret), and our joy is complete. "This day you shall know that the Lord will come and save us; and in the morning you shall see his glory" (introit). And now realizing better the internal birth that should take place in the celebration of the great feast, we pray "that the birth we have reviewed of thine only begotten Son on whose heavenly mysteries we are fed, may be our very breath of life" (postcommunion).

III. THE CHRISTMAS OCTAVE

Finally the day has arrived. The first part of Advent had told us of our redemption and who he is that is to redeem us. The second part told us that he is near, and prepared us for his immediate coming; the vigil itself trembled in the anticipation of the joy that was to come. Christmas itself announces the arrival. The promised sanctifier is now here, vested with the sublime dignity of the sonship of God, creating other children for his divine Father. So much suffices to see how far from the truth is the statement of the modernist, who judges the world from the angle of his own little ideas and makes his pronouncements with such supreme self-confidence: "The Christmas festival belongs, of course, essentially to the people and the fireside. The churches hold services on the morning of December 25, in which there is probably more singing and less preaching than usual, but what the congregations mean by the holiday is not and does not need to be celebrated in any ecclesiastical building." [2] Christmas celebration for us does indeed belong to the people—as also all the liturgy, like Christ's redemption, is for the people; but it is truly understood and expressed and enacted only around the altar of Christ in his Church.

In the darkness of the longest night, in the night of the year, the midwinter season when all the earth is dead and darkness is preponderant, in the darkness of the day of human existence when man was still enshrouded in the obscuring veil of Satan, God "made this most holy night to shine forth with the brightness of the true light" (collect, midnight Mass). Then was realized in time what had been true in all eternity: "The Lord said to me: thou art my Son, this day have I begotten thee" (introit); it was the God-man come to save us: "He who was born man shone forth also as God" (secret, second Mass). This is indeed a great grace for all of us, as St. Paul tells us in the epistle for midnight: "Dearly beloved: The grace of God our savior hath appeared to all men instructing us" how to live, so that we may calmly look forward to the ultimate "blessed hope and coming of the glory of the great God and our savior Jesus Christ" on the last day of judgment. The gospel tells us the simple story of the birth of the Child, but shows the glory of the event

[2] *The New Republic*, December 31, 1925, p. 130

in the incidents of the shepherds and the angels. Good
tidings indeed: So "let the heavens rejoice, and let the
earth be glad before the face of the Lord" (offertory·).
The time of our own regeneration, too, has come with this
feast, and lovingly does the Church pray to God "that
by thy grace, through this sacred intercourse, we may be
found like unto him in whom our nature is united to thee"
(secret).

The message of the first, the midnight Mass, is repeated
in the second, the Mass of daybreak. Like the sun that
is just about to rise, so "a light shall shine upon us this
day; for the Lord is born to us" (introit); and we pray
to God "that we, who are bathed in the new light of thy
Word-made-flesh, may show forth in our actions what by
faith shines in our minds" (collect). St. Paul tells us
that our justice comes not from ourselves, but that we
have received the Holy Ghost, whom God poured forth
abundantly upon us through Jesus Christ (epistle). Thus
we have an increasing understanding of that which our
poor minds could not grasp at once, and the marvel of it
grows upon us. He who came is indeed "the Wonderful,
God, the Prince of Peace, the Father of the world to
come: of whose reign there shall be no end" (introit).
With Mary in the gospel we ponder the words in our
heart, and with the shepherds we glorify God and praise
him for all the things we have heard and seen. "This
is the Lord's doing: and it is wonderful in our eyes. Alleluia, alleluia" (gradual). Truly "may the new sacramental life which this birthday feast specially brings us
ever revive us, O Lord, whose wonderful birth hath
banished the old man" (postcommunion).

The third Mass is celebrated in the full light of day

and with the fullest realization of what has transpired. "A Child is born to us, and a Son is given to us," but it is he upon whose shoulders rests the government of us (introit). He is indeed true God (epistle) and Savior of all men. Today "all the ends of the earth have seen the salvation of our God"; therefore "sing joyfully to God, all the earth" (gradual). And celebrating "the new birth of the only begotten Son," we pray with increasing fervor for the abundant birth of Christ also in our souls, which alone "may set us free, whom the old bondage doth hold in thrall under the yoke of sin" and alone may "sanctify" us and bring "to us the giver of immortality" (collect, secret, postcommunion). The Christmas message of the Mass is echoed out farther in the divine office that follows. "With the Lord there is merciful forgiveness; and with him a plentiful redemption," sings an antiphon of the vespers psalms, and the antiphon of the Magnificat sums up the universal joy: "This day Christ is born; this day the Savior hath appeared; this day the angels sing on earth, the archangels rejoice; this day the just exult saying: Glory be to God in the highest, alleluia."

Of the feasts immediately following Christmas, those of St. Stephen and St. John have the principal liturgical value. In the protomartyr Stephen we see the first full attainment of the glory of Christ, the first stone of the living edifice of the growing Church of God. Christ's birth is but a prelude to, and for the sake of, his fuller, more glorious appearance after the battle of this life. St. Stephen, on the point of martyrdom for his faith, "looking up steadfastly to heaven saw the glory of God, and Jesus standing on the right hand of God" (epistle, also communion, and alleluia verses), while the gospel again speaks of the final coming of the Lord. In St. John we see realized the burning love of Christ, the perfect presence of Christ in his disciples. Hence St. John even on earth receives a special foretaste of eternal bliss in resting on the bosom of his Master, who says of him: "So I will have him to remain till I come" (gospel). The feast of the Holy Innocents commemorates an historical incident connected with the birth of the Savior, but it also gives us the lesson of Christ, that we must die unto ourselves in order to live to Christ. "O God," prays the collect, "whose praise the martyred innocents confessed this day, not in speech but in their death: destroy in us the evil of all vice, that our lives may show forth in our deeds that faith in thee which our lips profess."

The Sunday within the octave of Christmas re-echoes the thoughts of Christmas, but with further development. In the gospel the high priest Simeon and the prophetess Anna publicly recognize the Child and preach the Redemption, indicating the unworldly nature of his kingdom. We also read there that Christ "grew and waxed strong, full of wisdom"; and we pray to God: "Do thou direct our actions according to thy good pleasure: that we may deserve to abound in good works in the name of thy beloved Son" (collect). Even now the first fruits of Christ's manifestation are showing themselves in us and in the world: "God hath sent the Spirit of his Son into your hearts" (epistle); and "they are dead that sought the life of the Child" (communion). The feast of the Circumcision reveals to us further the true character of the Redeemer, the God-man. The epistle tells us that the Savior "gave himself for us" and in the gospel we see the first shedding of his divine blood. His submission to the Mosaic law is an example of obedience for us, and brings Christ closer to our human conditions of life. "O admirable interchange!" says the first antiphon of Lauds. "The Creator of mankind, assuming a living body, deigned to be born of a virgin; and becoming man without man's aid, bestowed on us his Divinity." This sums up the message of Christmastide.

IV. THE EPIPHANY

In the feast of the Holy Name we see manifested to us the glory of the name of the Redeemer: "In the name of Jesus let every knee bow of those that are in heaven, on earth, and under the earth; and let every tongue confess that the Lord Jesus Christ is in the glory of God the Father" (introit). The vigil of Epiphany recalls the mysteries of Christmas in the words of the Sunday within the octave, and leads to the second great feast of the Christmas period, the Epiphany, or of the appearance of the Savior in the world. It is celebrated with an octave, and is followed by an aftermath of six Sundays. Epiphany is the feast of the manifestation of the divine character of Christ. But again it commemorates not merely the historical manifestations, it implies also the continuous revelation, the development of Christ in the souls of the faithful.

The words of Isaias in the epistle of Epiphany are addressed to all of us: "Arise, be enlightened, O Jerusalem; for thy light is come, and the Lord is risen upon thee. For behold darkness shall cover the earth, and a mist the people: but the Lord shall arise upon thee, and this glory shall be seen upon thee." "Behold the Lord," the introit announces, "the Ruler is come," who must govern also our hearts. Hence we pray God that "we may be led on to contemplate the beauty of thy majesty" (collect). May we too follow the star like the Wise Men of the gospel and say with them the words which the Church uses as her alleluia and communion verses: "We have seen his star in the East and are come with gifts to adore the Lord. Alleluia." The Epiphany, as the feast of the appearance of the Divinity in the form of man, is the feast of the union of God and man, therefore also of our union with God through Christ. This union became reality in the liturgical mystery, and so the mystery of Epiphany is also that of the Church and of ourselves in special degree. At the very dawn of day the Church exultantly chanted the canticle of the Benedictus to the following antiphon: "This day is the Church united to the heavenly Spouse, for Christ in the Jordan washes away her sins: the Magi run to the royal nuptials with their gifts: and the guests of the feast are gladdened by the water changed into wine, alleluia." The Magnificat antiphon mentions the same happenings in other words. Thus celebrating the manifestations of the divine powers of the God-man and realizing our own union with him in greater degree, we shall be better prepared to walk with him in the way that will be pointed out so soon in the second period of the liturgical cycle.

In the Sundays after Epiphany the commemoration of the appearance of God among men is continued and the manifestations multiply. The Sunday within the octave shows us the Christ as a boy of twelve revealing his divine wisdom in the temple and entering upon his God-given work. "Did you not know," the communion verse quotes from the gospel, "that I must be about my Father's business?" On the octave day John the Baptist tells us of the testimony of the Father and the Spirit at the baptism of Christ; and the postcommunion prays for the increasing manifestation of Christ in us: "That we may discern with a pure vision and receive with worthy affection the mystery in which thou wouldst have us partake."

The following Sundays continue the manifestations of the divine power of Christ. We have the miracle performed at the marriage of Cana (second Sunday), the healing of the leper (third Sunday), Christ calming the waves (fourth Sunday). The nature of the kingdom of Christ is exemplified in the gospel parables telling us of the growing together of wheat and cockle, and of the mustard seed growing into a tree (fifth and sixth Sundays).

At the end of the Christmas period the feast of the Purification is celebrated, also called Candlemas. It commemorates in one and the same feast the purification of the blessed Virgin, the presentation of Christ in the temple, and the meeting of the Christchild with the prophets Simeon and Anna. Today the Mass is preceded by the blessing of candles and the procession, the liturgical texts of which mingle with the theme of the feast also the liturgical meaning of light and candles. A collect of the blessing asks God "that by the light of thy grace we may inwardly attain to that which thou grantest us outwardly to venerate by this yearly service." The Christmas atmosphere is specially preserved by using the antiphons of Lauds of the feast of the Circumcision for the first Vespers of this day. The text of the Mass is replete with allusions to the temple event and the *Nunc dimittis* of Simeon,

"Now dost thou dismiss thy servant, O Lord, according to thy word in peace; because my eyes have seen thy salvation," occurs both in the ceremony of blessing and in the tract of the Mass. The keynote of the celebration is indeed the verse: "A light to the revelation of the gentiles, and the glory of thy people Israel." It is a further manifestation, greatly enhanced by the liturgical ceremony surrounding the celebration of the feast. In the Mass we apply the theme to our own spiritual life beseeching God that "as thine only begotten Son was this day presented in the temple in the substance of our flesh, so thou wouldst grant that we too, with purified souls, may be presented unto thee" (collect).

Therewith the Christmas period is ended. It is primarily a growing manifestation of the divine character of the Redeemer, and so it also prepares for a better understanding of the significance of the coming events of his passion and death. The Easter period brings these before us together with the mysteries of the Resurrection and Ascension, and thus presents us with the complete messianic work of Christ. In a way we may say, therefore, that the Christmas period is but preparatory to it while being at the same time its true beginning, just as the incarnation is the preliminary step to the passion and resurrection and at the same time the real beginning of the messianic work of redemption.

CHAPTER VII

THE EASTER PERIOD

I. Remote Preparation

THE liturgy of the Christmas period was filled with the glory of the Christchild, the God-man. Once the preparatory season of Advent was over, a note of jubilation ran throughout, and it was enhanced by the richer melodiousness of the chant in comparison with the more sober melodies that initiate the Easter period. For the members of the mystical body of Christ, Christmas was filled with joy, for they were in intimate possession of their true happiness. Christ had again come to all with the charming lovableness of innocent childhood.

In the light of what is now to follow, we can very well compare the atmosphere of the Christmas liturgy with the experiences of the soul that in the first transports of a life given over to Christ tastes of the sweetness of the heavenly bridegroom. No note of sadness, no real sorrows, mar the joyful flow of Christmastide. But as every soul that experiences the first joys of devotion to Christ must still go through the crucible of fire, must stand the test of spiritual dryness, of renewed temptations of all kinds, of the ordinary practices of Christian asceticism, or of a dryness in which all the consolation of spiritual joy seems to have fled from these practices, so too the first joys of the liturgical year with their happy faith must stand this test of Christ.

In the second period of the liturgical cycle we have left the sweet dreamland of the divine Christchild, and in the mature Man we must now face the grim reality of life. There our faith must meet its true test. We see Christ stripped of all the glory of his divinity, dragged into the lowest mire of earth. Like him we, too, must realize that the unalloyed joy, the honeymoon, of our renewed union with him is ended. We must still do our part to merit an increase of Christ in ourselves. The old man is not stripped off at one resolve. We must still show the stuff we are made of by practicing the conquest of self for Christ, curbing the desires of the flesh, doing violence to ourselves, even as Christ suffered violence. Only then shall we have shown that we are indeed firmly engrafted upon Christ and merit to be children of his resurrection and finally to be sharers of his return to the throne at the right of his Father.

In the Easter period, then, we meet the mature Christ entering upon the actual accomplishment of his bitter, but still glorious, mission; and we see the Church calling to us to enact in ourselves, in a mystical but real manner, this same mission. We are now called to realize in a special manner the truth preached by St. Paul, that we must all suffer and die with Christ so that we may also rise with him. The Easter period presents to us the double aspect of Christ's missionary career, that of his humiliation and that of his glory, the one ending with Christ's burial and the other beginning with his resurrection. In each of these stages, again, we have two steps. With his resurrection Christ's exaltation still remains incomplete. The feast of the Ascension, when Christ again enters into the realm of his celestial glory at the right of the Father, where he sits as judge, gives us the final stage in what we might call the personal rehabilitation of the divine Son of the eternal Father. In the same way we have the completer humiliation in the passion and death of Christ in Holy Week, which is preceded by the minor humiliation from Lent to his passion.

But there are three other weeks preceding Lent and commencing with Septuagesima. These are preparatory to what follows. On the other hand, the Easter period is not ended with the full personal triumph of Christ on Ascension day. We have seen that the Holy Ghost must descend upon the Church, which is then to enter upon her career as the continuer of Christ and his mission through all time. Pentecost sees the Holy Ghost come down upon the Church, and then the Sundays after Pentecost commence, which in point of time occupy about half the year. In these Sundays we have the Church, the kingdom of God on earth, performing her messianic mission. Near the end of this time we have most appropriately the feasts of All Saints and All Souls, both being feasts of the final realization of the plenitude of Christ—and the feast of Christ the King, who will reign triumphantly for all eternity over his glorified Church, as he reigns now over the Church as she is still passing through her earthly sojourn.

The Easter period is introduced by the three Sundays of Septuagesima, Sexagesima, and Quinquagesima, in which the austere melancholy of the chant of the introits admirably renders the required setting for the sacrifice. The liturgy again harks back to the time previous to the

coming of the Redeemer, particularly in the lessons of
the divine office. But this is by no means a mere echo
of Advent: it has a deep purpose of its own. While the
liturgy of Christmas has spoken and prayed for the development of Christ in us, the Easter period now enters
like Christ himself more especially upon its messianic
mission of transforming the man of sin into the member
of Christ.

Hence the three figures of Adam, Noe, and Abraham
are brought before us in the office of the first three weeks.
In Adam we are reminded of the fact of original sin
and its consequences both in the history of mankind and
in our own lives. In the story of Noe we see the terrible
wickedness of actual sin, its visitation by God in the deluge,
and the protection of God over those who conform to his
will. In Abraham we see the promise of the Redeemer
given to him whose seed will remain faithful to God, the
type of the sacrifice of Christ in Isaac, and Abraham's
presence at the unbloody sacrifice of Melchisedech the
priest, who is likewise a type of the eternal Priest to come.
We are thus at once made conscious of the great need
of our salvation, and in the types of sacrifice we are prepared for the bloody immolation of the divine Son of
God and the continued unbloody sacrifice of his Church.
Both the great cause and its means are thus held out to us
by the liturgy at the very beginnings of this period.

Well does the liturgy of the Mass echo this. "The
groans of death surrounded me," exclaims Christ, the
Christian soul, the entire Church, in the introit of Septuagesima, "the sorrows of hell encompassed me: and in my
affliction I called upon the Lord, and he heard my
voice. . . . I will love thee, O Lord, my strength . . .

my refuge and my deliverer." Touchingly does the Church pray for us "that we, who are justly afflicted for our sins may be mercifully delivered for the glory of thy name" (collect), while St. Paul tells us plainly in the epistle: "So run that you may obtain." The tract again cries out: "Out of the depths I have cried to thee, O Lord: Lord, hear my voice," while the secret prays that we may be cleansed. The gospel, telling us of the hiring of the laborers at different hours, gives us to understand that the redemption of Christ is for all time. Whether our time is the sixth or the eleventh hour, we know not; but of this we are certain: that all of us can obtain the full reward if we work faithfully for the Lord.

When Sexagesima Sunday arrives we have gone the first remote step. We can confidently remind God "that we put not our trust in aught that we do of ourselves" (collect), and hence we do not hesitate to call upon him with full confidence in the words of the introit: "Arise, why sleepest thou, O Lord? arise, and cast us not off to the end. Why turnest thou thy face away, and forgettest our trouble? Our belly hath cleaved to the earth: arise, O Lord, help us and deliver us." In the epistle St. Paul gives us a detailed picture of his sufferings for Christ, of his reward even in this life, and tells us that the Lord wills us to suffer the sting of our infirmities here on earth. The gospel is that of the sower of the seed. It reminds us that the seed was for all and that the seed in our heart must bear fruit, despite temptations. For this the postcommunion prays: Refreshed by the Sacrament, therefore by Christ, may we serve God by a life well pleasing unto him!

The Quinquagesima Mass continues to pray for God's

protection and delivery of us from the bonds of sin (introit, collect) and asks that the Lord teach us his justification (offertory). The epistle gives us St. Paul's sublime passages on charity, which endureth all things and never falleth away. The gospel most beautifully tells how Christ spoke to the apostles of his coming passion, how they understood not and were blind, and how Christ thereafter healed a blind man who had cried for mercy from Jesus. We are now upon the threshold of Lent. May we, through the mercy of Christ, be healed from our blindness, so that we may see and understand!

II. Lent to Passion Sunday

Lent calls us to a special practice of the Christian life, a sort of renewal in which the Church leads us nearer to her ideal. The liturgy traces out a program of penance for us, a minimum of which is demanded of all by the Church, while more than the minimum is urged upon us. Lent is for all Christians a sort of official time of retreat or spiritual exercises, in which the whole army of the Church militant, like our worldly armies, enters in a body upon a period of special drill and training. The model is Christ, and the drill master also is Christ speaking in the liturgy.

Of old this was the official time for preparation of the neophytes or catechumens for baptism, which would then take place on Holy Saturday. Again Lent was a special time for penance on the part of public sinners. They had ashes imposed upon them at the beginning of this season and went through special works of penance until the public reconciliation took place on Maundy Thursday.

The liturgy of Lent shows distinct traces of these two aspects of the season, but especially of the former and of the progressive preparation of the candidates for baptism unto a state of soul more worthy of the great grace that was to be theirs. In later times this has come to be a call to all the faithful for the renewal of their baptismal vows, a renewal of the spirit of which the liturgy of baptism is eloquent. Thus Pope Leo the Great addressed the faithful in the fifth century: "When have we more cause for recourse to the divine means of salvation than when the very mysteries of the redemption are brought before our souls in the recurrent flow of time? In order that we may celebrate them more worthily, we should prepare for them by the wholesome fast of forty days. But not only those who are to attain the new life through the mystery of Christ's death and resurrection in the rebirth of baptism, but likewise all people who are already reborn, will necessarily and with much profit take up the defensive arms of this sanctification: the former in order to receive what they do not yet possess, the latter in order to preserve what has already been received."

We are initiated into the spirit of Lent by the imposition of ashes on our heads in the form of a cross, with the salutary advice taken from Genesis: "Remember, man, that thou art dust, and into dust thou shalt return." Ashes have in all times signified penance and compunction, as the various prayers at their blessing on this day also remind us. One prayer recalls the repentant Ninivites and asks God that "we may so imitate them in our attitude as to follow them in obtaining forgiveness." We have now entered upon a holy war and the closing prayer of the ceremony reads: "Grant us, O Lord, to begin with holy fasts the exercises of our Christian warfare: that, as we do battle with the spirits of evil, we may be protected by the help of self-denial." From now on the Church leads us more directly and her liturgy becomes richer. Now there is a different Mass formulary for every day of the week, and regularly do the prayers of the liturgy touch upon the practice of fasts and penance. In these lies our hope of grace with the Lord.

On Ash Wednesday the epistle tells us to rend our hearts and not our garments and in fasting to turn truly to the Lord. The gospel likewise warns against fasting in sadness or for the sake of being seen. The gospel of Thursday shows how Christ answered the appeal of the centurion who confessed that he was not worthy to have Christ come under his roof. The reward of humility and penance is thus assured. The collect of Friday asks that the fasts that have been begun, "we may be able also to practice with sincere minds." Both epistle and gospel stress the indispensability of the true love of neighbor, without which fasting and penance will be of no avail. Saturday's gospel shows Christ calming the seas and healing blind and lame. Christ is also our physician as well as our medicine.

The whole Christian community is always assembled in greater numbers on Sundays, and so on the first Sunday in Lent we have a sort of solemnized opening of the season of penance and fasting. Then, in the words of the secret, "we solemnly offer up the sacrifice of the beginning of Lent" and ask God to help us observe our Lenten program. The introit tells us of God's promises: "He shall call upon me and I will hear him: I will deliver him and I will glorify him." And the epistle reminds us appropriately: "Behold, now is the acceptable time, behold,

now is the day of salvation." The gospel, however, gives
us the keynote: We there have the example of Christ
fasting forty days and his subsequent resistance to the
temptations towards inordinate appetite of sense, pride
of life, and lust for possessions—the three great enemies
of human salvation.

The Monday Mass makes the first reference to the
candidates for baptism. The epistle tells how the Lord
hunts the lost sheep and the gospel addresses them: "Come,
ye blessed of my Father, possess you the kingdom prepared
for you." The Tuesday gospel shows us Jesus purging
the temple of all that is not God's, just as we must now
also purge the temples of our bodies of all that is not of
Christ. On Ember Wednesday the Mass has two lessons or epistles. One shows us Moses retiring to the
mountain in solitary communion with God for forty days.
The other shows Elias fasting forty days and forty nights.
The gospel foreshadows the three days of Holy Week in
the figure of Jonas. Ember Friday tells us: "If the wicked
do penance for all his sins which he hath committed and
keep all my commandments and do judgment and justice: living he shall live, and shall not die. I will not
remember all his iniquities that he hath done" (epistle),
and the gospel shows us that the sick are made strong by
Christ. Similar wholesome instructions are given on Ember Saturday, while the prayers characteristic of Lent are
continued: "O Lord, the God of my salvation, I have
cried in the day and in the night before thee (offertory)
. . . Sanctify, we beseech thee, O Lord, our fasts by
these present sacrifices, that what our observance professes
outwardly it may effect inwardly (secret) . . . O Lord
my God, in thee have I put my trust: save me from all

them that persecute me and deliver me (communion)
. . . May our vices be cured by thy sacred mysteries"
(postcommunion).

The Ember Saturday Mass was formerly celebrated
early Sunday morning and the present Mass of the second
Sunday is a later insertion. It continues the prayers and
exhortations of Lent. In the epistle St. Paul exhorts us
to walk the way of God and abstain from various kinds
of sin. "For God hath not called us unto uncleanness, but
unto sanctification: in Christ Jesus our Lord." The gospel, as on the previous day, is that of the transfiguration
on Mount Tabor—a distinct foreshadowing of the coming glory of Easter, as also of the intervening suffering
since the apostles are bidden to "tell the vision to no man
till the Son of man be risen from the dead."

In connection with the lessons of the divine office of
this day Abbot Marmion has indicated the possible treasures hidden in the liturgy and often passed by unnoticed.
The lessons give the story of Esau and Jacob, of the selling
of the birthright, and of the clandestine obtaining of Isaac's
blessing by Jacob. "Like Esau has the race of Adam pre-
varicated and saddened its Father. But like Jacob in turn
Jesus Christ, sweet and innocent, takes upon himself the
garments and the flesh of his brother. He has clad himself with our human nature, with all its weaknesses and
miseries, except sin, 'being made in the likeness of men,
and in habit found as a man.' " [1] Again, Christ the first-
born is Esau, and we are Jacob together with all mankind.
We go to the Father in the guise of Christ, in his name.
In his death and resurrection we take part through baptism
and become like him. As Christians, other Christs, we are

[1] Phil. 2:7

like him, we are vested with the grace and the Spirit of Christ. Thus transformed into the person of Christ we present ourselves to the Father.[2]

As Lent marches on the ideas of the passion become more frequent. On Monday the gospel speaks of the time when the Son of man shall be lifted up, and on Tuesday it tells us that humility alone counts and that the greatest of us shall be as servants. The liturgy continues to pray that God may "mercifully work sanctification with us, which may both purify us from earthly vices and lead us to heavenly gifts" (secret, Tuesday). The Wednesday gospel distinctly tells of the betrayal, passion and crucifixion, connecting it with the mission of Christ to give life to many. Friday narrates the killing of the son and heir of the householder, and Saturday the reacceptance of the Prodigal Son by the father, thereby referring both to Christ and to sinful mankind. The epistle of Saturday, then, narrates the event of Esau and Jacob.

The third Sunday goes a step farther and presents the sacrifice of Christ, wherewith we were brought to light from darkness, so that evil things should now not so much as be mentioned among us (epistle). The gospel shows us the power of Christ in the casting out of devils, and ends with words meant for all of us: "Blessed are they who hear the word of God and keep it." Monday's epistle indicates the mission of Christ to the gentiles (Naaman—the catechumens), and the gospel speaks of the rejection of the prophet by his own people and mentions the first attempt to apprehend Jesus. On Wednesday the catechumens are instructed in the ten commandments (epistle) and told how the service of God must be also

[2] *Semaine liturgique de Maredsous,* pp. 8–10

interior (gospel). Friday is replete with the theme of the living waters that truly quench thirst (epistle, gospel, communion), while Saturday has a special message for the public penitents and for all of us in the judgment passed upon the hardened reprobates who tried to seduce Susanna (epistle).

A Christian Lent can never be entirely sad. The *Benedictus* antiphon of Ash Wednesday has from the start emphasized the very first gospel words of Lent: "When ye fast, be not as the hypocrites, sad." With the fourth Sunday the pent up spiritual joy in the true member of Christ bursts forth in anticipation of the Easter joy to come (Laetare Sunday). "Rejoice, O Jerusalem, and come together all you that love her; rejoice with joy, you that have been in sorrow" (introit)—a note re-echoed in the gradual and the offertory. The melody of the introit also is significantly that of the first Easter alleluia, *i.e.*, of Holy Saturday. This was the day when the catechumens were decked with roses and when roses were mutually exchanged. Thence comes the custom of the rose vestment.

On this day the epistle, contrasting the Old and New Testaments, likewise bids the latter rejoice, while the gospel shows how the people, who have nothing to eat, are miraculously fed by Jesus. In the same way will Jesus relieve our want by his coming resurrection and its perpetuation in the continued eucharistic sacrifice and sacrament. Wednesday was the day for examining the catechumens. The introit and the first lesson of the Mass say to them, to the public penitents, and to us: "When I shall be sanctified in you, I will gather you from every land: and I will pour upon you clean water, and you shall be cleansed from all your filthiness: and I will give

you a new spirit." And the second lesson: "Wash your-
selves, be clean, take away the evil of your devices from
my eyes: cease to do perversely, learn to do well, etc."
The gospel shows us the blind man who, washing in the
pool of Siloe, went away seeing and believed and adored
Jesus. On Saturday the same motive continues. The
catechumens, and we with them, are addressed in the introit: "You that thirst, come to the waters saith the Lord;
and you that have no money come and drink with joy
. . . incline your ears to the words of my mouth." The
gospel declares that Jesus is "the light of the world: he
that followeth me walketh not in darkness but shall have
the light of life." And in the prayers we ask again that
"the fasts we have undertaken become profitable to us"
(collect), and that God "mercifully compel our rebellious
wills to yield" to his divine will (secret).

III. PASSIONTIDE

With the fifth Sunday we enter upon Passiontide, the
second and more acute stage of Lent and of the humiliation
of Christ. The note of his suffering and of our penance
becomes more emphatic, although references to the catechumens and public penitents also continue. The lessons
of the office are taken from Jeremias whose Lamentations
strike such an emphatic note in the Tenebrae of Holy
Week. The Church, to show her retirement in sorrow and
penance, veils her statues and crucifixes, she suppresses the
hymn of praise to the Trinity contained in the *Gloria
Patri's* of the Mass, foreshortens her liturgy by suppressing
the initial psalm of the preliminary prayers. In the introit and the gradual of the Sunday she prays with Christ:

"Judge me, O God, and distinguish my cause from the nation that is not holy; deliver me from the unjust and deceitful man." The tragedy approaches. In the gospel Christ vindicates himself before his accusers who cannot convict him of sin. He proclaims his priority over Abraham, and they take up stones to kill him, whereupon, he leaves the temple. The death of the Old Testament is nigh! The epistle tells us of Christ's coming bloody oblation of himself for us, and the communion verse uses the words: "This is my body which shall be delivered for you, etc." The Vespers contains the beautiful hymn to the cross, "on which the Life himself died and by death our life restored." It is the famous *Vexilla regis* sung again on Good Friday in Holy Week. In it we have placed before us the whole of the passion of Christ, but not without a note of joy for what it brings to us.

The rest of the week continues in the ideas of the Sunday. In the Monday gospel Christ tells his apostles: "Yet a little while I am with you," and proclaims himself as the source whence the thirsty may drink. On Tuesday the God of Daniel is glorified, "for he is the Savior, working signs and wonders in the earth" (epistle); and the Jews try to kill Christ whom the world hateth (gospel). And so the theme continues, Jesus proclaiming himself constantly as one having divine power and the pharisees becoming ever more hateful; Jesus confounding them, they devising more and more how to put him to death, for "it is expedient . . . that one man should die for the people" (Friday gospel). On Saturday Christ again reveals the whole design of God to his disciples: "The hour is come that the Son of man should be glorified. Amen, amen, I say to you, unless the grain of wheat falling into the ground die, itself remaineth alone. . . . He that loveth his life shall lose it. . . . And I, if I be lifted up from the earth, will draw all things to myself" (gospel). With Palm Sunday the real passion of our Lord, liturgically, has its beginning.

The liturgy of Holy Week in particular contains all the mysteries of our redemption in concentrated form; it is a compendium of the entire liturgical year, of all of Catholic theology, of the entire sacramental life of the Church. This is specially true of the last three days, the *Triduum*. If it is impossible to give an adequate picture of the true significance of the liturgy of the church year in short form, the task becomes a matter of despair in regard to Holy Week. Only a few salient features can be touched upon in these pages. But everywhere we have the basic message of Christ: *Through death to life.* The two are inseparable, and if there is one idea outstanding in the liturgy of this time, we have it in the persistent connecting up of the passion and death with the resurrection. Without the resurrection the passion has no meaning, and so even in the darkest hour of the passion and death on Good Friday there is no complete suppression of the triumphant joy of the resurrection.

The blessing of the palms on Palm Sunday begins with the joyful cry of praise: "Hosanna to the Son of David; blessed is he that cometh in the name of the Lord" (antiphon). In the prayers, lessons and responses that follow during the blessings, this song recurs time and again, but not without touches reminding us of Christ's suffering and death. The liturgy of the blessing is elaborate. Of its significance one of the collects says: "The palms represent his triumph over the prince of death, and the olive branches proclaim in a manner the coming of a spiritual unction. For that multitude knew that by them was signified that our Redeemer, compassionating the misery of mankind, was to fight for the life of the whole world with the prince of death, and to triumph over him by his own death." Of the olive branches it prays that they may bring salvation as one time the dove by them proclaimed peace to the world. The procession being about to begin, the Church prays in words expressing an essential note of the liturgy: "Grant that the bodily service with which thy people honor thee today may be perfected spiritually by the utmost devotion, by victory over the enemy, and by the ardent love of works of mercy." The faithful have indeed freely accepted the blessed palms, the signs of Christ's triumph through his suffering and death, and by carrying them aloft they profess their participation in him and his works. During the procession prayers and songs glorify Christ and narrate his entry into Jerusalem. Amid the jubilation is it not significant that the crucifix heads the procession, and that the church as the heavenly Jerusalem is opened only when the cross has knocked at its door? We may get an answer by listening to the mysterious melody of the chant of the *Pueri Hebraeorum* of the procession.

The Mass itself is given over wholly to the passion of Christ. It commences with a cry for deliverance from the lion's mouth (introit) in the words of psalm 21, the psalm of the crucifixion. The collect asks that we may "deserve to have fellowship in his resurrection" after having mentioned the death on the cross. The epistle states that Christ was obedient unto death, but speaks also of the consequent glory of his name in which all beings shall bend the knee. The gradual commences calmly with "Thou hast held me by my right hand," but then suddenly the restraining spell is broken and the tract cries out despairingly: "O God, my God, look upon me; why hast thou forsaken me?" Therewith the passion commences in earnest. The theme of the tract continues and is followed by the gospel of the passion. Offertory, communion verse, hymn and verses of the Vespers and the antiphon of the Magnificat —all continue the tragic note. The abandonment is complete, "I looked for one that would grieve together with me, and there was none" (offertory).

Monday's gospel mentions the anointing for the coming burial and the betrayal of Judas, Tuesday and Wednesday narrate the entire passion, and then the great three days are at hand in which the tragic drama enacts itself in full. It contains a complete picture of the passion and death as historically enacted, of the sacramental enactment at the Last Supper, and brings these in their liturgical inseparability before us for our participation. The liturgy of these days is better known to the faithful at large than any other part of the year, and so a rapid survey of outstanding features shall have to suffice here.

The liturgy of the Triduum is both the end and the climax of the preparation for Easter and at the same time part of the "paschal mysteries" or Easter celebration. For just as with the passion the idea of the resurrection is always connected, so the resurrection is the triumph of the suffering Christ over sin and death. The height of the Triduum celebration naturally falls on Good Friday after Thursday has given us the Lord's last testament of love in the institution of the Eucharist. On Good Friday all bells are silent, altars are stripped except for the service which for once is but a commemoration and not a real enactment of the sacrifice. For the Host was consecrated the day before—whence the name of the Mass of the Presanctified. There is a progressive theme in the liturgy of these days, not only in the morning services but also in the Tenebrae (as seen, for instance, in the responsories after the lessons). If we combine the two services in their temporal sequence the progressive theme would be as follows: (*a*) Wednesday Tenebrae: Death Agony of Christ; (*b*) Thursday Mass: The Eucharist and the Passion; (*c*) Thursday Tenebrae: Death on the Cross; (*d*) Friday Mass of the Presanctified: Triumph of the Cross over Sin; (*e*) Friday Tenebrae: Rest in the Grave; (*f*) Saturday Ceremonies and Mass: Baptism and Resurrection.

The Benedictus antiphon of the Wednesday Tenebrae reads: "But the traitor gave them a sign, saying: He whom I shall kiss, that is he; hold him fast." The third nocturn lessons had been St. Paul's narrative of the institution of the Eucharist, the same as the epistle of the Mass of Thursday. This Mass re-enacts the sacrifice of Christ's passion in the background of the institution, thus combining the thoughts expressed in the official prayer of the Eucharist: "O God, who in this wonderful sacrament has left us a memorial of thy passion . . ." (Corpus Christi, and benediction of the Blessed Sacrament). Formerly there were three Masses on Maundy Thursday for the following purposes: reconciliation of public penitents, consecration of the holy oils, and commemoration of the Last Supper (with Easter Communion of the faithful). The one Mass of today is a mixture of joy and sorrow. The introit begins: "It behooves us to glory in the cross of our Lord Jesus Christ . . . in whom is our salvation, life, and resurrection"—as always we have the double aspect of death and resurrection. The color is the joyful white, and the bells resound at the Gloria, only to be silent thereafter till Saturday morning. After the Mass there is the procession to the side altar in which the *Pangue lingua* to the Eucharist is sung, while the return theme on the morrow will be the *Vexilla regis* of the cross—Eucharist and passion again. The stripping of the altar, the undecking of the eucharistic banquet table, follows and in some places the washing of the feet.

The Benedictus antiphon of Thursday evening is penetrating in its simplicity: "They put over the head his cause written: Jesus of Nazareth, King the Jews." Friday morning begins with a silent prostration of all the ministers, a mutely eloquent gesture in the face of the awful tragedy now realized. The Mass of the Presanctified divides into three parts. The first is the Mass of the Faithful in the most ancient style with its litanical series of prayers for all the intentions of the Church. Then comes the ceremony of the adoration of the cross, and then the communion service, which itself is very abbreviated from the ordinary communion part of the Mass.

The height of the Friday service is the second part. In it the cross is unveiled and presented to the people with the words: "Behold the wood of the cross, on which hung the Savior of the world. Come, let us adore!" During the adoration or kissing of the cross that follows, Christ himself addresses us through the liturgy with the touching words of the *Reproaches* that must melt even the coldest of hearts: "O my people, what have I done to thee? or in what have I afflicted thee? Answer me. What ought I have done for thee, and did not do it?"

We must all indeed strike our breasts in true compunction of heart and acknowledge our frequent ingratitude to our Savior, who has truly done so much for us: "I have exalted thee with great strength: and thou hast hanged me on the gibbet of the cross." Heartily should we enter into the prayer of the *trisagion:* "O holy God. O holy strong one. O holy immortal one, have mercy on us!" The procession for getting the presanctified Host for the communion service follows with its anticipating of Easter in the intimations of joy it also contains.

The Mass of Holy Saturday is understood only if we remember that the present service formerly commenced on Saturday night, the night of the baptism of the catechumens, which was then followed by Mass at dawn on Sunday. The whole liturgy is permeated with the symbolism of the light of Christ in reference conjointly to baptism and the resurrection. Light is struck out of a rock, even as Christ arose out of a stone tomb. It is indeed the *Lumen Christi,* the Light of Christ. The paschal candle is blessed, which will be lit daily until the gospel of Ascension Thursday. The long lessons of Holy Saturday were formerly the last instructions of the catechumens, whereupon the baptismal water was blessed for their baptism. Catechumens and faithful together sing while proceeding to the baptismal font: "As the heart panteth after the fountains of water, so my soul panteth after thee, O God . . ." One of the collects asks God: "Be present at these mysteries, be present at these sacraments of thy great goodness: and send forth the spirit of adoption to regenerate the new people, whom the font of baptism brings forth." A long preface follows that is as rich in meaning as was the previous preface for the blessing of the Easter candle if not also the famous *Exultet* of that ceremony. After the litany the Mass itself begins, which is in reality the ancient Mass of Easter morn.

The Mass begins abruptly with the collect, which reflects the ancient circumstances of the service: "O God, who dost illumine this most holy night by the glory of our Lord's resurrection, preserve in the new offspring of thy family the spirit of adoption which thou has given, that renewed in body and soul, they may give thee a pure service." This prayer is now applied to all of us who are renewed by the bath of Lenten penance and the resurrection of Christ. The epistle contains a final admonition: "If you be risen with Christ, seek the things that are above, etc.," whereupon the joy can no longer be contained and the celebrant intones the inspiring triple alleluia, so eloquent also in its melody. The remaining parts of the Mass sing a jubilant praise, the gospel announces the resurrection officially, and the Church, tenderly looking forward, prays in her secret "that what we have begun at these paschal mysteries may, by thine operation, obtain for us an eternal remedy." The alleluias continue to ring in the Vespers. Lent is over, and Easter has entered in almost before its time.

IV. EASTERTIDE

On Easter Sunday the joy of the Church is unbounded; and the Easter theme re-echoes throughout the octave. The mystical union of the Church with Christ in his risen splendor puts her in a transport of joy that continues to vibrate through the liturgy of the whole of Eastertide till the very consummation of this union on Pentecost Sunday. It is especially present in the first week, in which there is a proper Mass formulary for every day. Throughout these days the words recur: "This is the day which the Lord hath made: let us be glad and rejoice therein. Alleluia." The newly baptized, who for this week will wear the white garment of their new bliss, rejoice at their rising with Christ to the new glory. The Church rejoices at the signal transformation of Christ, which is also hers by her renewed participation in the liturgical mysteries. Christ himself, speaking in the liturgy, rejoices because of these things, and because the bitterness of his passion is over, and his love for man is now in part satisfied.

It is indeed Christ who in the transports of joy remains our guide. In the Sunday introit—something very rare—he himself addresses words of grateful acknowledgment to his Father, words that are also in turn addressed to Christ himself by the Church: "I arose and am still with thee, alleluia: thou hast laid thy hand upon me, alleluia: thy knowledge is become wonderful, alleluia, alleluia. . . . Lord, thou hast proved me and known me." The collect asks God's grace on our vows, which were indeed anticipated by God, who through Christ did "on this day overcome death and open unto us the gates of everlasting life." The epistle reminds us that we must "purge out the old leaven," in order that we may be "a new paste . . . for Christ our Pasch is sacrificed"; hereafter we must feast ourselves "with the unleavened bread of sincerity and truth." The sequence, the famous *Victimae paschali* with its wondering melody and its charming simplicity of language and dialogue is an unexcelled dramatization of the Easter sentiments and of the event of the morning: "Christ innocent and undefiled, sinners to God hath rec-

onciled. . . . In this great triumph death and life together met in wondrous strife. The Prince of Life, once
dead, doth reign. Say what thou sawest, Mary, say. . . .
I saw the tomb wherein the living one had lain; I saw his
glory as he rose again. . . . We know that Christ indeed
is risen. . . . Alleluia." Secret and postcommunion, repeating the words of the Holy Saturday Mass, ask that the
paschal mysteries enacted on the altar may be to all of us
"a healing remedy" and make us "to be of one mind" in
Christ our head.

During the week the liturgy addresses in turn the newly
baptized, or again all those who have been regenerated by
the liturgical mysteries of Christ's resurrection. Again it
prays that the eternal fruits bought by the resurrection
may be attained by us, and gives indications of the work
the Church is soon to commence. "The Lord hath brought
you into a land flowing with milk and honey," says the
introit for Monday; and on Tuesday: "He gave them the
water of wisdom to drink"; while on Wednesday comes
the significant invitation: "Come ye blessed of my Father,
receive the kingdom, alleluia, which was prepared for you
from the foundation of the world, alleluia, alleluia." In
the epistles the theme is the resurrection preached by the
apostles, chiefly Peter, who properly takes the first word.
We also see Philip instructing and baptizing the eunuch
of Ethiopia, an indication of the coming work of the
Church among the gentiles. The gospels narrate how
Christ showed himself to the apostles: first to the two
disciples at Emmaus, then to the others at various occasions, also to Mary, until on Low Sunday, the octave day,
he shows himself also to the doubting Thomas and in him
gives us all an exhortation to faith. The graduals and

alleluia verses continue to sound the note of joy and rejoicing. The collects ask that the servants of God "may hold fast in life to the sacrament which they have received by faith" (Tuesday), "may be worthy to attain to eternal joys" (Wednesday), that "all who are born again in the font of baptism may be one by faith in their minds and by love in their good deeds" (Thursday), "that what we celebrate outwardly we may imitate in our deeds" (Friday), "that we who have reverently celebrated the Easter festival may deserve through it to arrive at eternal joys" (Saturday). Saturday, we may say, ends with good emphasis. The secret prays that we may "ever rejoice in these paschal mysteries, that the continued work of our redemption may be to us a source of perpetual joy," and the postcommunion, "that quickened by the gift of our redemption, true faith may ever prosper within us by this help to eternal salvation."

The second Sunday after Easter presents the beautiful picture of the Good Shepherd who gives his life for his sheep. The third Sunday announces the coming mysteries of Ascension and Pentecost: "A little while and now you shall not see me; and again a little while, and you shall see me; because I go to the Father" (gospel); while the Church lovingly continues to think of us, praying that God "grant that all who are counted of the Christian faith may abhor whatever is contrary to that name, and strive after that which becomes it" (collect). The fourth Sunday consoles the disciples for the coming departure and enlightens their understanding: "For if I go not, the Paraclete will not come to you" (gospel). This is the first intimation at this time of that second regeneration in the Holy Ghost, which is to occur in order that the Church may be the full-fledged continuer of Christ's mission. On the fifth Sunday the Lord speaks still more plainly and the disciples understand (gospel). The vigil of Ascension, finally, contains the wonderful last prayer of Christ preparatory to his entering upon his glory in heaven.

The liturgy of Ascension is full of this glory of Christ as God dwelling on high (alleluia verse, offertory, communion verse). The introit announces the future coming as judge, and sounds the note of joy that permeates the day: "O clap your hands, all ye nations; shout unto God with the voice of joy." The Church, however, never forgets her sanctifying mission, and so she prays in the collect "that we, who believe thine only begotten Son our redeemer to have this day ascended into heaven, may ourselves dwell in mind amid heavenly things." The Sunday within the octave continues the joy over Christ's ascension, but now the Church also feels her loneliness: "I have sought thy face, O Lord . . . turn not away thy face from me" (introit). And beautifully does the gospel answer by recalling the promise of the coming of the Paraclete.

The time of fulfillment has arrived. Altar and ministers are clothed in red to indicate the flame of love that perfects the work of Christ and is to burn in the hearts of the Church. "The Spirit of the Lord hath filled the whole earth, alleluia," sings out the introit of the Mass. The epistle tells us the story of this coming of the Spirit of Christ, and of its immediate effects in the gift of tongues, and the gospel again gives us its significance for the Church and for us. In her prayers the Church asks that the light of the Holy Spirit may have its full effect in the hearts of her children—a sentiment wonderfully rendered in the chanted sequence, *Veni sancte Spiritus*. Filled with the plenitude of the Spirit, the Church, as it were, needs a week of liturgical texts to unfold its riches. A touching array of prayers throughout the week of Pentecost asks for the fruits of the Holy Ghost upon the children of the Church, while the epistles, taken from the Acts of the Apostles, show us the Spirit of God working in the new Church, the apostles working through the efficacy and the promptings of the Spirit that is now theirs. The new Church has been launched upon her enduring mission.

V. The Time after Pentecost

The Sunday after Pentecost is Trinity Sunday, the celebration of which was introduced into the universal Church only in the fourteenth century. It emphasizes the mystery of the triune God, which, however, permeates the entire liturgy of the Church. The preface of the Trinity is also said on all ordinary Sundays of the year, these being days of the Lord and therefore appropriately commemorating the full Godhead in the Trinity. Because of the absence of a special theme there is little deserving of particular emphasis in the liturgy of the day. "Blessed be the holy Trinity, and undivided Unity," the Mass text begins, and this is its recurrent thought.

On the Thursday following, the feast of Corpus Christi is celebrated. This too is a late accession, dating from the thirteenth century. The texts of Mass and office are the work of Thomas Aquinas, and are remarkable for their qualities of unity and theological profundity. The collect of the feast is the famous prayer so expressive of the spirit of the entire liturgy: "O God, who in this wonderful

Sacrament hast left us a memorial of thy passion: grant us, we beseech thee, so to venerate the sacred mysteries of thy Body and Blood that we may ever feel within us the fruit of thy redemption." Epistle, gospel, and the sequence, *Lauda Sion*, are a digest of the theology of the Eucharist. The latter especially, with its rich variety of melody, gives us also a faint glimpse of the great treasure of joy that the mystical union with the sacramental Christ may effect. With a fine sense of what is meant when the Eucharist is called the sacrament of the mystical body of Christ, the secret asks the Lord: "Grant to thy Church the gifts of unity and peace, which are mystically shown forth in the offerings we make to thee"; and the postcommunion: "Grant us . . . that we may have to the full that eternal enjoyment of the Godhead, which is prefigured by thy precious Body and Blood which we receive in this present life." Since Easter, especially, the thought of these eternal effects has been more frequent.

The Sundays after Pentecost, occupying about half a year, show us the ordinary life of the Church, receiving its vigor from Christ, the head of the mystical body, and growing as the kingdom of Christ on earth is destined to do. The gospels show us the continuous healing power of Christ in the Church. The man born dumb is healed (eleventh Sunday), also the leper (fourteenth), the men afflicted with dropsy and palsy (sixteen and eighteenth), and the son of the captain of Capharnaum (twentieth). Nay, Christ even restores the dead to life (fifteenth and twentieth). It is he through whom the fishers of men make their great catch (fourth), and he provides for all by his miraculous feeding (sixth), looking even for the lost sheep (third). He calls us to be perfect as his Father (first). He tells us we cannot serve mammon and God (fourteenth), and ruthlessly he cleanses the Church of its mercenary adherents (ninth). We must pray in all humiliation like the publican (tenth); but we must also do more than pray for it is not enough to say Lord, Lord, without doing the will of the Father (seventh). Above all, is the rule of love expressed in the two great commandments of love (seventeenth), of which the Samaritan is so noble an example (nineteenth), and without which no offering made to God is acceptable (fifth).

The epistles of these Sundays give a most profound and comprehensive series of instructions on the true Christian life, and the Church in her prayers asks with the efficacy of Christ's mediatorial power for our attainment of this true life. Living still on earth, she asks that we may use the temporal goods in such a manner as not to lose the eternal goods (collect, third Sunday), that the holy Sacrament, central source of Christian life, may help even the needs of our bodies (postcommunion, eleventh and sixteenth), that our wills, in thought and action, may be sunk in God's (collect, eighth), that he may give us ever increasing fervor and watch over it (collect, sixth), so that the Eucharist may ever "be for the healing of our ills" (secret, tenth), and that "its effect, and not our own senses, may ever have dominion with us" (postcommunion, fifteenth)—in short, that "as often as this memorial sacrifice is celebrated, the work of our redemption is wrought" (secret, ninth) and we thus become truly sharers in it (secret, eighteenth). Nor is the Church as such forgotten, the organic fellowship and unity of the brethren. The liturgy prays, for instance, "that what each does offer to the honor of thy name may avail for the salvation of all" (secret, fifth and seventh), that the "church may rejoice in quiet devotion" (collect, fourth), that God cleanse and fortify his Church (collect, fifteenth), and finally, may give ear to the fervent prayers of this his Church (collect, twenty-second).

The Ember days of the September harvest time occur after the seventeenth Sunday. While the spring Ember days had to do with asking God's blessing for an abundant harvest, the September days are those of the gathering of the fruits, and they point to the final consummation of things. The harvest in time directs the Christian mind to the eternal one. With the eighteenth Sunday a new note begins to be heard at times, while the general trend of the previous Sundays continues. After the harvest come the last days of the year. And with all the yearning of souls faithfully tested for months and years, the Church begins to look to the last end, longing for the final glory of Christ. It is within these last Sundays that the feasts of All Saints and All Souls occur, which are distinctly feasts of the next life, and likewise the feast of Christ the King, of which the papal encyclical instituting the feast says: "The last Sunday of October seemed far more appropriate than the rest for the celebration of this feast, because it approximately marks the end of the liturgical year. Thus the solemn festival of Christ's kingship will be a completion and consummation of the mysteries of the life of Jesus already commemorated during the year; and before we celebrate the glory of all the saints, his glory will be proclaimed and extolled, who triumphs in all the saints and the elect." [3]

The introit of the eighteenth Sunday cries out: "Give peace, O Lord, to them that patiently wait for thee," and

[3] *Quas primas*, Dec. 11, 1925

the epistle ends with a reference to "the day of the coming of our Lord Jesus Christ." The gospel of the nineteenth Sunday tells us how all that have no wedding garment will be cast into exterior darkness. On the twenty-first Sunday we are told that "the kingdom of heaven is likened to a king who would take an account of his servants." Then, on the twenty-fourth, the last Sunday of the year, we have the imposing picture of the last days, when we "shall see the Son of man coming in the clouds of heaven with much power and majesty"; and we pray in the secret to God: "Be propitious, O Lord, to our supplications, and receiving the prayers and offerings of thy people, turn the hearts of all of us to thee: that, being delivered from the greed of earthly treasure, we may pass on to heavenly desires."

With the last judgment comes the end of all time. But the Christian pilgrim on earth may have to wander the liturgical itinerary of the Church for many cycles to come. If so, the transition to the next liturgical year will not be abrupt for him. The picture of the final judgment of the world, as we have seen, is also presented on the first Sunday of Advent, so that it furnishes a common link between the two annual cycles, as it were, over which the transition from one to the other is made without too complete a break.

Reviewing the liturgical cycle as a whole, we see how the divine seed, alone containing the powers of true life, appeared in mid-winter. It was in the springtime that the seed was planted in deepest degradation, for the seed must decay in order to sprout new life, as Christ himself has said. Out of the death of Calvary came the life of Easter and Pentecost, which in the long summer grew into an

abundant harvest, to be gathered in the late fall, where-
after the eternal seed is to appear anew. In this spiritual
pathway there are many feasts of saints, of which we said
almost nothing, feasts of apostles, confessors, virgins, martyrs, rich and poor, lowly and great. All of these are so
many examples of the rich fruit of the divine Christ, and
they play their part in helping to attain the development
of Christ in our hearts. They are so many guides on the
way that is Christ. But the way itself is paved with the
mysteries of the divine Savior; it is through them that we
partake of his life and go with him along the journey.

Thus indeed "the liturgical year is a supernatural school
of piety, which the Church has opened to her children for
completion of their religious education according to a divine
method, namely, that of making the activities of his
disciples converge in the sacred person of Jesus Christ,
and of copying his life, of expressing his virtues, participating for time and eternity in his salutary merits." [4]

[4] Caronti, *The Spirit of the Liturgy*, pp. 53–54

CHAPTER VIII

THE LITURGICAL SACRIFICE

I. Mass and the Liturgy

WITHOUT the Mass, the liturgy of the Church would be about what many now think it to be—an empty shell of external forms. The Mass is the center and core of all the liturgical worship of the Church, so much so that all the other liturgical aspects have their true meaning only from their relation to and connection with the Mass. All the other aspects of the Church's liturgy revolve about the Mass as around their center and source of inner vitality. Whatever has been said about the liturgy as being the embodiment of the Divine, as being the essential worship of God by man, as being man's way of salvation and sanctification, as being the spiritual pathway of the continued growth and perfection of the mystical body in Christ—all this holds primarily of the liturgical sacrifice of Christ and only derivatively of all the other elements of the entire liturgy.

At the beginning of his exposition of the Mass, Dr. Pius Parsch alludes to the gospel of the buried treasure as narrated in Matthew.[1] Christ here refers to the kingdom of God which is hidden to many. "I should like, however," writes Dr. Parsch, "to compare this treasure with another

[1] 13:44

precious good that lies hidden to so many Christians, with
the holy sacrifice of the Mass, a really great treasure in the
acre of the Church, but for many remaining unknown and
buried." [2] There is hardly any exaggeration in the statement that for many Catholics even today the Mass is little
more than something that must be attended once a week.
For these the Mass is primarily connected in mind with
an obligation that is imposed upon all Catholics under pain
of mortal sin. But Church law as such is not meant to be
a definition of what things are. In fact, as with prescriptions
of the Church in regard to liturgical action, we can say that
the Church law was merely a conclusion drawn by the
Church from the true nature of the Mass or the liturgy.
The Mass is not so much a means of exercising our religion
because the Church has so prescribed; but rather it is so
essential to our holy religion, to the following of Christ,
that the Church declares anyone neglecting a minimum
participation of Mass no longer a true child of hers, a
brother of Christ, a living member of his mystical body.

Even with some Catholics who are more thoughtful in
the practice of their religion, the Mass may be merely an
occasion for performing a set of favorite private prayers of
their own, or pious readings. The Mass is thus the occasion
for the recitation of several rosaries, or litanies or the reading of morning prayers or occasional devotions out of some
prayer book; or it may be the reading of the "prayers for
Mass" out of some book but without much relation to the
progress of the sacrifice, so that a person may finish two
such prayer-book "Masses," or only half a one, while the
priest completes the enactment of the holy mystery on
the altar. Again, the Mass may mean for some chiefly the

.[2] *Messerklaerung*, p. 7

occasion when the consecration of bread takes place for
the sacrament of Communion, or as the time for private
preparation and thanksgiving in connection with the sacramental reception of Christ. Or one may more correctly
surmise in a general way that the Mass is really a living
presentation of a divine drama before our very eyes, in
which Christ in some manner enters as the chief actor.
Persons inspired with this view know that the Mass must
be something ineffably sublime, something of greatest
value also to them; but they stress the ineffability of it,
and are vaguely content with their state of mind, since
the ineffable is also taken to be not further intelligible
to limited human understanding. Yet the service Christ
desires of his brethren, we know, is eminently an intelligent service, on a level with the high dignity of creatures endowed with reason and free will and raised to
the high status of sharers in Christ.

Some persons, again, have tried to enhance the dignity
of the Mass or the devotion of the faithful by showing how
the Mass is a symbolical repetition of the life of the Savior,
how the Gloria recalls the shepherds at the manger of
Bethlehem, the epistle and the gospel the public teaching
and life of Christ, the Sanctus his triumphal entry into
Jerusalem, the Consecration the institution of the Eucharist
on Maundy Thursday, the breaking of the Host the suffering, and the Communion the death of Christ. There is no
need to comment on such a forced interpretation of the
Mass. Historically it arose and grew in popularity in the
centuries in which the liturgical sense of the people began
to wane and was lost almost completely. The parallel does
connect up the Mass in some way with the mysteries of the
life of Christ, but any detailed exposition of it not only

distorts the theological truth of the Mass but also hides altogether the true sacramental nature of the sacrifice of the altar in which the people should participate actively.[3]

II. THE MASS AND CALVARY

The sacrifice of the Mass is, according to the Council of Trent, the same as the sacrifice of the cross on Calvary insofar as the same priestly powers of the one Highpriest offer it and the same divine Victim is offered up to God on high. In both the sacrifice of the cross and that of the altar, Jesus Christ is the officiating priest and the sacrificial victim. The Mass receives all its infinite dignity from this fact, all its true meaning. It is indeed the realization or continuation or enactment or representation (making present again) in an unbloody manner of the sacrifice at one time offered on Calvary in a bloody manner. That is what makes the Mass the supreme act of divine worship, and gives to all the liturgy of the Church its high dignity because of its essential connection with the oblation of Christ on the altar and on Calvary. "By its very nature," says Dom Vandeur, "the sacrifice of the cross is *par excellence* the act of the virtue of religion. It expresses the fourfold end of religion: adoration, thanksgiving, petition, and propitiation. Its positive institution by Christ, furthermore, makes it an act that is essentially social, and hence eminently *liturgical*. Every cultual act performed by sinful man, from the very beginning to the end of time, has no value except through its relation, close or remote, to

[3] For a brief discussion of this parallel, see an article on "Mass and the Life of Christ," in *Orate Fratres*, Vol. IV (1929–1930), pp. 72ff.

the oblation of Christ on Calvary." [4] In the liturgy itself we find the Cross and the Mass spoken of as one and the same sacrifice. Thus the secret for the feast of St. Gregory the Great asks in reference to the Mass that "we may benefit by this sacrifice, by the offering of which thou didst vouchsafe to forgive the sins of the whole world"; and the secret for the feast of St. Paul of the Cross calls the Mass "these mysteries of thy passion and death," and that of the feast of the Most Precious Blood asks that "through these mysteries . . . upon thine altars, O Lord of hosts, may we renew the sprinkling of the Blood."

   Just what this should mean for us, we can well see in connection with a principle mentioned above. The liturgy is to apply through all time the fruits of the redemption, which Christ made possible for all men by his personal suffering and death, by his personal sacrifice on Calvary. "May this sacrament, we beseech thee, O Lord, bestow on us the fruit of our redemption," asks the secret of the third Tuesday of Lent, and that of Saturday in Easter week calls "these paschal mysteries . . . the continued work of our redemption." The Mass is in the truest sense the continuation of the redeeming sacrifice of Christ, nay, its greater completion. Only in this sense can we find any intelligible meaning in the prayers of the Church just quoted, or in others speaking of the Eucharist as "the spotless Victim by which we renew the work of the boundless love of our Lord Jesus Christ" (secret, St. Camillus), or as "the gift of thy Church . . . in which he whom those offerings signified is immolated and received" (secret, Epiphany). The most telling prayer in this regard is undoubtedly the

[4] *Semaine liturgique de Maredsous,* p. 57

oft-quoted secret of the ninth Sunday after Pentecost: "As often as this memorial sacrifice is celebrated the work of our redemption is enacted." It is therefore the Mass that gives its fullest efficacy to the sacrifice of Calvary; "it is the Cross put within reach of souls in every country and through all ages." [5]

The Mass is therefore more than a mere commemoration of the event that took place on Calvary. It is indeed a memorial celebration, for it was instituted by words of Christ indicating this character, "Do this for a commemoration of me," which words are quoted daily in the consecration prayer. It is a memorial celebration of Christ's death, of his passion and the shedding of his blood, which was also foreshadowed in Christ's words of institution quoted in the Mass: "This is my blood which shall be shed." But the Mass is also a celebration of Christ's entire life-work, and so the mysteries of the resurrection and ascension are mentioned in the Mass in union with that of his passion. It is therefore a memorial sacrifice of the entire work of the redemption, and that, after the unique manner of the liturgical mysteries by which is really made present what is signified by the external rites.

III. The Externals of the Mass

Like all liturgical functions the Mass is enacted by a series of external acts that progressively develop the internal action thereby realized. The nucleus of this external action was received from Christ himself, and it also finds expression in the very words of the institution quoted at the consecration. Also these externals, then, are in obedi-

[5] Dom Lefebvre, *Catholic Liturgy*, p. 71

ence to the behest of Christ when he commissioned the apostles to "Do this for a commemoration of me." In the "breaking of the bread" the apostles remained faithful in detail to this command.

Nor has the external structure of the Mass, developing and growing in time, in any way changed this essential sameness. While the Mass is an external liturgical action unfolding in time, the true inner nature ever remains the same; it but receives further visible expression through the external garb. "There is nothing extrinsic, material mingled with this celebration. For behind the visible, objective action there is always a perfect spiritual reality. Christ, the Son of God made man, beneath the veil of the mystical forms ever accomplishes the same spiritual oblation of self to his heavenly Father. And the community, its spirit filled with and urged on by the Spirit of God, unites itself to the sacrifice of Christ and with him performs its total spiritual sacrifice unto God." [6]

The external action of the Mass is precisely for the purpose of our better participation in the sacrifice under the leadership of the official priest of the Church, and for our better collective co-operation in the action of the Mass. The Mass has been instituted that the mystical members of Christ's body may not only imitate him but live more intimately with him. Hence, what Christ did for individual and society on Calvary, that we must now, both individually and socially, join with him in doing by participation in the Mass. That is why the Mass has been instituted as a complex liturgical function, and much of its ritual development is understood only with this purpose in view that the members of the mystical body may in union with

[6] *Die Betende Kirche*, p. 183

their Head, being supernaturally one in mind and soul and body with him, offer up again and again the same sacrifice as that of Calvary.

Hence we have so frequently in the Mass the dialog form of prayer, and words and exhortations of the Mass text, and ritual gestures, which indicate the collective nature of the sacrificial action. It is by means of the external rites and ceremonies that the inner nature of the liturgical mysteries is presented to us, and it is by means of these visible forms that we unite our hearts and souls to the inner divine action presented in them. It is through them that the sacrifice of Christ continues to live down the ages in a form that enables the fellowship of Christ's members to participate. It is through them that the Mass becomes the intimate means of living the life of Christ for all the members of his body, essentially the means of the inter-communication of the divine life between Head and members. For through them the members are actively entering into that holy action in their totality, body and soul, heart and mind. The Mass essentially gives all men the opportunity of fellowship in the suffering and death of Christ, in his saving work of redemption. Through it above all does the liturgy perform its function of salvation and sanctification.

In view of this we should see more clearly the sublime truth of the words of Christ, who said that when he should be exalted on the cross, he would draw all men unto himself. "This grace of attraction proper to Christ crucified," writes Dom Ryelandt, "is found in all its totality in the Mass; and it is by virtue of this power that, drawn to Jesus, we learn to live of his life of holy victimhood. Mass is truly the daily means of renewal and intensification of the interior life by an intelligent and loving contact with the divine reality of the sacrifice of Christ."[7]

The externals are there to facilitate this intelligent contact, as we have seen. It is through them that we must attain to the true inner meaning of the liturgical mystery. But we cannot do this without an understanding of both of these aspects, exterior and interior; and we are now in the inheritance of centuries of a loss of the true liturgical spirit. "Day by day in the holy Mass the greatest miracle of God's love is wrought before our eyes—and we do not understand it. Do not say that we are creatures of the dust and that God's works are too high for us; for in this work God has stooped to our lowness. The truth is that the Mass represents a supernatural world and a supernatural concept of life and we have let it become strange and unfamiliar to us. We have lost the pass word that gives entry to the holy land."[8]

For proper participation in the sacrifice of Christ and the fuller derivation from it of the fruits of the redemption it is necessary both to understand more fully the inner nature of the Mass as a sacrifice in its relation to all of us as members of Christ, and at the same time to see how and where these ideas find their realization in the very text and gestures of the Mass. Without so much being known, the Mass will remain a sealed book rather than a palpable means of communion in the fellowship of Christ.

IV. Sacrificial Worship

Wherever we know of the practice of religion among peoples, we find also the notion of sacrifice, and in some

[7] *Pour mieux communier*, p. 20   [8] Kramp, *Eucharistia*, p. 43

form or other the practice of sacrificial worship. It has remained for the Protestantism of the Christian era to show us extensive peoples that consciously rejected the idea of a ritual sacrifice as the chief expression of their religious life. If sacrificial worship is an essential act of the virtue of religion, then we are justified today in pointing to its absence in Protestant denominations as one reason for the loss of religious vigor in their public services and of any substantial hold on their members by the different denominations. If such sacrifice is of the life of religion, then one is justified in saying that any religious fellowship that abolishes such sacrifice has unconsciously signed its own death warrant.

What is there in the idea of sacrifice that is so intimate an expression of the virtue of religion? In general sacrifice ever implies the offering up of some sort of useful object to the Deity. The rational creature, by some form of external action, takes things of his own that have value or meaning for him, sets them aside for God, and by some ceremonial action indicates his delivery of them to the divine Being as an act of homage to the latter. Religious sacrifice is offered only to the Godhead, for it has always meant the acknowledgment by man of the divine superiority of God; sacrifice has always been looked up as an open confession by man of God's dominion over him. Hence the offering of the chosen object is meant to be an acknowledgment of this dominion of God over his creatures, and therefore also of the obligation that man has to acquiesce in this dominion. In that way sacrifice is immediately seen to be a supreme act of homage, a proper service, a profession of dependence, a means of reconciliation and propitiation, that is, a most appropriate exercise of the virtue of religion, a deliberate placing of oneself into proper relation to God in both mind and action, an act of dedication of the creature to his Creator.

Among the pagans, whose gods were afflicted with real human needs, the idea of offering something useful to the deities could possibly be taken more literally than among the Chosen People, who had a proper understanding of the sublimity and majesty of Jehova and of the complete self-sufficiency of the infinite God. By reason of this better understanding of God's nature and of their relation to him, the figurative or symbolical element in the action of sacrifice was naturally uppermost in their mind. Man, acting after the fashion of man, offers a gift to God, not because God needs it or does not already possess everything there is, but in order to signify thereby his own personal relation to the supreme being. The gift is something useful to man, the product of his own energies or work, and ordinarily it has value for the sustaining of life. It is taken to stand for the giver's life, therefore. In depriving himself of this life-sustaining article and giving it up for God, the offerer indicates the giving over of himself, his own life, to God in the gift.

The rich meaning of this action is explained succinctly by a recent liturgical apostle: "Sacrifice consists in offering a gift to God. In the process of being offered this gift is so changed as to become more worthy of and acceptable to God. After being prepared and consecrated, it is definitively given to God. This is the external aspect of sacrifice, its outward symbol. According to its inner aspect thus outwardly symbolized, the sacrificial gift is a sign by which man gives himself to God. The offering of the gift signifies the sacrificer's oblation of himself. The preparation

and consecration of the gift is the expression of the interior
preparation of the sacrificer, of his betterment, perfection,
and sanctification. The final offering of tl : prepared gift
is the expression of the definitive oblation to God of the soul
thus prepared, in order to do honor to God and to become
united with him." [9]

Thus understood, sacrifice is the most perfect ritual practice of religion, truly a profession of dependence on God
and an acknowledgment of the propriety of our rational
subservience to him, nay, the very fulfillment of this
reasonable subservience or service. Thence we can understand not only the universality of the existence of sacrifice
among peoples, but especially also the high esteem in which
it was held by men, their attachment to their sacrificial rites.
How unwilling the early Christians were to offer incense
even when asked to do so only externally, we know. From
the standpoint alone of the religious value of sacrificial
action one can well understand the supreme importance
the Church has ever attached to her official sacrifice, apart
entirely from its true divine character which raises it so
supremely above any other sacrifice.

In every sacrifice we have the two aspects of the liturgical
action, the external and the internal. Because of the complex liturgical prayer and action by which the sacrifice of
the Mass is offered up, and especially because of the Protestant and the non-Christian mentalities of our recent centuries, which are quite anti-liturgical, it is curiously enough
the real internal element of the Mass that has been almost
entirely ignored. Consequently many of the faithful today
will still be unable to give more than a vague answer to
the question: Just in what way should the member of

[9] Kramp, *The Liturgical Sacrifice of the New Law*, pp. 33–34

Christ assisting at Mass enter actively into the sacrificial action there enacted? in what way is the sacrifice of the Mass also his sacrifice?

"The sacrifice that is offered outwardly," says St. Thomas, "represents the inward spiritual sacrifice, whereby the soul offers itself to God according to the words of the psalmist: A sacrifice to God is an afflicted spirit." [10] That the inward sacrifice is supreme in the Mass, follows not only from what we have said in general about the true nature of the liturgy of the Church, but especially also from the fact that the Mass is a holy action performed by virtue of the priestly powers of Christ vested in the ordained priest and that it has Christ himself present under the sacramental species. The Mass, then, must not only as a sacrificial offering show the general marks of all sacrifice, but must show these elements as clothed with a value to us that can come only from the Son of God himself. If this value is present it should show itself through the external forms in spite of its having been hidden to many persons for so long, and any examination or study of the progressive action of the Mass should have as a primary purpose the revealing of it to the inquiring mind.

V. THE PARTS OF THE MASS

For a long time the question of the division of the Mass into its important parts was answered by enumerating the offertory, the consecration, and the communion. This in itself may be a reflection of the purely legalistic attitude we have come to take over against everything pertaining to the liturgy. The answer is connected with the decision that

[10] Ps. 50:19

the Sunday obligation to attend Mass is fulfilled only if the attendance includes these three moments of the sacrifice.

From the earliest days on the Mass was divided into two distinct parts, called respectively the Mass of the Catechumens and the Mass of the Faithful. The very names of these parts would indicate a special purpose for each of them in relation to the groups named. The catechumens of old were allowed to attend only the first part named after them. When that was ended they were called upon to leave. The second part is the true enactment of the liturgical mystery of Christ's sacrifice. Only those who had received the gift of faith in baptism were formerly allowed to attend, only they were capable of entering into the intimate union of fellowship with their brethren and with Christ that the common participation of all in one and the same sacrifice demanded and entailed. It was the real Mass and was only for the members of Christ to be present at, for presence to the early Christians could only mean active participation.

In a previous chapter we mentioned the twofold aspect of all liturgical prayer, of all true prayer, the directing of mind and heart to God on the part of man and the descent of God's blessing upon men. In the one part man gives homage to God and in the other God gives grace to man. It is on this twofold aspect of prayer that the further division of each of the two parts of the Mass is made. This is explained tersely as follows: "The Mass is an interchange of gifts; we give to God and God gives to us. This double motive is the basis of the entire Mass-structure. It determines the division into two parts of both the Mass of the Catechumens and the Mass of the Faithful. In the

Mass of the Catechumens we first give to God, in the prayer-part, and then God gives to us, in the instruction-part. Likewise in the Mass of the Faithful, the sacrifice-oblation is our gift to God, while the sacrifice-banquet is God's gift to us. In both cases the interchange is effected through our intimate union with Christ who is both God and man, according to the ever-recurring phrase: *per Christum Dominum nostrum*: through Christ our Lord." Accordingly we have the following scheme: [11]

THE MASS	I. Mass of the Catechumens:	1. Prayer	
		2. Instruction	
	II. Mass of the Faithful:	1. Sacrifice-oblation:	Offertory & Consecration
		2. Sacrifice-banquet:	Communion

The Mass of the Catechumens ends with the gospel or the Creed and the Mass of the Faithful begins with the *"Dominus vobiscum"* of the offertory. The sacrifice-oblation continues from there on to the minor doxology at the end of the Canon; and the sacrifice-banquet begins here with the introductory exhortation to the Pater noster. As the names indicate, the former is the real sacrificial offering of the Mass, and the latter is the communion part. These two parts however form one integral liturgical prayer, the Mass of the Faithful. It is only through our loss of liturgical sense that the custom could arise of attending Mass without receiving Communion, or of receiving outside the Mass without grave reason. After a description of a "High Mass with St. Gregory Great" a modern author concludes with the following statement: "In two important respects social participation in eucharistic worship has diminished since the end of the sixth century; first, the

[11] Quotation and scheme are both from Busch, *The Mass-Drama*, pp. 11–12

individual worshipers no longer make a personal gift-offering of the sacrificial elements, and secondly, the reception of Communion is not now regarded as a necessary adjunct of assistance at the Sacrifice." [12]

The two parts of the Mass of the Faithful will receive separate treatment in the two following chapters. Here we shall confine ourselves to the Mass of the Catechumens. It is sometimes called the Foremass today, especially in other countries, since it is a sort of preamble or preparation for the sacrifice proper. Such is still the purpose of this part of the Mass today, even if the distinction between catechumens and faithful from the above-mentioned standpoint has disappeared long ago, in fact shortly after the ending of the violent persecutions of the early centuries. "The Mass of the Catechumens continues to retain its ancient character of being in part a sort of initiation into the truths of the Christian religion, especially through the epistles and gospels. More than the rest of the Mass it emphasizes the truths of religion connected with the special feast of the day, and it helps to link up the general celebration of the Eucharist with these divine truths." [18]

The Mass of the Faithful, as we have seen, is the common sacrifice of all assembled insofar as they have united themselves with the officiating priest. It is the holiest of holy actions, performed by the living members of Christ's body acting in unity of heart and mind with him. When they first assemble for this action, they are occupied each with his own affairs; the echo of the things of the world is still in their minds. For the worthy common celebration of the holy mystery of the Eucharist, they must not only

[12] Ellard, *Christian Life and Worship*, p. 130
[18] Michel, *My Sacrifice and Yours*, p. 53

be properly lifted up in mind above the things of earth, but also be joined together in a unity of holy sentiments and aspirations, so that they can in truth enter upon that oneness of action, which is called for in the nature of the Mass and is so pleasing to Christ. In this lies the preparatory task of the Mass of the Catechumens.

VI. Mass of the Catechumens

The fuller participation by members in the sacrificial action of Christ depends on the degree in which the members can attain to the disposition and the mind of Christ. One of the first prayers of the sacrifice-oblation makes mention of the "spirit of humility" and the "contrite heart' by reason of which God should receive us favorably. Again the first prayers of the sacrifice-banquet ask God to purify our minds. In all the main liturgical blessings, prayer for the positive grace of God is preceded by a petition for purgation from anything that may hinder the blessing of God. The Mass of the Catechumens begins with the same idea, purgation of mind from all that is not of God. It is the prayers at the foot of the altar that present this first, or negative stage of mental preparation, that of expurgation of any sins and faults which may be clinging to the soul. These prayers, also called preliminary prayers, were formerly recited in the sacristy by celebrant and assistants. They are now recited alternately by the priest and the servers, who are speaking in the name of the people. In the following pages we shall take for granted that the people are again taking part in the Mass and joining in the prayers set aside for them.

The Mass begins with the sign of the cross, which occurs

so often in the holy action, but only in this instance with formal accompaniment of the words. Thereupon follows the psalm *Judica*, the gist of which is contained in the confident declaration, "I will go in unto the altar of God: unto God who giveth joy to my youth." After this official statement of intention, and the versicle, "Our help is in the name of God," with its simple answer "Who made heaven and earth," the priest confesses his faults in general terms to God and his saints, and then asks the saints and the people to pray for his forgiveness. The people answer: "May almighty God have mercy upon thee, forgive thee thy sins, and bring thee to life everlasting." After the priest's "Amen," the people in turn confess their sins in the same general terms and the priest recites the prayer for forgiveness in their behalf. Then the priest asks officially for himself and the people: "May the almighty and merciful Lord grant us pardon, absolution and remission of our sins." This beautiful dialog prayer, a noble exchange of holy sentiments and true Christian charity, is typical of the collective nature of the sacrificial action, as of the solidarity of the Church militant with that of the Church triumphant. After a short continuation of the holy dialog, the priest ascends to the altar, reciting alone, as presiding official, another prayer for purification: "Take away all our iniquities, we beseech thee, O Lord, that we may be worthy to enter with pure minds into the holy of holies. Through Christ our Lord. Amen."

After a further prayer invoking the merits of the saints, the introit, formerly the entrance song, is sung. It gives the keynote of the special feast or mystery to be commemorated or attained in the Mass. Thus on the feast of the Assumption of our Lady: "Let us all rejoice in the

Lord, celebrating a festival day in honor of the blessed virgin Mary, for whose Assumption the angels rejoice and give praise to the Son of God"; or for Ascension Thursday: "Ye men of Galilee, why wonder you, looking up to heaven? alleluia. He shall so come as you have seen him going up into heaven, alleluia. O clap your hands, all ye nations; shout unto God with the voice of exultation." Upon the introit follows the Kyrie, the triple cry of mercy, first to the Father, then to the Son, and also to the Holy Ghost—an invocation of the three persons of the Trinity that is most fitting at the very beginning of the holy action of the Mass. It is followed by the sublime hymn of praise, which was begun by the angels on the first Christmas night. The Gloria is a true form of elevated prayer. In it there is little thought of ourselves; instead we praise, bless, glorify God the Father, sing the greatness of Christ who alone is holy, and properly conclude with mention of the Holy Ghost.

We have now arrived at a higher elevation of mind unto God. In the collect, which follows, the priest, inviting the people to join with him, asks God, in the name of all, for some spiritual fruit that the Mass is to bestow on the corporate body of those sacrificing. It is the first more conscious uniting of all minds in a special common sentiment under the official direction of the priest. The elevation and unification of minds continues in the epistle, which begins the second or receiving part of the Mass of the Catechumens. The epistle instructs the people through the inspired word of a prophet of the Old or an apostle of the New Testament. That the instruction may have its immediate fruit, that the heart may act upon the information thus received by the mind, the gradual, tract, or alleluia verse is sung. Taken from the psalms, these lift the heart up to God with the impelling inspiration of the divine word and with the contagious enthusiasm so characteristic of these unexcelled religious poems.

At this point the music of the Gregorian chant reinforces the holy words with all the effectiveness of the art that it embraces within its purpose and scope. Artistically, emotionally, the chant is perhaps at its height in this part of the Mass. And most fittingly so. For its purpose is not only to reinforce the living sentiments thus far uttered but to elevate the minds still more, to prepare them for what is to come. For after the prophet or apostle has spoken in the epistle, there comes One who is immeasurably greater. None other than Christ himself speaks to us in the gospel, in order to educate our minds and hearts to a state in which we can more worthily proceed with the performance of his own sacrifice. Even in a low Mass all must stand for this reading, as only a standing position will express properly the reverence we must feel for the divine word dropped into our hearts by our divine Master himself.

With this word of Christ the elevation and unification of hearts in the celebrating members of the mystical body is completed. The holy action of offering is now about to begin. As in other liturgical functions, however, a further summarizing action usually takes place, a fitting conclusion to this preparatory part of the sacrificial service. Before receiving the power of forgiving sins, the candidate for ordination to the priesthood publicly recites the confession of faith. The sponsors at baptism do the same in behalf of the infant candidate for baptism. Similarly in most Masses, and always in the more official celebrations, the beginning of the Mass of the Faithful is preceded by the common recitation of the official *Credo* of the Church. In the simplest phrases, the better expressing the unambiguous dogmatic character of the mysteries professed, are the great truths of our religion professed.

"I believe in one God, the Father almighty, maker of heaven and earth," the *Credo* commences. From the Father it proceeds to "the only begotten Son of God. Born of the Father before all ages . . . true God of true God . . . who for us men, and for our salvation came down from heaven." Then follow the mysteries of our Redeemer, the incarnation, the virgin birth, the suffering and crucifixion, resurrection and ascension, the glorious throne in heaven, and the future coming as judge and eternal king. The Holy Ghost is professed as "Lord and giver of life, who proceedeth from the Father and the Son." Most properly the greater number of phrases is given to the Son, around whom center the chief mysteries of our relation with God, and whose mysteries we are about to enact and share in the sacrifice. Likewise is the mention of the mysteries of the divine Godhead most appropriately followed by a confession of our belief in "the one, holy, Catholic, and apostolic Church," for the Church is the embodiment of the divine life on earth, and by our belief in "one baptism for the remission of sins," for the liturgy is the Church's manner of living her divine life. Upon this confession of the divine mysteries and their earthly extension comes that of the last truths, which are also the basis of our hope and our perseverance, "the resurrection of the dead, and the life of the world to come."

The *Credo* is truly the embodiment of the whole dispensation of God, an epitome of the life of God in heaven and on earth, of all time past, present and future. Thus in the meeting of time and eternity are the minds of the faithful and the priest made one in God, turned away from the affairs of the earth to those of heaven, cemented in one faith in the one God, and prepared for the unified enactment of the one great sacrifice. After the *Credo* the priest kisses the altar, *i.e.*, Christ, turns to the people with the greeting, "The Lord be with you," and commences the Mass of the Faithful.

CHAPTER IX

THE SACRIFICE–OBLATION

I. Offering of the Gifts

"THERE are two goods," says Dr. Parsch, "which the Christian dispensation offers to us: faith and grace; Christ can take possession of our souls in a twofold manner, through faith and through the divine life of grace. These two goods are constantly imparted and developed in us through the Mass. In the Mass of the Catechumens it is faith or Christ in faith—hence the gospel is the climax of the Foremass and the Credo its final expression. In the Mass of the Faithful, the sacrifice of Christ is made present, which purchases the divine life for us, and the Eucharist is bestowed, which contains and develops this life."[1] Having both informed their faith and professed it anew in the Mass of the Catechumens, the faithful are spiritually prepared to enter upon the essential sacrificial action of Christ in union with their fellow members and their divine Head.

After exchanging the beautiful spiritual greeting with the people in the words "The Lord be with you," to which they answer, "And with thy spirit," the priest turns again to the altar and exhorts all to prayer: "*Oremus:* Let us pray." This exhortation formerly introduced a series of

[1] *Messerklaerung*, pp. 52–53

intentions and prayers for them, of which the liturgy of Good Friday contains an ancient example. Today the priest at once recites the offertory verse. This is usually a verse from a psalm, the whole of which was formerly sung during the offertory procession. It was then the custom for all the people to bring a gift of their own in person to the altar at this time of the Mass, especially bread and wine. Part of the latter was set aside by the priest for the sacrifice and the rest was put on separate tables for dispensing to the poor. Thus the offering of bread and wine was really something that had been given by the people, and could more directly represent their very persons and their lives. In that way the conscious relation of the people to the Mass was brought out much more emphatically than today. The people went up to the altar of Christ, they placed themselves in their gifts on the very altar of the sacrifice as living oblations to God, and in the consecration they were most truly merged in the very passion and death of Christ, sharing fully in the redemptive action of Christ made really present in the liturgical mystery. Even today, however, we must see the whole purpose of the collection taken up at the offertory on Sundays in the light of its ancient predecessor. In this collection the people are giving up something that is their own, are giving up part of themselves to the Church, and their offering is used for the maintenance of the divine services, especially for the Mass. Today the gifts of bread and wine therefore represent the people as truly as of old, and it is with this in mind that the faithful should both contribute to the Church at the offertory and enter heart and mind into the action and prayers of offering in union with the celebrating priest.

The priest offers the bread with the prayer: "Accept, O holy Father, almighty and eternal God, this host for the all-holy sacrifice, which I, thy unworthy servant, offer unto thee, my living and true God, to atone for my numberless sins of wilfulness and neglect; on behalf of all here present, and likewise for all faithful Christians, living and dead, that it may profit me and them, as a means of salvation unto life everlasting. Amen." [2] An analysis of this prayer gives us a summary of the whole purpose and nature of the sacrificial offering. It is (1) rendered by the priest, (2) to God, (3) in atonement, (4) in behalf of all present, (5) for all the faithful of the Church, (6) unto salvation and eternal life. We shall meet with many statements in the Mass prayers that are expressive of the unity and solidarity of the whole Church as well as indicative of purposes of the Mass, which are as broad as the all-embracing sympathy and love of Christ.

While mixing water with the wine he has put into the chalice, the priest says one of the most beautiful and significant prayers of the whole Mass. It contains in a few phrases the whole essence of the Redemption as of the sacrifice of the altar. "O God, who hast established the nature of man in wondrous dignity, and still more admirably restored it, grant that through the mystery of this water and wine, we may be made partakers of his dignity, who has deigned to become partaker of our humanity, Jesus Christ, thy Son, etc." In the action the water stands for the people, the wine for Christ, says St. Cyprian. In the incarnation Christ had ennobled human nature and on Calvary he had renewed it. In the liturgy and especially

---

[2] The text of the ordinary is quoted from Goeb, *Offeramus* and was rendered into English by the Reverend Richard E. Power.

in the Mass we apply the fruits of this renewal, that is, we become renewed through union with Christ. This is symbolized by the union of water with wine, which becomes the more significant because the drops of water merge indistinguishably with the wine, all of which will then later become the real living Christ of the Eucharist. The prayer asks simply that the union thus symbolized may become a perfect reality through the liturgical mystery being enacted on the altar.

The chalice is offered up with the following prayer, addressed like the others to the Father: "We offer unto thee, O Lord, the chalice of salvation, humbly begging of thy mercy that it may arise before thy divine majesty with a pleasing fragrance, for our salvation and that of all mankind. Amen." This is a simple plea for acceptance, and another mention of the purpose of the Mass, namely, our salvation and that of the whole world! The latter thought again shows us how conscious the liturgy is of the mission of Christ, how it always looks beyond the individual or the assembled group to the entire mystical body, to potential as well as actual members.

The next prayers continue to ask for the favorable acceptance of the offerings. Significantly the priest asks in regard to ourselves the offerers: "In a spirit of humility and with a contrite heart, may we be accepted by thee, O Lord," and requests that we may be enabled so to offer our sacrifice that it will be pleasing in the sight of God. Then God as the divine ratifier of all the work of Christ and his Church is invoked to come down and to "bless this sacrifice prepared for the glory of thy holy name." During this prayer the priest makes the first of many signs of the cross over the oblation, thus by virtue of his priestly power, here officially exercised, actually bringing down the blessing of God. After this, in solemn Masses, the offerings are incensed. For us it is significant that the people present are also incensed, therefore both the gifts and all the people whom they represent, for the people are to be offered to the heavenly Father in the Mass by means of these gifts.

In imitation of the Hebrew highpriest of old after the handling of the sacrificial victim, the priest now washes his hands, reciting some verses of psalm 25, which indicate that the sacrifice must be offered up with innocence of heart and mind. After that comes the summing-up prayer, addressed to the Trinity: "Accept, most holy Trinity, this offering which we are making to thee in remembrance of the passion, resurrection, and ascension of Jesus Christ our Lord: and in honor of blessed Mary ever-virgin, blessed John the Baptist, the holy apostles Peter and Paul, and of these, and of all the saints; that it may add to their honor and procure our salvation; and may they deign to intercede in heaven for us who cherish their memory here on earth: Through the same Christ our Lord, Amen." Here we have a declaration that the sacrifice is in memory not only of Christ's passion but also of his resurrection and ascension, of the whole work of redemption. This declaration will significantly be repeated in the first words of prayer after the consecration has been consummated and Christ is sacramentally on the altar as the all-inclusive Gift. A great difference between Calvary and the Mass is that Christ is now also the risen and glorified Christ, Christ totally and undivided. Furthermore all our imitation and realization of Christ is also to be of his resurrection and ascension. That precisely is the purpose of all the liturgy, that we rise with Christ unto life everlasting. In the above prayer the great fact of the Communion of the Saints, the solidarity of the entire fellowship of Christ, is again drawn upon. We honor the saints unto our salvation, because in honoring them we please and honor God, and their intercession will greatly help us. Our whole purpose being to get nearer to Christ, we naturally approach those who are perfect members of the mystical body of Christ, through whom we find more ready entrance into union with our mutual divine Head.

II. OUR OBLATION

The offertory prayers we have been examining are practically all of relatively recent introduction into the Mass text. When the offertory procession was still the ordinary practice, it took the place in a graphic way of all verbal prayers of offering. After the gifts had been set aside for the sacrifice, *i.e.*, placed on the altar, the secret prayer was recited by the priest as the common oblation prayer of all. Today, especially where the offertory procession is not again in use, it is all the more incumbent on all the faithful to enter heart and soul in the recitation of the offering prayers in union with the priest. This is all the more true insofar as in our day we have allowed the custom to establish itself of having the faithful at this time sit down in the benches, a posture of receptivity and not of active participation, whereas one of the offering prayers still makes mention of the *circumstantes*, those standing about the altar and participating actively.

But the fine psychological sense of the Church is not yet satisfied with the prayers so far mentioned. The liturgy is enacting the noblest drama there is, and its specific aim is also to work up our minds into the most perfect disposition for deriving the best fruits from participation in the liturgical mysteries of the Mass. Hence the Church freely uses the principle of progressive repetition. The priest now turns to the people and exhorts them: "Brethren, pray that my sacrifice and yours may become acceptable to God the Father almighty." And the people answer: "May the Lord receive the sacrifice at thy hands, unto the praise and glory of his name, for our advantage and that of all his holy Church," to which the priest in turn gives his official "Amen." What a beautiful summary! Again the Father is the chief recipient of the sacrifice, the purpose of which is that of the entire liturgical worship, as it is of the creation and incarnation, namely, the praise and glory of God and the salvation of man. And the sense of the solidarity of the mystical body is again stressed in the praying for all the Church. Truly the Mass is the sacrifice of the people!

After this summary sacrificial prayer, the secret is said. It is a collect form of prayer, varying with each different Mass. It generally expresses some sentiment connected with the season or the feast or mystery being celebrated, and always refers to the oblations to be sacrificed, so that the sum total of the secrets of the missal would give us an admirable exposition of the significance of the sacrificial offering made in the Mass. Our connection with the gifts of bread and wine has already been mentioned. Hence we readily understand why the secret of Trinity Sunday, for instance, prays that God "sanctify . . . the victim of this sacrifice: and through its means make of us too an eternal offering to thee." The gifts are indeed ours and the sacrifice is also our offering: "Look graciously, O Lord, upon thy people, look graciously upon our gifts" (secret, thirteenth Sunday after Pentecost); in fact, in the gifts we are offering ourselves: "Receive the offering of this spiritual victim and make of us too an eternal oblation to thee" (Monday after Pentecost).

To realize the mind of the liturgy and of Christ in this regard, we must ever enter more deeply into the purpose of the action of the offering, we must consciously associate ourselves with the gifts on the altar and make of them and of ourselves one selfsame oblation. Nothing less will do for the member of Christ. "It is necessary," writes Dom Ryelandt, "that when the priest elevates the paten with the host, we in union with him also elevate our soul and our body, our whole life, in oblation to God: presenting our 'bodies a living sacrifice, holy, pleasing unto God.'" [3] The essence of Christ's sacrificial action was the complete subjection of his will to that of his Father; everything else was but the working out of this act of oblation. The essence of our sacrifice must likewise be an act of our will, performed in union with the priest, first of all at the official first offering we are now dealing with. We may take our cue from the atmosphere of the liturgical season, or from some special circumstances of our own life. But always should our offering also contain some personal element, something concrete, and perferably connected with the life of the day.

With the host we may place on the paten some special sorrow we have had, some recent difficulty, some current vexation, the failings or sins of which we are guilty and repentant, or again all our joys and hopes, our wants and

[3] *Pour mieux communier*, p. 18

desires, but above all our love and homage, so that with the host they may be offered up to God.

It is here that our action will be the more efficacious because we have joined it with that of the Church of Christ, with the divine depositary of Christ's priestly powers in all their efficacy, by uniting our action with that of her priest. Because the priest acts by official delegation, he acts in the name of the whole Church, and through him and her Christ himself acts. Thus our action becomes part of the action of the whole mystical body of Christ. We no longer stand alone, but act with the backing of the same irresistible power that wrought our redemption in the first instance, and our voices are merged in the pleadings of Christ and of all the friends of Christ, also of those already blessed in heaven and enjoying forever the intimate friendship of God.

With this, however, we have not yet exhausted the sublime transcendence of the liturgical sacrifice. Were ours but an ordinary offering, our action could end here, whereas it is in reality just beginning. The secret of the Epiphany asks God to "regard graciously . . . the gifts of thy Church, in which are offered now no longer gold, frankincense, and myrrh, but he whom those offerings signified is immolated and received, Jesus Christ thy Son our Lord." Other sacrifices must remain content with the purely symbolical offering of a gift to God. Ours begins therewith and is symbolical not merely after the manner of man but after that of the liturgical mysteries; it is truly a holy, a divine action unfolding itself, in which God himself lives and acts in all reality. The gifts will later be transformed into the divine victim, Christ himself; and this transformation gives to our present actions their full significance, their sublime spiritual value. It was Christ whose blood originally washed human nature into an acceptable purity. Now we have merged ourselves with all our weaknesses in the oblations. The more perfect this act of ours is the more perfectly shall we also be transformed into acceptable gifts, into possessors of the divine life, when the gifts are consecrated. Then we shall again come into direct contact with the saving flow of Christ's own blood and be purified unto a veritable share in the divine life itself. "O God, who by thy venerable intercourse with us in this sacrifice makest us partakers of the one supreme Godhead," says the secret of the eighteenth Sunday after Pentecost. Truly, words can hardly depict the rich bounty of this liturgical action. Only repetition of the action itself will through the divine light open our understanding gradually to the fulness of it.

The first prayers of the offering are therefore only a first step, but they foreshadow the greater things to come. The gifts have now been designated for a holy purpose, and a renewed offering more eloquent of their divine mission is to take place. Before entering upon it, the liturgy cannot refrain from giving voice to a sublime prayer of gratitude and praise for all the good things of God. After the customary salutation of "The Lord be with you," the priest exhorts the people to lift up their hearts and give thanks, and he enters thereby upon the singing of the preface: At all times and at all places is thanks to be given to God. And with the angels in heaven is the community to join its voice in humbly but joyously singing "Holy, holy, holy, Lord God almighty! Heaven and earth are filled with thy glory. . . . Blessed is he that cometh in the name of the Lord." With that we have again announced the coming of the Lord, and at the same time have entered into the holy of holies, the sacred Canon of the Mass, in which the liturgical Epiphany is to be realized.

III. THE CANON

After this common prayer of priest and people as an introduction the body of the Canon commences, in the climax of which Christ himself enters in sacramental reality. This is the most sacred action of the Mass, in which the intimate union of members and Head is to be consummated. Loud externals would only disturb the silent communion of the souls, and no words are really adequate to express even remotely the sacred event that is taking place. The Church emphasizes the mystic solemnity by prescribing the silent recitation of the prayers by her officiating priest. The Canon as it now exists dates from very ancient times. It is succinct in its expression and very definitely and symmetrically ordered. Its progress from the introductory preface to the concluding doxology to the Trinity can be divided as follows: (1) Three memento prayers commemorating the Church, the congregation and the Communion of Saints; (2) Two oblation prayers; (3) The Consecration, containing the effective narrative of the Last Supper and a memorial prayer; (4) Two oblation prayers; (5) Three memento prayers commemorating the dead, those present, and the gifts of the nature.

The drama of the Mass here begins by a renewed oblation of the gifts, which have now been sanctified by their holy purpose and which are offered in memory of the Church and the hierarchy: "And now, most gracious

Father, we humbly beg of thee and entreat thee, through Jesus Christ, thy Son our Lord, to deem acceptable and bless these gifts, now set apart for the holy and all-perfect sacrifice; which we offer unto thee especially for thy holy Catholic Church, that thou wouldst deign to keep it in peace and unity, to protect and sustain it throughout the world; together with thy servant N., our pope, and N., our bishop and all the bishops and their flocks, who cherish the catholic and apostolic faith."

Again the solidarity of the Church is uppermost. The offering is in the first place for the Church, for the visible universal head and for the local successor of the apostles, both of whom represent the Church and Christ for us. There is no saving sacrifice apart from communion with the Church, and in every official sacrifice the efficacious power of the whole Church is thrown into the balance in our favor. This prayer is followed by the memento for the living, for whom the Mass is to be offered in a special manner and who are rightly called servants of God, as well as for "all here present," who have by this time shown their mind, and "whose faith is known" to God. The sacrifice is offered in their behalf and they themselves also offer "this sacrifice of praise for themselves and all who are theirs, for the good of their souls." The prayer of priest and people is fortified by a third commemoration, that of the saints in heaven, headed by the Mother of God and the apostles. They are the more tested and tried members of the mystical body, already glorified and most intimately united to God. Hence we ask God that by their "merits and prayers . . . we may be always favored with the help of thy protection," but always "through the same Christ our Lord."

Encouraged by the assistance of the saints, we again address God with a special view to his acceptance of our gifts and their most holy purpose: "We further beseech thee, O Lord, to receive in atonement this sacrifice of adoration from us and from all thy household. Provide that our days be spent in thy peace and save us from everlasting damnation, and cause us to be numbered among those whom thou hast chosen." During these words the priest has held his hands extended over the bread and wine. It is a gesture apparently taken over from the ancient Hebrew sacrifices. We have not forgotten that the oblations represent ourselves, and that by action of our wills, we have united ourselves, our troubles and transgressions, with these gifts. Before the ancient offering, the Hebrew highpriest held his hands on the forehead of the oxen to be sacrificed so that his sins and those of the people might be thus transferred to the victim and washed away in its blood. So, too, at Mass the imposition of the priest's hands will signify the transfer of our burdens and failings into the oblations, so that the power of consecration may transfigure them and us into a state of purity and divine life.

With this action we are ready for the supreme moment of the consecration and in a final prayer of offering, we ask God's blessing in direct reference to the transformation of the gifts into the divine Victim. "Do thou, O God, deign to bless what we offer, and make it approved, effective, worthy, and pleasing in every way, that it may become for our good, the Body and Blood of thy dearly beloved Son our Lord Jesus Christ."

The moment has arrived, the consecration is at hand. The Canon continues in the gospel word narrating the institution of the Eucharist. This is the quintessence of the liturgical mystery. In form it relates a past event. But in the memorial enactment of it by the Church, the event itself becomes present in a most real sacramental manner, the past becomes present in all its divine efficacy and reality. The priest pronounces the formula of consecration in the first person, but the words are Christ's own. By virtue of his sacramental ordination he speaks for Christ. This is the distinctive nature of his certified official priesthood over against the general priesthood of all the faithful. In the act of the consecration the people have no co-operative part; it is there they are most purely witnesses of the mystery being enacted before their eyes for their good.

The consecration is God's acceptance of our gifts, and it is the most sublime acceptance that the mind can think of. Not only are the gifts received, but Christ himself comes down upon the altar and identifies himself substantially with them. In the divine mystery of the transubstantiation he has taken their place and has identified himself with us and our burdens and prayers, just as he did two thousand years ago in the great mystery of the incarnation.

As far as dignity of action is concerned, we are in the act of consecration at the supreme moment of the Mass. The divine is enacted before our very eyes. But as far as the sacrificial action of the liturgical mystery is concerned, we are only now entering upon its most efficacious moment, Christ, as it were, having come down to help us complete it, to complete it for us.

So far we have had a twofold action of offering. First

was the setting apart of the gifts for the purpose of sacrifice, their designation as objects destined for a holy action and their dedication to God. And then, in the part of the Canon so far analyzed, we had the more intimate offering of these objects to God for the special purpose of effecting the end of our liturgical sacrifice. In the whole text we have so far a progressive development by definite steps properly adapted to our nature. It expresses admirably our relation to God and addresses itself to the eternal Father as the fountain and source of the Godhead, of all divine life. The mediatorship of Christ is expressed repeatedly, it is never left out of mind. The Church also expresses her own share in the exercise of this mediatorship by repeatedly blessing the gifts on the altar with the sign of the cross made by her official representative. Very emphatic is the mention of the entire Church and the relationship of the Church militant to the Church triumphant in heaven. The bond uniting the two as different parts of the organism that is the fulness of Christ is rendered efficacious by their intercession. Through the solidary fellowship of all the faithful united in Christ, the individual lives the life of Christ, which by participation becomes his own. All of this shows us the profound richness of the liturgical worship of the Church; yet it all pales into insignificance in face of the divine fact that takes place through the consecration of the Mass. Here we have the realization of the divine mystery to the fullest extent, by which indeed "the work of our redemption is enacted." "What a sublime Mystery!" exclaims Dom Boeser. "The sacrifice of the eternal Highpriest on Golgotha and the sacrifice of the Mass on our altars — the identical sacrifice! The sacrifice of the eternal Highpriest, which was actually present nearly two thousand years ago, becomes actually present again today in every holy Mass." [4]

IV. The Divine Victim

By means of the consecration, then, the sacrifice of Christ has become real on the altar itself. The same victim as on Calvary is now on the sacrificial table. In the fullest sense possible a holy action has been performed; the divine act of redemption itself is re-presented, made present again. We are face to face with the same mystery as on Calvary; it is re-enacted in the way chosen and commanded by our divine Savior himself at the Last Supper. Even the death of the Redeemer is symbolized by the separated species. And as on the cross, so now has Christ drawn all unto himself, united all in him. Through the descent of Christ into the common gifts of the offerers, he has united them, his members, in a special way to himself as their head. It is a sublime exercise of the mediatory power of Christ, by which he unites all to himself so that they may thus become acceptable offerings unto his heavenly Father. Now is made possible the fulfilment of the prayer, which the Church so well expresses in some of her secrets: "We beseech thee, O holy Lord, Father almighty, eternal God, that our sacrifice may be made pleasing to thee through him who on this day taught his disciples to do this in commemoration of him" (Maundy Thursday), or again, "May thine only begotten Son, O Lord, . . . deliver us from our sins and make our offering agreeable unto thee."

There is a wide-spread belief that now the time has

[4] *The Mass-Liturgy,* p. 61

come for directing our prayers of adoration to Christ on the altar. Hence the importance some place on pronouncing the indulgenced formula "My Lord and my God!" while the consecrated Host is being elevated. This is indeed well and good, and has the full approval of the vicar of Christ. But it extends only to the moment of elevation, at which, however, the approved formula may not be said aloud. Formerly the Mass knew nothing of the elevation and of the ringing of the bell at the consecration. These practices were introduced only later, when heretics began to deny the doctrine of the Real Presence.

What action the Mass itself calls for after the consecration has been indicated above. Christ does not descend on the altar in the resplendent glory of our king or judge, but still as the divine mediator. If anything, the mediatorial character of Christ has grown doubly emphatic by reason of the consecration. It is precisely now that, humanly speaking, he attains an opportunity more nearly equal to the one he used so well on Calvary. The moment is indeed unique in the liturgy, and the Church loses no time in making fullest use of it. Having received the divine Redeemer as victim of her sacrifice, she immediately offers him up to the heavenly Father as the one fully acceptable gift of oblation.

Attached to the consecration formula is the prayer that follows, which is a memorial prayer or memorial offering in expansion of the preceding. At the genuflection after consecration of the chalice the priest says: "As often as you shall do these things, in memory of me shall you do them." Hence the next prayer calls to mind the redemptive mysteries being enacted: "Wherefore, O Lord, we thy servants, and likewise thy holy people, calling to mind not only the blessed passion of the same Christ thy Son, but also his resurrection from the dead, and finally his glorious ascension into heaven, offer unto thy supreme majesty, of thy gifts bestowed on us, the pure, the holy, the all-perfect sacrifice of thanks for our redemption— the holy Bread of life eternal and the Chalice of unending salvation." After this eucharistic commemoration, *i.e.*, a thanksgiving memorial-offering, the Canon proceeds to the two formal offering prayers. In the first God is asked "to regard with gracious and kindly attention" the gifts just mentioned, and to accept them even as he accepted the sacrifices of Abel, Abraham, and Melchisedech.

The question might arise here, why we should at all offer to God his only begotten Son, who long ago ascended to heaven and who sits forever at the right of the Father, and especially why we should pray so solicitously for the acceptance by the Father as if the Father could refuse to accept his own divine Son. If the Mass were a literal repetition of the circumstances of Calvary, the question might have some force. But in the Mass Christ is no longer making the offering alone. The whole Church now unites with him, and especially those present and actually participating. They are joined to Christ both as offerers and as victims offered. This is the new aspect found in the sacrifice of the Mass: the conscious association of the faithful with the sacrifice of Christ. It is just this that makes of the Mass the fuller development of Christ, the actual application of the fruits of Calvary to all who have part in the Mass. Now the association of the members of Christ's body with him and his sacrifice is dependent on the perfect state of their minds and wills. Christ will undoubtedly be accepted by the Father, but the acceptance of the members is in so far less certain as they may not perfectly unite their wills with that of their divine Head, may still suffer human weaknesses that prevent them from entering fully into the action of their Head. The collect petition for the feast of the Purification might well be applied to the offering of Christ to the Father after the consecration: "We humbly beseech thy Majesty that, as thine only begotten Son was this day presented in the temple in the substance of our flesh, so thou wouldst grant that we too, with purified souls, may be presented unto thee."

It is then for the acceptance of the wider Christ, of the entire mystical body, of ourselves with Christ, that the last set of oblation prayers is recited. From this standpoint the reference to Christ's passion, and especially to his resurrection and ascension, becomes significant. The members of the mystical body here on earth must still perfect themselves in the passion of Christ and they must still achieve their final resurrection and ascension. This resurrection and ascension we hope for through the sacrifice, and we shall the more surely attain them, now in part and then fully, the more acceptably we can unite ourselves with our Head in the oblation of the Mass.

The second prayer of offering gives us an indication of this. It asks for a ratification of the gifts, that the gifts be carried by the hands of "thy holy angel unto thy altar above, before the face of thy divine majesty." This time a purpose is expressed which relates specifically to those who are participating in the sacrifice: "that those of us who, from this sharing in the heavenly sacrifice, shall receive the most sacred Body and Blood of thy Son, may be filled with every grace and heavenly blessing: Through the same Christ our Lord. Amen." Primarily the prayer asks for the full reception by the offerers of the benefits of their act of offering themselves with Jesus. The text, however, also shows us the common understanding of a former day, namely, that those attending the Mass receive Christ sacramentally in communion.

Having united themselves more intimately with Christ in the sacrifice, the members of the Church militant make a memento for their fellow-members of the Church suffering "who have gone before us with the sign of faith, and rest in the sleep of peace." This is a touching example of how the Church in union with Christ has imbibed intimately of the divine sympathy and thoughtfulness of her Head. But the Church goes farther in cementing her union with her divine Head. There follows a memento prayer for the members in attendance—"To us also, sinners"—asking for closer fellowship with the "holy apostles and martyrs" and all the saints of God. This time, the prayer is not for their intercession but for union with Christ through them, "into whose company we implore thee to admit us, not weighing our merits, but freely granting us pardon." A closer union with the saints in heaven necessarily means also a closer union with Christ in whom alone they live and have their bliss.

This last prayer, like so many others of the Mass, closes with a mention of the mediatorship of Christ, "Through Christ our Lord." From this phrase the following prayer, acknowledging the universality of this mediatorship, takes its cue: "Through whom, O Lord, thou dost ever provide, make holy, fill with life, make fruitful of good, and bestow upon us all these thy gifts." The reference here is to the gifts brought up to the altar in the offertory procession, of which some were set on side tables and some placed on the altar to be used in the sacrifice. With this third memento prayer, which commemorates the gifts of nature, therefore all nature, the union of all things in Christ is accomplished. There remains only the small doxology which ends the Canon of the Mass as well as the sacrifice-oblation.

"Through him, and with him, and in him, is to thee, God the Father almighty, in the unity of the Holy Ghost all honor and glory, for ever and ever. Amen." This hymn of praise to the most holy Trinity, accompanied by five signs of the cross with the consecrated Host, and a minor elevation of Host and Chalice together, ends the first part of the Mass of the Faithful. A "sacrifice of praise" it was called at the beginning of the Canon; and with a note of praise the sacrificial action concludes. The latter has unfolded itself with constantly increasing understanding of its sublime nature in an ascending action that is marvellous both for its simplicity and its rapidity of progress. The liturgical drama, however, is not yet ended. We now stand before the final consummation of the sacrificial oblation rendered by the mystical body of Christ, the eucharistic communion or repast, which is an integral part of the liturgical mystery of the altar.

CHAPTER X

THE SACRIFICE-BANQUET

I. THE DIVINE REPAST

THE ascending action of the Mass of the Faithful, the sacrificial offering is over, and now the descent from God to man is entered upon. "In the sacrifice," says Dr. Parsch, "is embodied the longing of man to unite himself with God. Man enters into God through the offering and immolation of his sacrificial gift, and God imparts himself to man through a gracious acceptance and especially through the sacrificial repast."[1] The intimate relation between the two actions is thus quite evident.

It is not without its significance that the Eucharist was both foretold and instituted by Christ under the picture of a banquet. "I am the living bread which came down from heaven," Christ said. "If any man eat of this bread, he shall live for ever; and the bread that I will give, is my flesh, for the life of the world. . . . Except you eat the flesh of the Son of man, and drink his blood, you shall not have life in you. . . . For my flesh is meat indeed: and my blood is drink indeed."[2] When the first realization of this astounding prophecy took place, it was naturally in the setting of a supper. The institution of the Last Supper took place in connection with the eating of

[1] *Messerklaerung*, p. 15   [2] John 6: 51–56

the Jewish Pasch. It was at once the sublime realization of what the Pasch had prefigured, the official abolition of the Old Testament figure and substitution of the reality in its place. But the supper or banquet idea was retained by Christ as could be expected from his prophecies regarding the Eucharist. The very words of the institution give expression to this aspect: "Take ye all, and eat of this: for this is my body. . . . Take ye all, and drink of this, for this is the chalice of my blood" (text of consecration).

There was a special significance given in older times to the fact that persons ate at the same table. It established a bond of friendship between them that could not lightly be broken. Admittance to the table of the king, for instance, was a sign of special royal favor. It was in memory of his friendship with Jonathan that David decided: "Miphiboseth the son of thy master shall always eat bread at my table," [3] and in a similar way he provided for friends in his dying statement to Solomon: "Show kindness to the sons of Berzellai the Galaadite, and let them eat at thy table." [4] And in regard to the treachery of Achitophel, David's high reproach was based on the same idea: "For if my enemy had reviled me, I would verily have borne it. . . . But thou a man of one mind, my guide, and my familiar, who didst take sweetmeats together with me. . . ." [5]

In the Orient in particular the admittance of a guest to the family table gave him all the protection and immunity of a member of the house. The eating of the same food by all, its absorption into their very flesh and blood, was considered a special connecting link between them. It created an intimate bond between the table com-

[3] 2 Kings, 9:10   [4] 3 Kings 2:7   [5] Ps. 54:14-15

panions that was given spiritual significance. Eating at a common table symbolized the close union of minds and hearts; it was a pledge of friendship and fidelity.

From this the practice of eating of the sacrificial victim also receives added meaning. Not only did it constitute a special bond of union between all those who partook of the same sacrificial food; but it set up in particular a close union of these persons with the object of the sacrificial offering. In the Old Testament sacrifices the animals were killed in the act of their oblation to God. As a symbol of their having been given up for God, moreover, part of the animal was burnt up in holocaust. But the rest, which also belonged to God and was sanctified by his acceptance, was eaten by the people. God was thus the divine Host at the sacrificial banquet, and the people, having given themselves to God in their gifts, assimilated themselves more fully unto him by eating of his food at his table. They received back their own gifts from God but as imbued in some degree with the stamp of God's own sanctity and goodness.

In the light of this conception it is more easily intelligible why St. Paul should forbid the early Christians in such severe terms to eat of the meat that had been slaughtered at the heathen religious rites. "But the things which the heathens sacrifice, they sacrifice to devils, and not to God. And I would not that you should be made partakers with devils. You cannot drink the chalice of the Lord, and the chalice of devils: you cannot be partakers of the table of the Lord and of the table of devils." [6] Partaking of the table of the Lord meant partaking of the body and the blood of the Lord, but it was always

[6] 1 Cor. 10:20–21

the body and blood as effected in the sacrifice of his passion. And so partaking of Christ's body and blood was an intimate participation in this same sacrifice of his death. Therefore St. Paul could also say: "For as often as you shall eat this bread, and drink the chalice, you shall show the death of the Lord, until he come." [7]

The sacrifice-banquet is thus not a sort of additional ceremony attached to that of the sacrifice-oblation, or a minor appendix to the latter, but its real completion and fulfilment. The two intimately form one divine sacrifice after the manner symbolized in the sacrifices of the Old Testament, but realized in an infinitely higher degree in the one sacrifice of the New Law. "Having partaken of this saving victim," the postcommunion for the feast of St. Augustine (May 28) begins. In the sacrifice-banquet we receive back from God the gift we gave to him in the sacrifice-oblation but in the meantime it has been consecrated into the living Christ. Our acceptance of it is in the form of the Bread of Life. We thus assimilate ourselves most intimately with God, by uniting ourselves with the sacrificial victim. It is an assimilation to the cross of Calvary. We receive back our original gifts, but in a divinized or deified form. We receive of the very strength of God to live after the manner promised in the sacrificial action in which we have participated.

"Holy Communion is the answer to the prayer said at the mixing of wine and water at the offertory, even as it is the answer to every offering prayer of the entire Mass. Those who share in the heavenly sacrifice, by receiving the most sacred Body and Blood of our Lord, are filled with every grace and heavenly blessing. They are, indeed,

[7] 1 Cor. 11:26

'made partakers of his divinity who has deigned to become partaker of our humanity' (offertory prayer)." [8]

II. AFTER THE CANON

The silence and reserve of the Canon is ended with the Canon itself. The priest again chants audibly so that the people may join more fully in the banquet-action that is theirs as well as his. The familiar exhortation of *"Oremus: Let us pray"* leads on to the Our Father, the prayer that Christ himself taught us as the perfect type of prayer. It was introduced by Christ's "thus shall ye pray," and this is echoed in the introductory words of the Mass text: "Directed by saving precepts and prompted by divine instruction, we make bold to say: Our Father, etc."

Many Christians may have recited the Our Father thousands of times without adverting fully to the perfection with which it gives expression to the true sentiments that should be ours in all prayer. It addresses itself first of all to God as our divine Father and for his own sake. It praises him, wishes for the increase of his kingdom on earth, for the fulfillment of his will in all the world, and therefore for his greater glory. And only after that does it turn to thoughts of self, petitioning for the daily bread of life, for forgiveness, and protection. It is a perfect prayer, indeed, both in its acknowledgment of the dominion of God and in giving the proper perspective to thoughts of divine praise and human petition. In its twofold structure it is admirably suited to form a sort of connecting link between the sacrifice-oblation and the sacrifice-banquet, its first part being an echo of the theme of

[8] *Through Christ Our Lord*, p. 88

the former, and its second part indicating the trend and action of the latter.

The Our Father is here the community table prayer before the eucharistic banquet. We have, especially since the consecration, entered intimately into a close union with Christ. What is more natural than that we should now cement this union by means of the sacrament of Christ's body and blood, and that we should address God as *our* father, *i.e.*, as the common father of Christ and ourselves? The Father had been presiding at the sacrificial altar to receive our homage and now he is to preside also at the sacrificial table to give us life. The Our Father moreover asks God "to give us this day our daily bread," a phrase that has from time immemorial and especially by the Church Fathers been interpreted as referring first of all to the divine Bread of Life. In its petitions it also brings back our thoughts from the mystical union with Christ and our intercourse with God on high back to the realities of our daily life and of our own needs and the battle that is still to be ours before we can enter forever into the full peace of the heavenly union with God.

With a fine practicality the Our Father calls for the divine help we shall ever need amidst the temptations of this life, and it asks at the very moment when it can receive that help together with the divine Helper. "Forgive us our trespasses, as we forgive those who trespass against us," we dare to pray. It is almost a challenge to God to judge us by our love of neighbor; and its boldness is an excellent expression of the sincerity with which we are seeking full union with God. In praying for God to help us by purifying our minds from sin and temptation, it recalls the initial purgative stage of the Mass of the

Catechumens. Approach to God is always conditioned on our part by a stripping off of the old man of sin, and its realization is in proportion to the success we have in purging ourselves of all that stands between God and us. This success depends on the grace of God, and so the last thought of the Our Father is continued in the prayer that follows: "Deliver us, O Lord, we beseech thee, from all evils, past, present, and to come." The intercession of the blessed Mother and of all the saints is appealed to, and the specific purpose mentioned: "Grant in thy goodness, peace in our days, that aided by the riches of thy mercy, we may be always free from sin and safe from all disturbance,"—all of this ever "through the same Jesus Christ thy Son, etc." The petition for the peace of Christ is the first mention of the theme that is soon to dominate.

After this prayer the priest breaks the sacred Host into two halves, and from one of these breaks off another particle. This is a remnant of the former practice of breaking up the bread at this part of the Mass for distribution to the assisting ministers and the faithful. It is the first step of banquet: the dividing up of the food, the apportioning, after the saying of the table prayer. With the small particle the priest makes the sign of the cross over the Chalice saying to the people: "May the peace of the Lord be always with you," to which they answer with the customary "And with thy spirit." This is the motive of inner peace among the members, which is one of the most beautiful preparatory actions for the common communion. It was foreshadowed in the words with which we asked forgiveness in the Our Father. Before the reception of Christ by the mystical body, the members unite themselves more firmly in mind and soul, and prepare themselves by mutual prayer for interior peace, the peace of Christ, as the most fruitful disposition for receiving their Lord and Head sacramentally.

Dropping the small particle into the chalice the priest continues: "May this mingling and hallowing of the Body and the Blood of our Lord Jesus Christ help us who receive it unto life everlasting." This is as it were the announcement that the moment of communion has arrived. It is continued in the Agnus Dei, in the very words of John the Baptist, announcing Christ when he was about to enter upon his active mission as the messiah. Now he is about to perfect that mission in our regard. "Lamb of God, who takest away the sins of the world," the Church prays three times; twice the answer is "Have mercy on us," while the third time another reference to the peace of Christ is made: "Grant us peace." The latter phrase is again taken up by the priest in the next prayer, which asks for the fulness of this peace in the entire mystical body of Christ: "O Lord Jesus Christ, who hast said to thy apostles: Peace I leave unto you, my peace I give unto you, regard not my sins but the faith of thy Church, and deign to keep it in peace and unity, according to thy will, who livest and reignest God through all eternity. Amen." Significantly this prayer, like the preceding petition and the two following prayers, is no longer addressed to the Father, but to the sacramental Christ himself, who is so soon to enter the hearts of the faithful.

After the prayer just quoted an action takes place in solemn Mass which formerly occurred in every Mass and extended also to all the faithful. It is known as the kiss of peace. The celebrant gives the deacon of the Mass the paternal embrace with the words, "Peace be with you," to which the deacon answers, "And with thy spirit." This is now repeated between deacon and other clergy present, and the ministrants at the altar. While no longer extending to the people, the rite retains its old significance and is the official exhortation to a mutual renewed act of forgiveness and charity among all the members before the sacramental reception of Christ their common head. Thereupon follow two prayers in which the priest prays for the reception of the full benefits of the body and blood of Christ which he is about to receive, and for the permanence of the fruits thereof, so that it may be for him a permanent "safeguard of both soul and body, like a well-taken remedy."

The priest now takes the sacred Host in his hand with the words: "I will take the bread of heaven, and call upon the name of the Lord." And striking his breast, he repeats three times the well-known words: "Lord, I am not worthy that thou shouldst enter under my roof: say but the word and my soul shall be healed." Making the sign of the cross with the sacred Host, he says the words, "May the Body of our Lord Jesus Christ preserve my soul unto life everlasting. Amen," and then consumes it. After a short act of recollection, he gathers up the particles from the corporal with the paten, saying at the same time words that are striking in their profound simplicity: "What return shall I make to the Lord for all that he hath given me? I will take the chalice of salvation, and I will call upon the name of the Lord. Praising I will call upon the Lord, and I shall be saved from my enemies." He then consumes the precious Blood with the words, "May the blood of our Lord Jesus Christ keep my soul unto life everlasting. Amen."

III. THE COMMUNION

After the communion of the priest comes that of the faithful. Special prayers were introduced for it about the thirteenth century, therefore fairly recently. These prayers consist of the confession of faults and the petitions for forgiveness exchanged between priest and people at the foot of the altar in the preliminary prayers of the Mass. In our analysis of the first part of the Mass of the Faithful we had some indication that the text of the Mass, as well as the progressive development of the action, points to the communion of all who take part in the sacrificial offering. The whole sacrifice is an action that expresses and effects an intimate union between the members of the mystical body and their Head, and the sacramental communion is at once the supreme symbolization as well as the supreme realization of this union. It is therefore the natural and logical outcome of the foregoing action of the Mass.

We have seen that the priest used the plural number in offering up the gifts to the heavenly Father and in offering up the consecrated Host, and was speaking and acting for all the congregation assembled and in the name of the entire Church. No change takes place in this regard when the action of the eucharistic repast commences. The table prayer is still in the same plural, and so are the other prayers asking for purity of heart and fruitful reception of Christ, down to the moment when the kiss of peace is given. No distinction is made in this regard between priest and people. Keeping that in mind, we shall better understand all that was germinally contained in the decree of Pius X for the promotion of frequent communion among the faithful. The Church has indeed defined officially that the sacrifice of the Mass is complete without the communion of any of the faithful (but not without that of the celebrant); but that in no way detracts from the propriety and fruitfulness of communion by all the faithful in connection with the hearing, that is, the co-offering of the Mass. The Council of Trent had expressed the keen desire of the assembled Fathers that the faithful present at any Mass should also communicate not only spiritually but also sacramentally so that they might gather more abundant fruit from the sacrifice; while the Catechism of the Council says that the faithful who can communicate sacramentally at Mass but do not do so are robbing themselves of heavenly treasures.

Moreover the communion of the faithful belongs properly in the Mass and not before or after it, or entirely outside the Mass. The *Roman Ritual* says in this regard that "the communion of the people should take place in Mass right after the communion of the celebrating priest (unless Communion is sometimes to be received immediately before or after a private Mass for a good reason), since the prayers ["Orationes"] which are said in Mass after communion regard not only the priest but also the faithful." [9] This statement refers particularly to the postcommunions, any number of which refer to the reception of the Eucharist by all the faithful. Thus on the fifth Sunday after Epiphany we pray: "We beseech thee, almighty God, that we may obtain the effect of that salvation, of which in these mysteries we have received the pledge," and on Sexagesima Sunday the prayer refers to us "who have been refreshed by thy sacraments." Oc-

[9] Tit. iv, cap. 2, n. 11

casionally a secret prayer, which ordinarily gives the specific purpose of the sacrificial offering, makes a similar reference. The secret for the feast of The Exaltation of the Holy Cross begins with: "We are about to feed on the body and blood of Jesus Christ our Lord. . . ."

Such prayers, then, as well as the very nature and meaning of the entire action of the Mass of the Faithful, and the ancient tradition of the Church, point to two things: The ideal of general communion by all who are attending a Mass, and the place of the communion of the faithful within the Mass itself. There is no doubt that the practice, still greatly in vogue, of receiving Communion outside of Mass is usually an abuse of the mind of the Church. Least of all can some of the excuses given therefor be considered as "good reason." No weight, for instance, can be attached to reasons drawn from the fact of having more time for prayers of preparation or of thanksgiving, if Communion is received after or before Mass. There is no better preparation for the reception of Communion than the progressive action of the Mass such as we have analyzed it.

Only too often people who give such excuses think of a thanksgiving or preparation that gives personal satisfaction to themselves. Thereby they set up their own subjective reactions above the action of the Mass, which is the official action of the mystical body in regard to the Eucharist, the official way of celebrating the Eucharist for all the members of Christ. The attitude here censured has undoubtedly been inspired by the individualism of our time, which has entered also the spiritual domain under the Protestant influence of so many centuries. Even a cursory examination, on the other hand, of the dispositions mentioned by the decree of Pius X as sufficient for the daily reception of communion will show that they are best attained through an intelligent participation in the sacrificial prayers of the Mass. As to the thanksgiving, we may indeed and should derive added benefit out of fervent solitary prayer after the Mass, even though a more lasting thanksgiving is the more permanent one of living the life of Christ also during the rest of the day, and of cementing the bonds of members and Head by a constant exercise of divine charity to all men, as well as by the recitation of occasional prayers such as the divine office calls for or the frequent momentary contacts with the many sacramentals that should accompany us on all our daily life.

In this regard Father Kramp has given the following admirable advice: "In giving yourself up to participation in the offering of the Mass, do not be too anxious lest you seem to abbreviate your preparation for holy Communion. It is a wrong sort of piety, it is religious self-deceit, to make of the Mass, which is our sublimest act of divine worship, a work of anxious self-concern. God wants of us in the Mass the sublime expression of the deepest and truest self-oblation and thanksgiving. And we are all absorbed in the thought of how we shall get our share of merit and grace. Give glory to God; and he will take care of your soul." [10] All of this does not of course argue in any way against the performing of private preparation and thanksgiving, and most certainly not against these when performed before and after the Mass. What is opposed is the attitude that wishes to substitute the private devotions of the individual during the Mass for

[10] *Eucharistia,* p. 45

the official ones of the Church on the supposed ground of their greater benefit to the spiritual life.

IV. After Communion

While the priest receives wine and water into the chalice for its purification after the communion of the faithful, he recites the following two prayers in a subdued tone for the full efficacy of the sacramental reception: "What we have taken like bodily food, may we treasure in a pure heart; and may what is given us in time be our provision for eternity"; and "May thy body, O Lord, which I have eaten and thy blood which I have drunk, affect me to the depths of my being, grant that no taint of sin be found in me, whom these pure and holy mysteries have renewed: who livest and reignest through all eternity. Amen." After this the action again becomes more public. The priest reads the communion verse aloud, the remnant of a text that was sung in full formerly while the faithful marched in procession to the altar-table for communion. Like the introit at the beginning of the Mass it changes with the different seasons and feasts, and is a reflection usually of the spiritual theme of the day. At Christmas, for instance, it reads: "All the ends of the earth have seen the salvation of our God" (third Mass); on Palm Sunday, the beginning of Holy Week: "Father, if this chalice may not pass away, but I must drink it, thy will be done"; and on Easter Sunday: "Christ our Pasch is immolated, alleluia: therefore let us feast with the unleavened bread of sincerity and truth. Alleluia, alleluia, alleluia."

Now the priest again faces the people and giving the customary greeting bids them all pray with him. There follows the postcommunion prayer. This is one of the customary collective prayers of the Mass to which the people give their assent by the answer of "Amen," and which varies with the different Mass formularies. Yet practically all the great numbers of postcommunions have a common note. They pray in the name of the congregation, they refer unqualifiedly to the common reception of the Eucharist that has just taken place in the sacrifice, and they pray for the greater efficacy of this sacramental mystery in the lives of the faithful.

The continuity and compact unity of the two parts of the Mass of the Faithful is also brought out by the unity of thought that we find in particular in many of the Mass prayers for special occasions. There all the prayers of the Mass refer more specifically to one and the same motive, so that what we pray for in a general way in the collect of the Mass, we pray for in the secret as the effect of the sacrifice to be offered, and in the postcommunion as the effect of receiving the sacred mysteries. Thus, for instance, in the prayers "For One in Prison or in Captivity," the collect asks God to "loose the bonds of thy servant now in captivity," the secret prays for God's "abundant blessing on these offerings; may it loose the bonds of this captive," while the postcommunion asks the Lord: "Through these sacraments which we have taken, free thou thy servant from captivity's bonds."

If one were to take the entire series of postcommunions and set them in a logical order, one would get not only a complete program of life to be led as the effect of sharing in the sacrificial altar and table, but one could get also a complete scheme of the various special fruits that are to be derived from the eucharistic sacrifice-sacrament.

A few instances may help to bring out the rich content of these postcommunion prayers. The Eucharist:

(*a*) Gives us a share in the divine Victim: "Having partaken of this saving Victim . . ." (St. Augustine, May 28).

(*b*) Is a pledge of our salvation: "Grant that we may obtain the fruit of that salvation, of which we have received the pledge in these mysteries" (first Tuesday of Lent).

(*c*) Is our heavenly food and refreshment: "May the sacraments which we have received . . . be unto our souls a quickening food, and to our bodies protection and aid" (third Sunday after Easter).

(*d*) Cleanses us from vices: "May our vices, O God almighty, be healed by thy holy mysteries" (seventeenth Sunday after Pentecost).

(*e*) Gives growth in sanctity: "Grant that as we frequent this mystery so the work of our salvation may advance" (fourth Sunday of Advent).

(*f*) Gives growth in love of God: "While we receive thy gifts in our tribulation, may we through our consolation grow in thy love" (Rogation days).

(*g*) Brings unity among men: "May the communion of thy sacrament . . . be to us the source of purity and unity" (ninth Sunday after Pentecost).

(*h*) Increases membership in Christ: "Grant . . . that we may be numbered among his members in whose body and blood we have communicated" (Saturday, third week in Lent).

(*i*) Gives the Holy Ghost: "May our hearts be cleansed, O Lord, through the inpouring of the Holy Ghost" (Pentecost).

(*j*) Makes us sharers in the divine nature: "Grant . . . that the sacrament of the Body and Blood, which we have received, may sanctify our minds and hearts so that we may deserve to be made partakers of the divine nature" (St. Cyril, March 18).

(*k*) Makes our whole life a continued thanksgiving: "Grant . . . that we who are nourished with the sacred gifts may ever abide in thanksgiving" (Sunday in octave of Ascension).

After the postcommunion prayer the priest at the center of the altar turns to the people with the words of dismissal: "*Ite, missa est*—the Mass is ended." The real interpretation of this phrase has been much discussed. Dom Boeser writes of it: "*Ite, missa est* is usually translated: 'Go, the Mass is ended.' But it admits of another interpretation. Its liturgical import is better understood when we translate it: 'Go forth! The hour of your mission is come. . . .' Now he (Christ) appears before us and charges us with the commission: *Ite, missa est*—'As the Father hath sent me, I also send you.' I send you out into my vineyard. The liturgical sacrifice is over. Now begins the extra-liturgical sacrifice of your daily occupation." [11]

Formerly the Mass ended here, and the following parts were added only in later centuries. Today the priest, facing the altar, addresses to the holy Trinity a prayer for the full attainment of the sacrificial purpose: "May the tribute of my worship be pleasing to thee, most holy Trinity, and grant that the sacrifice which I, all unworthy, have offered in the presence of thy majesty, may be acceptable to thee, and through thy mercy obtain forgiveness for me and all those for whom I have offered it." Thereupon follows the

[11] *The Mass-Liturgy*, pp. 126 and 129

official blessing and then the last Gospel of St. John. Most fittingly does the latter now conclude the liturgical sacrifice, for it is an inspired hymn of the glory of the mediatorial Christ, who is the Alpha and Omega, the Beginning and the End. "All things were made by him and without him was made nothing that was made. In him was life, and the life was the light of the world." Today again, on the altar, "the Word was made flesh, and dwelt among us: and we saw his glory, as it were the glory of the only begotten of the Father, full of grace and truth," and today it was again verified that "as many as received him, he gave them power to be made the sons of God."

The Mass is truly a liturgical drama. As such it is a preeminent fulfillment of the aim of all liturgy, of the mission of Christ, which is the glorification of God and the sanctification of man. The Mass is truly a "sacrifice of praise"; and like the Our Father, it directs its thought first of all to the glory of God, whence comes all good, and not to the creature. The Mass is dramatic in its development. While the principle of repetition is abundantly used, since the Mass aims at the formation of mind and soul, there is no lagging in its action. It proceeds rapidly from offering to offering, unto the reception of the fruits thereof in communion, after which the close comes in a few rapid steps. The action of the Mass is essentially collective. It knows no silent or passive witnesses. The hearts of all present must speak up with the official leader, pray with him, and act with him. The Mass properly prayed is the highest form of the living of Christ by his members, and the highest form of the unified life that makes of all members living branches of one and the same divine Vine.

CHAPTER XI

THE SACRAMENTAL INITIATION

I. The Liturgical Sacrament

In the chapters on the sacrifice of the Mass we became acquainted more intimately with the liturgical action as it unfolds itself in the central act of the entire liturgical worship. The study of the liturgical year had given us some indications of the wonderful spiritual richness of the liturgy as a guide in the daily lives of the faithful members of Christ. However, it is the Mass that gives its full efficacy to the spiritual treasury of the liturgical cycle, and it is under the inspiration of the Mass and by means of the divine energies derived from participation to the full in its sacrificial action, that we can effectively take up the program of the liturgical cycle and make it the itinerary of our continuous journey through life with Christ.

In the sacrifice of the Mass we meet the action of Christ in the official acts of his Church not only in the same manner as this happens in the other liturgical functions, but we meet Christ himself. And in the sacramental reception of the Eucharist it is he in person who comes into our hearts, to whom we are joined, in order to live and to act out the Christ-life in our every word, thought, and deed. As the memorial celebration of the Lord's passion and death, from which as from its unique source all divine life comes for man, and as the re-enactment of the whole work of Christ's redemption in the manner peculiar to the liturgical mysteries, it is also the source of all the spiritual energies and divine life that are bestowed through the other liturgical acts of the Church. Hence the unparalleled position of the Mass in the liturgy.

It cannot possibly be a depreciation of the other parts of the liturgy to say that they radiate about the Mass as about their center, that they are in one way or another paths leading to or streams flowing from the Mass. That in fact is their true glory. Just as it is the true glory of man and an indication of his high dignity, that he is a creature of God endowed with intelligence and free will for the purpose of freely rendering the homage of praise and obedience to his Maker, so the intimate relation of the other liturgical functions to the Mass is really an indication of their supreme value, their exceptional character. Outside the liturgical life of the Church of Christ, there are no actions connected with the life of man that can compare in dignity and in spiritual reality to them. Within the field of the liturgy, in turn, those liturgical functions are the highest that are most intimately connected with the sacrifice of the Mass itself or have their whole being and function in relation to it, just as the highest choirs of angels stand nearest to the throne of God.

The first rank among these liturgical actions, in relation to the Mass, is held by the sacraments. Strictly speaking, indeed, the sacraments include the Mass as their very sun and center, since the Eucharist is inseparably both sacrifice and sacrament, or sacrament-sacrifice as it has been happily called. In former times the connection of the sacraments with the Mass was better understood than now, and it was better expressed even externally, insofar as the sacraments were conferred only in connection with the sacrifice of the Mass. This is still true today of Holy Orders, and to a great extent at least of Confirmation and of Matrimony. The fact that so many of us see no incongruity of any kind in the reception of the latter two sacraments outside of Mass is but a further indication of our lamentable loss of liturgical sense. Certainly the intention of the Church has never been other than that these sacraments should be administered in connection with the sacrifice of the altar from which they derive all their efficacy. Formerly the sacrament of Baptism was also conferred in connection with the celebration of Mass on certain days, especially as we have seen, on Holy Saturday night. The fact that the question of receiving Communion at Mass rather than outside of Mass needs defense at all again indicates to us how custom may gradually depart from the original position of the Church in such matters. Whenever persons are sponsoring this practice without good reason or considering it spiritually neutral and indifferent, it is a case, we may hope, where their ignorance is their bliss. Far from being a practice expressive of the true Christian spirit, the separation of communion from the Mass reflects the attitude of the Protestant reformers, who not only minimized but abolished altogether the liturgical sacrifice, while attempting to retain communion as an independent supper service.

Next to the Mass itself the sacraments are the most intimate expression and enactment of the power of Christ entrusted to the Church. In them Christ himself acts in the truest manner. As a consequence the Church rightly teaches and emphasizes the fact that they produce their effect *ex opere operato, i.e.,* by virtue of their being correctly and officially administered to persons having the right preparatory disposition. So little does the personality or human character of the ministering priest count in their dispensation, that the moral status of the human agent through whom they are being performed can hinder their true efficacy as little as it can cause their effects. It is not the person of the priest in any way that causes the sacramental effects, it is the person of Christ operating in and through the actions of the priest.

The sacraments are thus true liturgical symbols in the sense claimed for this term in chapter three. They are therefore anything but a mere close-to-hand indication of something happening far away, say, in the distant heavens; nor are they a mere interpretative symbol of the fact that something immeasurably higher is occurring somewhere or somehow. Their performance is ever the dispensing here and now of the Divine unto men. They are therefore most genuine performances of the mission of Christ in his Church and by his Church. Where they occur, there the work of the redemption is become present and is being fulfilled. This aspect of the sacraments has been called their impersonal character. "The very impersonal and objective character of the sacrament," writes Karl Adam, "like the impersonality of the Church's teaching activity, expresses that profoundest claim of the Church, her most intimate union with Christ, her working purely out of the fulness of Christ, her sanctifying through the might of Christ alone. . . . It is not the human element in her which sanctifies men, but the power of Christ alone."[1]

[1] *The Spirit of Catholicism,* p. 27

II. The Means of Life

In their general nature the sacraments well portray the universality, the catholicity, of the mission of Christ. Like the latter they are for all times and places, for all men of all ranks and conditions. Some of the sacraments exist for the general exigencies of human life and spiritual growth, and they are for all men indiscriminately. Others are for special occupations in life, that is, for special functions in relation to the wider mission of Christ among men. In their totality the sacraments accompany the individual human soul from the cradle to the grave, ever ministering unto man the healing or invigorating medicinal food of the Light and Life of the world, making the lame again to walk on the path of Christ, restoring to the blind their ability to see the Light and thus follow it, giving the deaf of soul again the power to grasp the true meaning of the Word of God, indeed calling back to life those that have died the death of sin.

Thus the sacraments will also continue to accompany men through life as long as the mission of Christ in the Church endures, which is as long as men will live in time. Some of them are for special emergencies, or again for frequent and, as it were, wholesale dispensation, and for these the ceremonial rite is shorter. Others are for more exceptional solemn moments in life, and for these the rite is more imposing and impressive, more emphatic in its development and more instructive in its messages. In all of the sacramental rites, however, we have something of the progressive unfolding of the inner action as expressed in the outer ceremony, such as we saw so strikingly present in the liturgical sacrifice. Again, whether we view them from the standpoint of individual repetition of the same sacrament, or of the successive reception of several different sacraments, we find in them the aim also of the progressive interior development of the Christian soul living the life of Christ.

Because the sacraments are the essential means of our spiritual growth it is all the more important for us to develop the proper attitude of active participation in regard to them. They produce their effect *ex opere operato,* it is true, but this means chiefly that the seed of sacramental grace is *ipso facto* planted in our souls when we receive them properly. But whether this seed of divine life will flourish in us and bear rich fruit depends on the disposition with which we receive it and the consciousness with which we try to develop its growth in our daily actions. Now the sacramental rite has for one of its purposes the better development in us of what might be called sacramental consciousness; it should help to give us a better understanding of what the sacraments mean in our life and to inspire us with a greater will towards attaining their fruits to the full. The text of the rite, if actively and intelligently participated in by us, should help to give us more of the mind of Christ in general and of the mind of Christ in regard to the particular need supplied by the sacrament, and it should be a means of greater worship of God. Active participation means intelligent submission to God and his power as exercised in the sacraments. It should therefore be for us a high type also of homage to our Creator and of worship that we try to live true to in all the actions of our life.

Thus the performance of the sacramental rites, the distribution of the sacramental grace and life of Christ, is one of the chief functions of the Church, as it should be one of the most important elements in our daily life. It is the ordinary means, willed by God, for rendering the energies of Christ effective in the life of man, for the elevation of man into the life of the divine love. The sacraments are most effective, official means for stripping off the old man of sin ever more and more, and more perfectly putting on the new man Christ. They are the effective means by which we truly die unto ourselves and to sin, and learn to live ever more and more for God. They enact in us the death of Christ unto sin and the resurrection of Christ unto true life. They are the official channels by which members are united to the mystical body of Christ.

All the sacraments, as we have hinted in another chapter, are intimately related to the life of Christ in his mystical body. It is through them that we first become engrafted upon the Vine as living branches; that the branches are given an increase of strength and vigor, are pruned of all injurious blight and insects, are in fact restored to life when dead, and receive the daily flow of divine sap without which they could not live. Hence a contemporary Catholic apologist could say with true mystic appreciation and beauty: "The sacraments breathe the very spirit of primitive Christianity. They are the truest expression and result of that original and central Christian belief that the Christian should be inseparably united with Christ and should live in Christ. In Catholic sacramental devotion Christ is immediately conceived and experienced as the Lord of the community, as its invisible strength and principle of activity. In the sacraments is expressed the fundamental nature of the Church, the fact that Christ lives on in her and that the divine is incarnated in human form." [2]

The initiation into the sacramental life of Christ takes place in baptism. In the rite of this initiation we have a more elaborate ceremony, both as better befitting the uniqueness of the occasion, which occurs but once in a lifetime for each member of Christ, and as better impressing upon us the importance of the occasion. For baptism introduces us into the fellowship of the members of Christ. It effects our entrance into the ranks of the mystical body of Christ. It is baptism that enables us to become intimate partakers of Christ in the Eucharist. As Dom Grea says, "To nourish oneself on the Eucharist is the proper act and the exercise of the rights conferred in baptism. Baptism creates a permanent state. . . . The Christian is washed in the blood of Jesus Christ only to be in him and live by him. And the right he has acquired in baptism and the virtue itself of baptism is realized and exercised through the holy Eucharist. By the relation he has assumed to the immolated flesh of Christ in baptism, he has already acquired, as it were, a habitual and permanent state of union with Jesus Christ." [3]

Only too often we think of our baptism merely as a fact that occurred long ago, and not as a reality that should continue to live and develop in us as time goes on. And still this is the true nature of the baptismal state. Those who enter the religious state, or the priesthood of Christ, make certain promises and acquire a certain state. Have these promises and this state achieved their full possibilities with this initial step? By no means. The first

[2] Adam, *The Spirit of Catholicism*, p. 20
[3] *L'Eglise*, I, pp. 84–85

step was only the beginning of what is to continue to increase throughout life. The actual living out of these
promises and this state ever gives them more and more
actuality; they are an increasing production of the fruit
whose seed was planted by the first step. So it is with
baptism, and so it was well understood by the first Christians, who were blessed with such a profound understanding of the things of Christ, with such an abundant and
fruitful liturgical sense. "In primitive Christianity," says
a scholarly writer of today, "baptism occupied a much
more central position in the religious life than today.
Then to be a Christian meant nothing less than to desire
to be wholly what one had become in baptism: free from
sin, consecrated to God, a child and image of God, a temple of the Holy Ghost, an heir of heaven. Thus the early
Christians lived more consciously in the central and basic
ideas of Christianity, in the high appreciation of sanctifying grace and of a living union with the triune God.
Thence sprang the great joy of faith and the profound
inner life that characterized the first Christians. They
were proud to be Christians; and as Christians they were
also ready to go into imprisonment and death for their
faith." [4]

Since the baptismal ceremony is one of initiation into a
permanent new state, we should expect it properly to look
forward and to concentrate on the present and future rather
than on the past. In germ it contains the whole plan of
the Christian life, so that the life after baptism is indeed
but the increasing realization of the vows then taken and
of the grace then infused into the soul. It is the beginning
of the contact with the priestly power of the Church, which

[4] Bichlmair, *Urchristentum und katholische Kirche*, p. 87

is to accompany us through life. Hence, too, our own baptism should ever be for us not merely the past performance of a set of external ceremonies, but our first union with the living divine energy of Christ. It is the inner soul of baptism, as we have seen in regard to all the liturgy, that gives the external rites their true significance. A very great change takes place through baptism, a change that is well symbolized in the various rites of exorcism, anointing and ablution. The inner change, as we have seen, is a dying to self and a rising to the life of the new man in Christ, the burial of the old man of original sin, a real participation in the divine resurrection of Christ as well as in his passion and death. And so the spiritual growth achieved at the inspiration of and by participation in the liturgy throughout our life is but a continuation of our new spiritual birth in baptism. In all the liturgy actively lived by us, and in all our daily life of fruitage unto Christ, it is the baptismal grace that continues to live and grow, so that our baptism is ever a living fact in us, and becomes in a sense ever a greater reality as time goes on.

III. The Baptismal Rite

The liturgical rite of baptism now used for infants was formerly applied to adults. Its general dialog form is a striking illustration for us of the mind of the Church in regard to active participation of the faithful in her liturgy. The questions and answers speak for themselves. Since baptism is now ordinarily administered to infants a few days after their birth, the answers are given by sponsors in the name of the child. The dialog form is prominent at various stages and helps to indicate the progressive

steps leading up to the climax by which the entire ceremony so beautifully expresses the internal action that is
being performed and the rich meaning that baptism should
have in the life of the Christian. A preliminary question-
ing introduces the ceremony. This is followed by a remote
preparation both of expurgation and elevation of mind
and then by a more immediate preparation. When these
are accomplished the solemn moment arrives of the application of matter and form in the ministration of the sacrament. After the climax, in the characteristic manner of
the liturgy, a few short but meaningful prayers bring the
ceremony to a close. Formerly the candidates, even as
catechumens, had assumed a new name to indicate that
they were saying farewell to their old pagan selves and
entering upon a new life in Christ. Even today the rite
uses the name from the very beginning in addressing or
speaking to God of the candidate.

The priest meets the child and the sponsors at the entrance of the church. Since the candidate is still in original sin and under the domain of Satan, he cannot enter
without further ado into the holy of holies, which is truly
the house of God. The priest is vested in surplice and
violet stole, therefore wearing the official insignia of the
priestly power that is to be exercised. And the questions
with which he begins indicate at once the fact that the
Christian life is one of personal responsibility. The true
member of Christ must know what he is and what he is
about in the liturgy; all his service should be a conscious
and willing service of God, nothing mechanical or forced
upon him by external circumstances. In the initial liturgical rite this is emphasized time and again, as if the Church
could not tire of bringing home to the candidate that he

is responsible for the growth of the seed of divine life she will implant into his soul, and that no one not even the Church herself can take away, or substitute herself for, his own personal responsibility.

"N, what dost thou ask of the Church of God," is tne first question.

"Faith," is the reply.

"What does faith bestow upon thee?"

"Life everlasting." [6]

There is no hesitation in question or answer, and so the Church proceeds at once with her God-given task. The priest gives a preliminary counsel, which in the words of Christ himself contains all the law. The entire life of the candidate will be nothing but a growing realization of it: "If then thou wilt enter into life, keep the commandments. Thou shalt love the Lord thy God with thy whole heart, and with thy whole soul, and with thy whole mind; and thy neighbor as thyself." In order to live this life of love the Spirit of divine Love must infuse the soul and the power of Satan must be broken. The priest indicates this by breathing upon the face of the child and then saying: "Depart from him, thou unclean spirit, and give place to the Holy Ghost the Paraclete." This is, in the words of the Church herself, a statement of what is to be achieved by the holy sacrament.

At once 'the Church begins to take possession in the name of God and through Christ by putting the stamp of the Redeemer on the child. Signing the forehead and breast with the sign of the cross the priest says: "Receive the sign of the cross upon thy forehead and upon thy

[6] The English text is taken from the translation of the Reverend Richard E. Power, *The Gift of Life*.

heart; take unto thee the faith of the heavenly commandments, and be thou such in thy ways that thou mayest be fit henceforth to be a temple of God." It is only the ordained priest whose hand can thus sign with the efficacy of Christ himself. And the signing is not only externally symbolical of what is happening. The living body, therefore body and soul together, receive the sign of the cross, since both together are to be the temple of God. To strengthen action and word the priest now addresses his first prayer to God: "Graciously hear our prayers, we beseech thee, O Lord, and protect by thy unfailing might this soul of thy choice, N, now marked with the sign of our Lord's holy cross, that holding to his first knowledge of thy infinite perfection, he may deserve, by keeping thy commandments, to come to the glory destined for those who are born anew: Through Christ our Lord. Amen."

The priest lays his hand upon the head of the child. The gesture signifies the conferring of spiritual strength. It is the same by which in the sacrament of Holy Orders the bishop gives of his priestly power to the candidates for priesthood. "Look down with favor upon thy servant N," God is asked. "Heal him of all blindness of heart; sunder all the snares of the enemy in which he has been entangled; open to him, O Lord, the gate of thy fatherly love, that signed with the seal of thy wisdom, he may be free from the corruption of all wicked desires, and under the blessed influence of thy commandments may serve thee gladly in thy Church, advancing in perfection from day to day." Advancement from day to day is indeed to be the happy privilege of the newly baptized, and the advancement is to take place under the guiding hand of the Church.

Next a bit of salt is placed in the mouth of the child. Salt is used for the preservation of foods; it prevents decay. It is also used to make foods tasty and agreeable. The salt of baptism was blessed in the name of the living God "that it may become to all who receive it an effective remedy, working ever within them." It is the salt of the wisdom of God, by which human beings are to become acceptable to God. "N, receive the salt of wisdom," says the priest, may it be unto thee an earnest of God's favor unto life everlasting. Amen." The beautiful Christian greeting of "Peace be with thee" is given, and the prayer following asks for the efficacy of the ceremony pointing also to the coming new birth. "O God of our fathers, . . . most humbly we pray thee, of thy goodness, to look with favor upon thy servant N, and permit not that he, who now tastes this first morsel of salt, should hunger any more, but rather may he abound in heavenly food, that he may be always fervent of spirit, joyful in hope, always honoring thy holy name. Lead him to the font of the new and better birth, that as one of thy faithful he may deserve to win the everlasting reward which thou hast promised."

A formal exorcism is now pronounced: "I bid thee begone, unclean spirit, in the name of the Father, and of the Son, and of the Holy Ghost; that thou depart and keep far from this servant of God N, for he commands thee, accursed reprobate, he who trod the waves under foot and extended a helping hand to Peter about to sink. Therefore, accursed fiend, acknowledge thy doom and give honor to the living and true God, give honor to Jesus Christ, his Son, and to the Holy Ghost, and keep far from this servant of God, N, because Jesus Christ our Lord and

God has been pleased to call him to his holy grace and blessing, and to the font of baptism."

A second time the child is signed by the priest: "And this sign of the holy cross, which we trace upon his forehead, do thou, accursed fiend, never dare to violate." A second more emphatic imposition of the hand concludes the remoter preparation of the child for the great grace it is about to receive. "Holy Lord, . . . I earnestly call down upon this thy servant thy eternal and holy love, that thou wouldst be pleased to guide him with the light of thy wisdom. Make him pure and holy, give him skill to learn the truth, that having been deemed worthy of the grace of thy baptism, he may persevere in firm hope, right purpose, and holy doctrine: Through Christ our Lord. Amen."

IV. Birth in Christ

The preliminary preparation of the candidate for baptism is now over and the more proximate preparation appropriately commences with his introduction into the house of God. So far he has had to remain outside or in the vestibule. Now the priest places the end of his stole on the child. It is the Church's official act through her minister of taking possession of her new child to be. "N, enter into the temple of God," says the priest, "that thou mayest have part with Christ, unto life everlasting. Amen." It is a formal declaration, not only an invitation; and it expresses the essence of the life everlasting that the baptismal faith is to bestow, namely, "part with Christ," a real sharing in the true life divine of Christ, by becoming a member of his mystical body. Christ himself is making the declaration through the liturgy.

While proceeding to the baptismal font the candidate (through the sponsors) appropriately makes a confession of faith by reciting the official formula of the Church, the Apostles' Creed, and adds to it the prayer that Christ himself taught us as the model form of prayer. It is the first action of the candidate in his capacity of prospective Christian. It is a statement of his will to adhere to Christian truth and life and at the same time his first act of worship in the house of God. The Church immediately goes on with the work of taking fuller possession of him in the name of Christ. Halt is made at the door of the baptistery for a final exorcism. In the name of the three divine persons the unclean spirit is adjured to "keep far from this creature of God's making, N, whom our Lord has been pleased to call to his holy temple, that he also may be made a temple of the living God, and that the Holy Ghost may dwell within him." For this purpose, the entire person must belong to God, and so possession of his senses, which are the gateway to his soul as well as the soul's means of expression, must be taken in the name of God. The priest moistens his thumb with spittle and touches the ears and nostrils of the child, saying in the very word of Christ: "Ephpheta, which is, be thou opened unto the odor of sweetness. But thou, spirit of evil, begone; for the judgment of God is at hand."

The exorcism is now complete, the senses have been snatched from Satan and opened to the things of God. But in the true spirit of the liturgy the candidate must himself express his willing participation in this happening, thereby also using his blessed senses for the first time unto God.

"N, dost thou renounce Satan?"

"I do renounce him."

"And all his works?"

"I do renounce them."

"And all his pomps?"

"I do renounce them."

A holy unction completes the preparation of the child. With the oil of the catechumens breast and shoulders are anointed in the form of a cross: "I anoint thee with the oil of salvation in Christ Jesus our Lord, that thou mayest have life everlasting. Amen."

Everything is now ready except, so to say, the Church herself. She realizes the great importance of the step better than anyone else, and she must assure herself doubly of the worthiness of the candidate and of the full responsibility which each member of Christ must have for his own salvation through Christ. And so she patiently inquires further, demanding a final declaration of faith and good will and firm resolution from the candidate.

"N, dost thou believe in God the Father almighty, Creator of heaven and earth?"

"I do believe."

"Dost thou believe in Jesus Christ his only Son, our Lord, who was born and suffered for us?"

"I do believe."

"Dost thou believe also in the Holy Ghost, the holy Catholic Church, the Communion of Saints, the forgiveness of sins, the resurrection of the body, and life everlasting?"

"I do believe."

Satisfied again, the priest asks the final momentous question: "N, wilt thou be baptized?" And immediately upon the answer, "I will," follows the baptism, the new birth in water and the Holy Ghost. With the catechumens of old, whose baptism took place by stepping down into a pool of water, being immersed completely and rising washed anew, the present child also dies completely unto self and Satan and comes forth from the holy action born anew, instinct with the divine life of Christ himself. The priest has poured water on the head of the child in the form of a cross at the mention of each of the three divine persons, while pronouncing the words: "N, I baptize thee in the name of the Father, and of the Son, and of the Holy Ghost." There is no "Amen" given here by the candidate. His consent is a precedent condition for the efficacy of the liturgical action, and this he has given repeatedly in the previous part of the ceremony.

The remainder of the rite is short but expressive. Anointing the head of the child with holy chrism in the form of a cross, the priest says: "May God almighty, the Father of our Lord Jesus Christ, who has given thee a new life by water and the Holy Ghost, and granted thee remission of all sins, may he anoint thee with the chrism of salvation in the same Christ our Lord, unto life everlasting. Amen." The beautiful greeting of "Peace be to thee," is given with renewed significance, since the baptized member is now through Christ fully capable of the peace that only Christ can give.

Finally two symbolical actions take place in the conferring of a white garment and a lighted candle. The first is reminiscent of the old practice in which the newly baptized wore white garments during the octave week of their baptism. The second is reminiscent of the lively sense with which the new members had participated in the blessing of the fire and the paschal candle on the night of their baptism and had understood and accepted so fully the message of the "Light of Christ" on Holy Saturday. Today a white cloth is laid upon the head of the child with the words: "Receive this white garment, which mayest thou wear without stain before the judgment seat of our Lord Jesus Christ, that thou mayest have life everlasting. Amen." The shining whiteness of baptismal innocence is indeed a treasure that should be born unsullied through life to the day of judgment. How truly liturgical is the reference here to the last days, to the final goal and end of all life! So also is the summing up that takes place in the prayer said at the giving of the lighted candle. With a stroke of artistic perfection it takes up the thought with which the entire ceremony was begun: "Receive this burning light, and safeguard thy baptism by a blameless life; keep the commandments of God, that when our Lord shall come to claim his own, thou mayest be worthy to greet him with all the saints in the heavenly court, and live forever and ever. Amen."

Thereupon the dismissal follows: "N, go in peace and may the Lord be with thee. Amen."

Now the child is a member in the fellowship of Christ. He has part with Christ even unto a share in his divine priesthood. By virtue of the latter he is now able to take part in the official worship of the Church, in the daily sacrifice of the mystical body, and to share also in the other sacraments as need and occasion demand, for the ever greater development of the Christ-life in him until the fulness of his time.

CHAPTER XII

THE SACRAMENTAL LIFE

I. Food and Medicine

The newly baptized Christian has put off the old man of sin and put on the new man Christ. He has received a share in a new life through his birth in Christ, and he has taken upon himself to foster and cherish this life with all his abilities. It is destined to grow and flourish in his soul as long as he is here on earth. Like all life it must receive its regular exercise and nourishment, and it must be able to defend itself against untoward circumstances and hardships and use healing remedies if it has suffered from failing strength or malady. Like all life again it has not only its laws of growth and health, but also of reproduction, without which it could not carry on as it must in the Church down the ages to the very end of time. It is for all these vital needs of the life divine in the mystical body that the different sacraments were instituted by its divine Founder and Head.

First of all the new member must be able to exercise and nourish the life that is now in him. This he does through the holy Eucharist as both sacrifice and sacrament. Through the baptismal gift of faith he is now able to share actively in the celebration of the Eucharist, in offering with the priest and Christ and in completing his participation by partaking of the Bread of Life in communion. Enough has been said about this in the chapters on the liturgical sacrifice. The true member of Christ cannot be satisfied with a minimum participation in the Eucharist such as will keep him from being guilty of mortal sin: Sunday Mass and annual communion. He will need no impelling force of sanctions to unite himself more closely with his divine Head as far as circumstances allow. Nor will it be necessary to try to persuade him to receive the Bread of Life during the sacrifice, or to prepare himself by joining in the action of offering.

It is only for times when a person is too sick or feeble to attend the liturgical mysteries enacted upon the altar of Christ, that the Church has instituted an official rite for the reception of the Eucharist in the home of the person in question. When Communion is brought to a sick person at his home the priest greets the family with the words, "Peace be to this house," with its answer, "And to all that dwell therein." He then sprinkles the sick person and the room with holy water while saying the following antiphon together with the first verse of the Miserere psalm: "Sprinkle me, O Lord, with hyssop, and I shall be cleansed; wash me, and I shall be made whiter than snow. Ps. 50: Have mercy on me, O God, according to the greatness of thy mercy. Glory be to the Father, etc." The help of the Lord is then invoked and the people are asked by the priest to join in his prayer: "Holy Lord, Father almighty, eternal God, graciously hear us, and deign to send thy holy angel from heaven to watch over, encourage, protect, abide with, and defend all who have their home in this habitation: Through Christ our Lord. Amen."

Now the Confiteor is recited by the sick person and others present. It is the same humble confession of faults and invocation of the saints with which Mass begins, and which is always recited before the communion of the faithful no matter when this takes place. After the confession of faults the priest recites the two prayers of forgiveness, the Misereatur and the Indulgentiam, which regularly follow the recitation of the Confiteor. Then he announces the Lord as during Mass at the communion of the faithful: "Behold the Lamb of God; behold him who takes away the sins of the world," which is followed by the "Lord, I am not worthy" recited three times. For all ordinary communions, the Eucharist is given with the prayer: "May the Body of our Lord Jesus Christ keep thy soul unto life everlasting. Amen." But if the Eucharist is received as Viaticum, that is, by a person in danger of death, the formula reads: "Brother (sister), receive the Viaticum of the Body of our Lord Jesus Christ; may he shield thee from the malignant foe and bring thee to life everlasting. Amen." After the ablution of the fingers, a final prayer is recited by the priest: "Holy Lord, Father almighty, eternal God, we beg of thee in all confidence that the most sacred body of our Lord Jesus Christ, thy Son, which our brother (sister) has now received, may be for him (her) a remedy both of soul and of body unto life everlasting: Through him who liveth and reigneth with thee in the unity of the Holy Ghost, God through all eternity. Amen." With a final blessing in the name of the triune God the rite is ended.[1]

There is weakness and sickness, not only of body but also of soul, impairing the spiritual life. As long as we

[1] The text is quoted from the Reverend Richard E. Power, *God's Healing*.

are pilgrims on earth, the old man of sin will not be rooted out entirely; he will still be strong and at times also gain a victory over the life of Christ in us. But even if we be dead to God, the Church will still hold out her saving hand, for hers is the divine sympathy of Christ. In the sacrament of Penance we have a healing medicine that gives back the lost life, or renews our strength when we have grown weak. It must be administered often and to large multitudes individually. Hence the liturgical action is of the shortest, although even here we find in the very text of the sacrament a progress from preparatory stage to climax and the wider prayer of petition with which its liturgy closes.

The penitent enters the confessional asking for a blessing and the priest responds: "The Lord be in thy heart and on thy lips that thou mayest rightly confess thy sins, in the name of the Father, etc." The penitent confesses his sins. He has a part all his own to perform in this sacrament. It is a mysterious action, understood only if we remember the sacred official character of the confessor. No human lips will ever reveal what has transpired in that solemn moment. The act of confessing over, the liturgical action proper commences. With words already well-known to us, the priest recites the preparatory prayers: "May God almighty have mercy on thee, and forgive thee thy sins, and bring thee to life everlasting. Amen.—May the almighty and merciful Lord grant thee pardon, absolution, and remission of all thy sins. Amen." The circumstances of the liturgical mystery being enacted render these petitions of our loving mother the Church all the more significant here. There follows the solemn declaration which so well realizes all we have said about

the exercise of divine power in the official liturgical acts:
"May our Lord Jesus Christ absolve thee; and I by his
authority absolve thee from every bond of excommunica-
tion and interdict, as far as I am able, and thou hast need.
Moreover, I absolve thee of thy sins, in the name of the
Father, and of the Son, and of the Holy Ghost. Amen."

With these words and the sign of the cross the Spirit
of Christ enters into our hearts. It is a most solemn moment for us. It is the enactment of the living Christ
himself, a continuation of the mission he conferred when
breathed upon the apostles and said to them: "Receive
ye the Holy Ghost. Whose sins you shall forgive, they
are forgiven them." In the sacrament of Penance the
priest exercises this same power; there its life-giving energy flows to us. We are there revitalized with the life
and energies of Christ, and become more worthy members
of his mystical body, ready to bear richer fruits. This the
Church has fully in mind. And, as in other cases, the
penitent is not dismissed before she has prayed for a
greater abundance of the divine life in him. "May the
passion of our Lord Jesus Christ, the merits of the blessed
virgin Mary and of all the saints, whatever good thou
mayest do and whatever evil thou mayest have to endure,
profit thee unto the remission of sins, increase of grace,
and glory in the life without end. Amen." How well the
Church does her work! The sacrament of Penance engrafts us more firmly as living branches of the Christ-
vine, makes us to live more intimately in the mystical
body of Christ; and the Church in her closing prayer
mingles our merits with those of the saints of Christ and
of Christ himself, so that we may live the more abundantly
of his divine life.

II. Strength for Combat

The new-born child of God, even after being fed with the Bread of Life and healed with the saving ointment of the sacrament of Penance, may still have many difficulties of many kinds to conquer. Inexperienced as he is, he lacks the cool judgment and the skilful strength of the tried soldier. Hence the Church has another sacrament for him, one in which the divine energy of the Holy Spirit descends upon him in special abundance and makes of him a full-fledged member of Christ. The sacrament of Confirmation strengthens the branches of the vine Christ, so that they may withstand the onslaughts of wind and weather, and various blights and animal pests, and in the face of these live a fruitful life in Christ. Confirmation receives additional solemnity from the fact that the bishop alone ordinarily can confer the sacrament. For this ceremony of the coming of age of the Christian soul, a greater father of the family, a more powerful bearer of the energies of Christ, a direct descendant of the apostles, comes into the parish home. The ceremony itself, however, is appropriately short, since all the candidates of the parish receive the sacrament on the same day. Moreover, confirmation was formerly administered immediately after baptism, so that the preparation for the latter also held for the confirmation. The first collect prayer of the sacramental rite itself alludes to this close connection. Yet, short as the whole rite is, it nevertheless has its liturgical stage of preparation leading up to the real sacramental action in the manner we meet so frequently in the development of liturgical functions.

The candidates kneel facing the bishop who stands

before them with folded hands and vested in full pontificals. "May the Holy Ghost come upon you," he solemnly
prays, "and may the power of the Most High keep you
from sin."[2] To this we have the liturgical answer of
"Amen." "Our help is in the name of the Lord," the
bishop continues, and the customary answer is given: "Who
made heaven and earth." Therewith the new battle cry
has been announced to the soldiers of Christ, whose whole
life is to be led most truly "in the name of the Lord."
With the "*Oremus*" the bishop exhorts all to join in his
prayer, which he recites with hands extended over those
to be confirmed: "Almighty, everlasting God, who hast
deigned to bring these thy servants to a new life by water
and the Holy Ghost and hast granted them remission
of all their sins, send forth upon them thy sevenfold Spirit
of Holiness, the Paraclete from heaven." "Amen," is the
answer. "The Spirit of Wisdom and understanding."
"Amen." "The Spirit of counsel and fortitude." "Amen."
"The Spirit of knowledge and piety." "Amen."

The first part of the prayer links up with the last formal prayer of the baptismal rite, using the very same
phrases. A further continuation of the prayer points to the
indelible seal of the sacrament being conferred, the seal
of Christ the head and highpriest of the mystical body.
"Fill them with the Spirit of thy fear, and graciously seal
them with the sign of the cross unto life everlasting,
through the same Jesus Christ, thy Son, our Lord, who
liveth and reigneth with thee, in the unity of the same
Holy Ghost, God through all eternity. Amen."

Thereupon, dipping his thumb in the holy chrism, the
bishop anoints the candidates. It is the one time in the

[2] Power, *The Seal of the Spirit*

life of every Christian, that he comes in direct contact with the power of Christ in all its apostolic abundance. Making the sign of the cross on the forehead of each candidate with the holy oil, the bishop says simply: "N, I seal thee with the sign of the cross, and I confirm thee with the chrism of salvation, in the name of the Father, and of the Son, and of the Holy Ghost. Amen." This is followed by a slight blow on the cheek, the meaning of which is not definitely known, while the traditional Christian greeting is given of "Peace be with thee."

At the reception of the children of God into their full maturity, there is rejoicing in the Church and among all the faithful of the parish in particular. The choir sings out the following melody with a note of triumphant joy: "Preserve, O God, what thou hast wrought in us, from out thy holy temple which is in Jerusalem. Glory be to the Father, etc." With her customary solicitude and her fine sense of completeness the Church will not dismiss the newly confirmed soldiers of Christ without a final prayer and blessing. The first part of the prayer is an excellent declaration of the true powers residing in the Church and exercised in the liturgy. "O God, who didst give the Holy Ghost to thy apostles, and didst will that he should be given through them and their successors to the rest of the faithful, look with favor upon our lowly ministration, and grant that the same Holy Spirit, coming upon those whose foreheads we have anointed with the sacred chrism and sealed with the sign of the holy cross, may graciously consecrate their hearts as a temple of his glory by dwelling within them."

After this prayer, the newly confirmed are dismissed, but not without a final blessing. The bishop announces it in these words: "Behold, thus shall everyone be blessed that feareth the Lord." The blessing follows, which is instinct with a sort of prophetic vision of the reward of fidelity that shall be the lot of the new soldiers of Christ: "The Lord bless you out of Sion, that you may see the blessings of Jerusalem all the days of your life and may have life everlasting. Amen." Therewith ends the ceremony of the spiritual maturity of the member of Christ. How different, and how beautiful, in comparison with the cold dogmatic instruction that alone many of us received before the bishop visited us and imparted to us the fulness of the Holy Spirit! How solemn the moment must be for the Church, since she sends one of her very apostles to us to knight us for Christ! From him, indeed, it is most fitting that we receive the fulness of the divine life into our souls. The sign of Christ is now indelibly upon us a second time, and we must henceforth remain ever faithful throughout our journey on the way that is Christ.

We are knights of Christ. We must now do battle for him and his cause as occasion demands. But it must always be with the essential weapon of Christ, that of divine charity. We are now sharing doubly in the general priesthood of Christ and in his mission. Every one of us must therefore be a true light of Christ shining out into the darkness of the world, so that men may see the rays of this light of Christ reflected in every action and word of ours, and seeing may believe and praise and honor God. We are now, in the words of St. Thomas, *quasi ex officio* bound to help further the kingdom of God, to work for the fulfilment of the petition which Christ put in the Our Father immediately after the hallowing of God's name. It is thus, in fact, that we achieve the hallowing of God's name in truth; for without this battle waged in all charity for Christ, is not our profession of homage in danger of turning to the lip service that Christ condemned so strongly? Here, too, as in all the liturgy, what a task lies before us, in order that we may recapture for ourselves and for others the "true Christian spirit" that once before conquered a world-wide pagan civilization!

III. In Serious Illness

When the day's battle of the soldier of Christ is ended and the final bugle call of Christ summons him to his eternal reward, the forces of Satan will make a last effort to avenge on him the defeat they suffered through his faithful service in God's cause. For the special trial of any severe illness of body and consequent spiritual weakness, there is the sacrament of Extreme Unction, in which the priestly energy of the Church comes to the aid of the distressed member; and if his last moments have arrived the Church also puts the seal of her divine approval and efficacy on the closing earthly career of the Christian warrior. Of this sacrament some have the notion that it is a sure harbinger of death. Others, by force of habit perhaps, think of it mainly in terms of the externals belonging to a sick-bed outfit, knowing nothing of its inner beauty or of that of the liturgy as a whole. Yet the internal action is but a further wonderful example of the tender solicitude and consciousness with which the Church exercises the priestly powers entrusted to her by Christ. We have here a sacrament that is not necessarily of the dying at all, but is for all who are in serious illness. The word *extreme* may not be a happy one.

The progressive liturgical action in the sacrament of Extreme Unction commences with the same simple greeting that is recited by the priest when he enters a home to bring holy Communion to a sick person: "Peace to this house, and to all dwelling therein." The sick person is given a crucifix to kiss and holy water is sprinkled. Ordinarily the sacrament is preceded by confession and communion, in which case the priest begins the rite of Extreme Unction with the verse and answer: "Our help is in the name of the Lord.—Who made heaven and earth." [3] The first collect prayer is a beautiful expression of the true Christian atmosphere of the family home: "May there enter this house, O Lord Jesus Christ, with our unworthy coming, unending happiness, heaven-sent prosperity, joy undisturbed, practical kindness, and unfailing health; may the angels of peace come hither, and harmful discord of whatever sort depart from this house. Glorify thy holy name, O Lord, in our regard and bless what we are about to do; show forth thy power through our coming here, unworthy though we be; thou who art holy and gracious, and abidest with the Father and the Holy Ghost."

Another prayer continues the invocation of God's benison upon the household, asking for his abundant blessing upon all its members, for the protection of a guardian angel, for devotion of the members in the service of God, and for freedom from "all that might work evil against them" and "from all anxiety and distress . . . and from all harm." Thus the preliminary preparation has the same note of general protection and expurgation that we meet with so often in other parts of the liturgy. It ends with

[3] Power, God's Healing, pp. 24ff.

the following summarizing prayer: "Holy Lord, Father almighty, eternal God, graciously hear us, and deign to send thy holy angel from heaven to watch over, encourage, protect, abide with, and defend all who have their home in this habitation: Through Christ our Lord. Amen."

In the next stage of the liturgical action, the priest is concerned more immediately with the object of his visit. The Confiteor is recited by all present, and the priest recites the prayers of general absolution that always follow the liturgical confession of faults. Then he extends his hands over the head of the sick person while reciting a prayer that echoes the second part of the Confiteor by invoking the aid of the entire communion of saints, of all the members of the mystical body, in behalf of the member here in distress: "In the name of the Father and of the Son and of the Holy Ghost, may all power of the devil against thee be at an end through the imposition of our hands and through the invocation of the holy and glorious virgin Mary, Mother of God, of her most worthy spouse, Saint Joseph, and of all the holy angels, archangels, patriarchs, prophets, apostles, martyrs, confessors, virgins and all the other saints. Amen."

All being now in readiness, the Church enters upon the sacramental administration itself. Through it the power of Christ remits the punishment due to sins, and may restore bodily health and strength; and if the patient is in a state where sacramental confession is impossible, it remits also the sins themselves insofar as the proper disposition for sacramental efficacy is present. At baptism the taking possession of the senses of the candidate was accomplished in a gesture or two. Now the Church exerts more detailed care in the final purgation of the senses from whatever of evil they may have connived at or committed. Each sense organ is treated individually, one after the other, eyes, ears, nose, mouth, hands, and feet. Each of them is anointed separately with holy oil and for each the priest repeats the formula with no change other than in the mention of the name of the sense organ being anointed: "Through this holy unction and his most tender mercy, may the Lord forgive thee whatever sin thou has committed by the sense of sight . . . of hearing, . . . of smell, . . . of taste and the power of speech, . . . of touch, . . . by the power of motion. Amen."

In the anointing of the parts of the organic body the liturgical mystery is applied to the soul of the sick person, but to the soul precisely as the vital principle of the living person. Both soul and body in their living unity are anointed by the powers of Christ, even as both soul and body in inseparable co-operation performed whatever of evil was done by the person as well as whatever of good he accomplished in the name of Christ. It is in full accord with her liturgical appreciation of the value and meaning of the externals that the Church shows her tender care so constantly also for the body of the member of Christ. It is the body together with the soul, the entire integral man, that she accompanies with her ministrations from the cradle to the grave, showing her respect even to the dead corpse after the soul has fled, knowing well what part the body played in the religious life of the person on earth and what part it shall have in the great glory to come after the final resurrection. The anointing of the living body in the sacrament of Extreme Unction may be the last preparation of it for the glorified existence it is to have in the company of the saints in heaven.

When danger of death is imminent and the performance of the entire rite may take too long, the Church dispenses with all preliminary prayers. She is never a pharisee in her liturgical observance, and she knr vs well that the letter of the law may kill. In such circumstances a single anointing, that of the forehead, suffices with the formula: "Through this holy unction may the Lord forgive thee whatever sin thou hast committed. Amen."

As usual, the climax of the sacramental mystery is followed by some last prayers which ask for God's full blessing on what has been done and for the attainment of its fullest fruitage. These prayers begin in dialog form after the reciting of the Our Father: "Save thy servant: Who puts his trust in thee, my God. Send him help from the holy place: And from Sion come to his defense. Be thou to him, O Lord, a tower of strength: Against the face of the enemy. Let not the enemy prevail against him: Nor the wicked one have power to hurt him, etc." Then the people are asked to join in the following prayer: "O Lord God, who through Saint James thy apostle hast said: Is any man sick among you? let him call in the priests of the Church, and let them pray over him, anointing him with oil. . . . Cure, we beseech thee, O our Redeemer, by the grace of the Holy Ghost, the ailments of this thy sick servant; heal his wounds; and graciously bless him with perfect health within and without, that being made well again by the gift of thy goodness, he may be able to take up anew the duties of his state of life." Another prayer asks of God ". . . refresh the soul which thou hast created" and a final prayer ends the rite by having all present call upon the name of the Lord and ask him in behalf of the one anointed: ". . . do thou lift him up by thy right hand, sustain him by thy saving help, defend him by thy might, and restore him to thy holy Church with every advantage that could be wished for: Through Christ our Lord. Amen." Thereupon the priest departs, unless the person is in dying agony. Further prayers are provided by the liturgy for that occasion, but they are not part of the sacrament of Extreme Unction.

IV. HUMAN PARENTHOOD

The position of parenthood in our civilization and in the fellowship of Christ need not be dwelt upon here. No member of Christ's mystical body can be forgetful of the high privilege and dignity of co-operating with God in the creation of new prospective members of this same mystical body and of sowing in their souls the first seeds of the knowledge of God and of Christ. Nor need we dwell on the propriety of connecting the sacrament of Matrimony with the sacrifice of the altar, since it is well known that a Christian marriage is infinitely more than a human contract, as much more as the liturgical mystery of the New Testament stands above the purely human words and gestures of souls in no way united to God.

The union of man and woman in Christian marriage is effected through the priestly power of Christ himself. It is a union effected by God and in God. In the holy fellowship of husband and wife God is ever a third partner, and the union of all three is for the purposes of Christ and for no other. Husband and wife are destined each to serve Christ in special degree in the other. For both, their life is to be a mutual co-operative stripping off of the old man of selfishness and sin, and the common putting on of the new man Christ. And this mutual growth in Christ is made doubly possible through the birth of children and the serving of God in the care of his and their children. Both the sacramental enactment and the new life it has established is for each a continued sacrifice of self in union with Christ.

The sacrament is performed according to the mind of the Church immediately before the sacrifice and at the very altar of the Lord, and it is sealed by the merging of the common sacrifice of each to the other in the universal sacrifice of Christ through participation of husband and wife in both the sacrifice-oblation and the sacrifice-banquet. On the part of husband and wife, who are the ministers of the sacrament under witness of the official priest of the Church, it is a special exercise of the powers of general priesthood conferred on them in the sacraments of Baptism and Confirmation. So also is their later fulfilment of their state, in the education of their children, a special working out of their position as "other Christs," as both teachers and priestly sanctifiers and moral guides of their children.

At the foot of the altar the well-known question is asked of the husband and the wife, and their mutual answers of "I will" achieve the sacramental efficacy in the name and the power of Christ. Thenceforth they are joined by God for a common lot until parted by death. After the union is blessed in the name of the Trinity by the priest, the collect prayer for the blessing of the ring is recited: "Bless, O Lord, this ring, upon which we invoke a blessing in thy name, that she who is to wear it, being faithful in all things to her husband, may abide in peace according to thy will, and live with him always in well-requited af-

fection: Through Christ our Lord. Amen."[4] Like other
prayers to come in the Mass itself, the Church prays in
particular for the wife, who truly sets the tone of the
Christian home, who in fact is its true guardian angel and
priestess. The prayer, again, indicates another characteristic of the liturgy—the exhortation of the woman to fidelity
and the mention of the affection due her from her husband.
If the husband is to have a deciding voice in the direction
of some affairs of the home, it is always the voice of true
Christian love than which nothing can be more Christ-
like. If the two terms, fidelity of the woman and love
of the husband, are taken literally, then it is the husband
and not the wife who has the greater task enjoined by the
liturgy. After an extended dialog prayer the concluding
petition of the rite asks of God: "Look with favor, we
beseech thee, O Lord, upon these thy servants and deign
to watch over the provision of thy wisdom for the increase
of the human race, that those who are made one according
to thy will, may be kept safe by thy protection."

The mention of unity in God is taken up at once in the
Mass that now follows. "May the God of Israel make
you one," the introit begins. The collect asks for God's
blessing, and the epistle instructs us in the beautiful words
of St. Paul regarding the parallel between marriage and
Christ's union with the Church. The sacramental union
just enacted indeed foreshadows the union of Christ and
his Church, just as it has for its highest purpose the promotion of that union and of the mission of Christ. St.
Paul exhorts that the "women be subject to their husbands as to the Lord," for which purpose also the husbands
must love their wives, not stintingly, but as fully "as

[4] Power, *Marriage in Christ*

Christ also loved the Church, and delivered himself up for it." Surely a sublime task, almost impossible for men, though not for those living in Christ for they "are members of his body, of his flesh, and of his bones. . . . This is a great sacrament, but I speak in Christ and in the Church." The gradual then sings out in the rich imagery of the Orient: "Thy wife shall be as the fruitful vine on the walls of thy house . . . ," while the gospel repeats the words of Christ: "Therefore now they are not two but one flesh. What therefore God hath joined together, let no man put asunder."

Apart from the proper parts of the Mass text, the priest prays twice for the newly-married couple, each time interrupting the ordinary progress of the liturgical action of the sacrifice. After the Pater noster he turns to face them and recites a long prayer that recalls God's creation of man and woman, the symbolical meaning of marriage in relation to Christ and the Church, and he asks the special blessing of God upon the woman on whom the burden of the family life shall fall, praying for loyalty, patience, fortitude, long life and the peace of the blessed in heaven. Finally, just before the blessing of the Mass the priest again turns to them, takes up the last note of the preceding occasion and recites the concluding prayer of the Church's rite in behalf of the happiness of the couple: "May the God of Abraham, the God of Isaac, the God of Jacob be with you, and may he fulfil unto you his blessing; that you may see your children's children unto the third and the fourth generation; and thereafter enjoy forever eternal life, with the help of Jesus Christ our Lord, who with the Father and the Holy Ghost, liveth and reigneth, God through all eternity. Amen."

V. SPIRITUAL FATHERHOOD

The whole sacramental life of the Church is maintained only through the powers of Christ as transmitted to his apostles and to their successors. Foremost among these powers is the sacerdotal or priestly power of offering the sacrifice and administering the sacraments. This power together with those of teacher and ruler is transmitted by means of the sacrament of Holy Orders. While the Eucharist is the most important of the sacraments, if comparisons can be made at all between it and the others, because it contains the whole work of Christ's redemption from which all graces flow, there is a sense in which the sacrament of Holy Orders also may be called most important, *viz.*, from the standpoint of the mission of the Church as continuer of the work of Christ on earth. Without the transmission of the powers of Christ through Holy Orders there would be no Eucharist and no Church existing in time.

There are many steps in the whole ordination rite of the official priesthood of Christ. Each of these steps has a rite of its own, so to say, and may be conferred apart from the others, but not unless the candidate for any step has already received the others that precede in the series. First there is the initiation rite, the conferring of tonsure, or the "making of the cleric." Then there are the four minor orders of Porter, Reader, Exorcist, and Acolyte, successively approaching nearer to the altar. All of these constitute only sacramentals. After these come the major orders which are successively those of subdeacon, deacon and priest. Ordination to the priesthood confers the full priestly powers needed for the ordinary administration of the sacramental life of Christ to the faithful. The plenitude of apostolic power is transmitted in the consecration of the bishop. He alone can validly ordain other priests and ordinarily administer the sacrament of Confirmation.

The rites accompanying these various steps of Holy Orders follow a general pattern. They all begin with the calling of the names of the candidates who must singly answer their "Present." The ordaining bishop then gives them an exhortation to fidelity in the duties of the office they are about to receive. A symbolic action, conferring the right or the power to function in the new order, follows and then a prayer or series of prayers asking God's blessing and aid for the candidates. In the major orders there follows the ceremony of investment with the apparel distinctive of the respective order, and after the calling and answer the Litany is sung while the candidates lie prostrate before the altar.

In the ordination to subdeaconship the title (diocesan affiliation or religious order) under which the ordination takes place is mentioned. The subdeacon is definitely attached to the Church, must pray officially in her name, and can receive his support from the altar. Because of the importance of the step the candidates are asked "to consider attentively, again and again, to what a burden you, of your own accord, this day aspire. For as yet you are free and it is lawful for you at will to pass over to worldly pursuits." [5] They are told that "it is the duty of the subdeacon to prepare water for the service of the altar, to wash the altar cloths and the corporals, to assist the deacon and present him the chalice and paten used

[5] All quotations in this section are from Lynch, *The Rite of Ordination.*

in the sacrifice." And they must "study, therefore, whilst neatly and most diligently fulfilling these visible services which we have mentioned, also to perform those invisible offices of which these are the exemplars." They must "minister worthily in the divine sacrifices, and serve the church of God, that is, the body of Christ." A chalice and altar cruets are handed them as the insignia of their new office.

When the candidates for deaconship, which is definitely a priestly order, have been called, the further question is asked by the archdeacon: "Do you know them to be worthy?" and the bishop proceeds only after an assurance in the affirmative. The bishop formally chooses them for deaconship in the name of Christ. He tells them that "it is the duty of the deacon to minister at the altar, to baptize and to preach," and that they are the legitimate successors of the tribe of Levi of the Chosen People of old. They must "be clean, undefiled, pure, chaste, as becometh ministers of Christ and dispensers of the mysteries of God," and since they are "co-ministers and co-operators of the body and blood of the Lord," they must be estranged from every allurement of the flesh." Special prayers are said for them and a solemn preface is chanted, in the midst of which the bishop places his right hand on the head of each while saying most solemnly: "Receive the Holy Ghost, that you may have strength and be able to resist the devil and his temptations. In the name of the Lord." The deacon's stole is put on each and the dalmatic, then the gospel book is given.

In the final step, the ordination of the deacons to the priesthood of the sacrifice, the exhortations, prayers, etc., become more solemn and impressive as befits this greatest of steps. "It is the duty of the priest to offer sacrifice, to bless, to govern, to preach and to baptize. . . . Strive, therefore, to be such that by the grace of God you may be worthily chosen as helpers of Moses and the twelve apostles, that is, of the Catholic bishops." The exhortation contains the famous advice in regard to intelligent liturgical performance or participation: "Bear in mind what you do. Let your conduct be in conformity with the action you perform, so that celebrating the mystery of the Lord's death, you take heed to mortify your members from all vices and lusts." Prayers follow and a solemn preface, which says towards the end: "Bestow, then, we beseech thee, almighty Father, the dignity of the priesthood upon these thy servants; renew in them the spirit of holiness, that they may receive from thee, O God, this office next to ours in dignity, and that the example of their lives may be for others an incentive to virtue." The priestly stole and chasuble are conferred, and then the "Come, Holy Ghost," is joyously sung. The hands of the deacons are now anointed with holy oil in the manner prescribed, while the bishop at the same time asks of God: "Vouchsafe, O Lord, to consecrate and sanctify these hands by this unction, and by our blessing. Amen. That whatsoever they shall bless shall be blessed and whatsoever they shall consecrate may be consecrated and sanctified; in the name of our Lord Jesus Christ. Amen." A special rubric prescribes here that the candidate himself answer the "So be it." Chalice and paten are given with the words: "Receive power to offer sacrifice to God and to celebrate Mass, as well for the living as for the dead, in the name of the Lord. Amen."

The Mass, which had been interrupted for the ordination, now proceeds with the offertory prayers, and the candidates from here on concelebrate with the ordaining bishop, reciting all the prayers aloud with him. The special secret for those ordained reads: "Enable us, by thy mysteries, we beseech thee, O Lord, to offer with worthy souls these gifts to thee." The newly ordained communicate immediately after the bishop and without any intervening prayers. After the last ablution, the bishop reads a responsory relating to the conferring of the Holy Ghost, and when the newly ordained priests have recited the Apostles' Creed, he places both hands on the head of each while saying: "Receive the Holy Ghost; whose sins thou shalt forgive they are forgiven them; and whose sins thou shalt retain they are retained." A promise of obedience is made to the bishop and his advice is received in regard to faithful performance of the liturgical ceremonies, whereupon he gives his formal blessing in these words: "May the blessing of almighty God, Father, and Son, and Holy Ghost, descend upon you; that you may be blessed in the order of priesthood, and that you may offer, for the sins and offences of the people, sacrifices of propitiation to almighty God, to whom is honor and glory forever and ever. Amen." The communion verse is said, and after the blessing of the Mass the ordination rite ends with a final exhortation by the bishop: "Dearly beloved sons, consider diligently the order you have received and the burden that has been placed upon your shoulders; strive to live holily and religiously, and to please almighty God, that you may be able to obtain his grace, which in his mercy may he himself vouchsafe to

grant you." The Mass then ends as usual with the last
gospel of St. John.

After the analysis of the sacramental life of the Church
in this chapter and the preceding, there is no need to stress
further the important position of the sacraments in the
Church of Christ and in the life of the Christian. The sacraments are the indispensable means of living the life of
Christ here on earth. Through them alone can we partake of the divine energy that Christ imparts to us through
the liturgical ministrations of the Church he founded for
that very purpose. Wonderfully expressive is the whole
complex of words and actions by which the sacraments are
administered. But still more wonderful is their inner
meaning and soul, the mysterious enactment of the divine
life in the souls of the faithful, that constant rebirth in
Christ, that sublimest contact by which God himself deigns
to touch the soul to the quick with the divine energy of
his own being. Most truly can we apply to the sacraments
the words: Let him who can, understand. As our life in
Christ must be an increasing contact with the sacramental
action of Christ, so its fullest efficacy, our increasing spiritual growth, must also be and will logically be a growing
understanding of the wonderful treasure that Christ has
entrusted to his Church in her sacramental liturgy.

CHAPTER XIII

THE SACRAMENTALS

I. Nature of Sacramentals

In a preceding chapter the sacramentals were referred to as extensions of the sacraments. Thereby is meant that they are an extended application of the divine powers that the Church exercises in the sacraments, but with an important difference. As actions of divine grace centering immediately around the eucharistic sacrifice, the sacraments form a close inner circle of their own. In them alone does the divine energy of the priesthood of Christ take effect by the mere virtue of the ritual action—gesture and word, matter and form—of the sacrament, performed officially for the Church by some properly authorized person. In other words, the sacraments produce their effect *ex opere operato*. In the sacramentals the effects depend more completely on the disposition and intention, on the degree of active intelligent participation, with which the members of the Church use them. At the same time they do not get their efficacy merely from the intention of the person using them in co-operation with God's general graces. That would also be true of individual and private works.

The sacramentals have the special authorization, approval, and blessing of the Church. They are therefore instinct with the spiritual vitality of the Church and of Christ, but in a lesser degree than, or in a manner different from, that of the sacraments. Hence by their use of the sacramentals the faithful align themselves with the intention and the efficacy of the official Church of Christ; and their actions, in using the sacramentals, are accompanied by the efficacy of the sanctifying power of the Church herself. In them, as it were, the merits and appeasing powers of all the saints are joined to our own efforts. And behind our own prayers and efforts is the prayer-power of the Church, not the official declarative power that effects necessarily what it declares, but the petitioning power that has special appeal before the throne of God because it is the beloved voice of the Bride of Christ. The sacramentals are then for us a means pointed out by the Church and instituted by her, through which the members of Christ can live the Christ-life more also in the detailed circumstances and situations of life under the special guidance of the Church. They are so many ways of living in more faithful union with the mystical body and of developing ever more perfectly the complete mind of Christ in men.

Under sacramentals we may include everything connected with the liturgy of the Church, therefore everything found in the official liturgical books, missal, breviary, ritual, pontificals, etc., that is not essential to the sacrifice and the sacraments. In this sense Dom Lefebvre could speak of "the whole of the Mass, and more especially a high Mass, which, as the prayer of the Church, is the greatest sacramental," as being itself "made up of a series of sacramentals, from which we derive little profit since we are ignorant of their meaning." [1] He referred espe-

[1] *Catholic Liturgy*, p. 113

cially to the use of holy water, to the Confiteor, incense,
blessing, pater noster, the gospels, the sign of the cross,
tapers, lights, blessed bread, holy oil, etc. In the same
way Dom Festugière calls the whole of the liturgy a vast
sacramental: "Composed above all of the sacrificial rite,
the sacraments, and the sacramentals and inspired texts,
voice and action of the mystical body of Christ, the liturgy, taken in the fullness of its organic complexity, forms
a vast sacramental, which is—more or less strictly according to the elements considered—the bearer of grace. It
envelops in the folds of its grace all humanity, individual
and social; and it seizes and carries along all human existence in a single stream of grace." [2]

The sacramentals in general, then, include the prayers
especially approved by the Church, her divine office in
particular which we shall examine in the next chapters,
and the many blessings of persons and objects of all kinds,
in which the liturgy abounds. These blessings may be
divided into two classes, those which are in any way connected with religious practice or religious life, and those
which are concerned with the daily life of the Christian
in the world. Among the former blessings are above all
those connected with the enactment of the sacrifice and
the sacraments, or with the special states of religious life
or of clerical orders. In this class would come, for instance, the blessing of abbots, or of men or women embracing the religious state, and then of the many articles
used in the liturgical worship, such as the church building, the cornerstone, the altar and its equipment, vestments, organ, bells, holy water, incense, the cemetery,
likewise the ritual blessings of Ash Wednesday, Palm

[2] *Qu'est-ce que la liturgie?* pp. 79–80

Sunday, Feast of the Purification, Holy Saturday, etc.
The second class of blessings, those of articles used outside of specific liturgical worship or religious life, would
include all the blessing of sacred objects for the home—
medals, scapulars, pictures, candles, etc.; then blessings
of persons in particular circumstances, such as a mother
before or after childbirth, a sick child, an infant, and of
the home itself or the school, of implements of work such
as plow, telegraph, bed, books, airplane, or finally the
grave; and again of different foods and animals, as for
instance, bread, wine, beer, eggs, cattle, horses, bees, and
the like. The Church has her special ritual blessing for
each of these and for many more, so that the loving member of Christ may at all times live his daily life as a constant thanksgiving unto God for all the good things of the
redemption of Christ.

By means of these many blessings the Church accompanies the Christian into all the daily contacts of his life;
everywhere can he remain within reach of her blessing
hand and derive strength and help from her. He need
never feel himself abandoned by his loving Mother, or
left to his own weakness in any emergency. Through the
sacramentals he can always draw upon the treasure of the
Church's prayers and spiritual aids; they are ever within
his reach. The ordinary occupations of his daily life thus
can become part and parcel of the divine service he renders to God through the Church, he can at all times both
work and pray, he need never abandon the divine con-
versation which he experiences at its best in the sacrament
of the Eucharist in intimate contact with the altar of
Christ. The sacramentals extend the atmosphere of altar
and church, of the house of God, into all the wide world

and far beyond the direct reach of the official ministers of the life of Christ in the mystical body. Through them the entire world is reunited to God to take intimate part in the service at all times rendered to the Creator by the whole of regenerated creation.

In the sacramentals we have a special indication of the divine love with which Christ constantly pursues us. In them the Church shows the full delicate tenderness of her divine Bridegroom for all her children. In them "the voice of the Church, our mother, is not so loud, nor surrounded by such dignity, as at high Mass or the consecration of a Church, Baptism or Holy Orders. It is rather like a whispering breath. But here we can well discern her pulsebeat, her feelings and thought, her solicitude for the weal and woe of all her children. Wherever a Christian and his wife establish a home, she would pray for their happiness; she would share with them the burden and reward of toil whatever the work be, whether in competition with the machine and high power in the whirl of factory, or on the soil with horse and plow." [3]

It is for us and only for our spiritual good that the Church has developed her vast array of sacramentals. And their efficacy, as we have seen, the application or administration of the spiritual virtue put into them by the Church, depends particularly on our way of using them. The sacramentals are in a special manner designed for our intelligent participation. Yet it is just the idea of participation, of intelligent use of them that has been forgotten in our day even by Catholics otherwise known for their intelligence. Almost the whole ensemble of the sacramentals is unknown to most Catholics. They are well

[3] *Die Betende Kirche,* p. 459

nigh as ignorant of the great treasure of the Church's sacramental blessings and helps as are the unbaptized. Some few of the sacramentals are indeed in common use, but of these also it must be said only too often that they are not really used with intelligence or understanding. A simple question directed to those using holy water or blessed medals might prove enlightening if not shocking.

In fact, the loss of proper liturgical sense has brought us to such a pass that sacramentals are not infrequently used mechanically, or thought of subconsciously as if they were fetishes or magic formulae or objects. In some instances this state of affairs is hardly indistinguishable from the mental attitude or outlook that the heathen of old had in relation to his charms. Only the vague consciousness, perhaps, that the blessing of a supernatural Church has endowed things with some kind of efficacy, saves many persons from the attitude of pure superstition. An examination of the actions or of the fundamental concepts of some of the sacramental blessings should help much not only towards a better understanding of their true nature but also towards a better appreciation of the beauty and inspiration contained everywhere in the liturgy of the Church.

II. Consecration of Virgins

Among the ritual blessings having to do with the official worship of God or his special service, the consecration of a church and the consecration of the chosen spouse of Christ are most imposing. We shall examine the latter here in order to see how well the Church in her ceremonies shows her high appreciation of the event in question and of the state of virginity dedicated to God, and how the ceremony, like that of baptism, gives a plan of life for the future. Again, we shall see that what is done in the ceremony does not end therewith, but must continue to grow and to realize itself ever more. As with baptism, therefore, the renewal of the ceremony in mental analysis or in prayer is of itself most wholesome for those who have been the beneficiaries of it. For all readers it is a striking illustration of the rich beauty and the spiritual inspiration of the Church's liturgy.

The ceremony is presided over by the bishop himself, the highest liturgical dignitary of the Church, and it occurs in the Mass, so that the oblation of the virgin soul may be immediately united with that of the spotless Lamb on the altar. When the candidates have been solemnly accompanied into the Church by other dedicated virgins, the chief assisting priest sings out the antiphon: "Ye prudent virgins, prepare your lamps, behold the Bridegroom approaches, go to meet him." Thereupon he formally presents them to the bishop: "Most reverend Father, our holy mother Church asks that you deign to bless and consecrate these virgins here present, and espouse them to our Lord Jesus Christ, the Son of the all highest God." The bishop asks: "Do you know that they are worthy?" The answer is: "As far as human frailty can know I believe and testify that they are worthy." Then follow the spiritual nuptials in which various progressive steps of ascending action are discernible.[4]

The first step is the calling of the brides. The bishop seated at the altar in full pontificals says solemnly as the spokesman of Christ: "God and our Savior Jesus Christ

---

[4] Cf. *Die Betende Kirche*, pp. 448ff.

helping us, we choose these virgins, to bless and consecrate them and to wed them to our Lord Jesus Christ,
the Son of the highest God." In a most expressive melody
of the chant the call and its response is sung. "Come,"
sings the bishop. "Behold we follow," answer the virgins. Again the bishop sings: "Come." "We follow with
our whole heart." "Come, my daughters, give ear, I will
teach you the fear of the Lord." "We follow with our
whole heart, we fear thee and seek to behold thy face.
Lord, do not confound us, but do unto us according to
thy kindness and the greatness of thy mercies."

The next step is that of the promise of virginity. The
virgins approach nearer, and each one says aloud: "Receive me, O Lord, according to thy word, that the power
of injustice may not dominate over me." After asking
all of them together, the bishop asks each one individually: "Do you promise to preserve virginity forever?"
"I promise." The words have been given, and the bishop,
rejoicing with Christ and the Church, utters a simple
"Thanks be to God."

The third step is that of vesting for the spiritual wedding. "Do you will to be blessed and consecrated and
betrothed to our Lord Jesus Christ, the Son of the all
highest God?" "We will." The virgins prostrate themselves at the altar, and in the Litany of the Saints the
prayers and merits of all the saints in heaven are drawn
upon by the Church. The religious garments to be put
on are then blessed. In the prayers of the blessing they
are called "garments of salvation and of eternal joy . . .
signifying humility of heart and contempt of the world
. . . the habit of sacred chastity" whereby the virgins are
"vested with a happy immortality . . . so that when they

come to the perpetual reward of the saints, they may with the prudent virgins under thy guidance [*i.e.*, Christ's] enter into the nuptials of eternal happiness."

While the veils, rings, and wreaths are being blessed, the virgins go out to vest themselves in the new habits. Entering again in slow procession, two by two, they chant: "I have despised the kingdom of the world and all its adornment for the love of our Lord Jesus Christ. I have seen him and loved him, believed in him, chosen him. My heart has spoken a good word, I have promised my word to the King." While they kneel before the bishop, the latter prays over them, and extending his hands sings the special preface. It is a solemn hymn of thanks, like that of the Mass, and is like the latter the introduction to the fulfilment of the holy action of sacrifice. It is a wonderful tribute from the mouth of the Church to the state of virginity, in which human substance, "still in the fetters of mortality, has been raised to the similitude of angels"; and most earnestly is God petitioned to guide and guard the virgins in order that "a hundredfold fruit may be crowned by the gift of virginity."

In the next step the virgin is wedded to Christ. "Come, my chosen one," the bishop sings; "thy King longs for thee. Hear and see, incline thine ear." The virgins answer: "I am a handmaid of Christ, therefore am I vested in servile habit." A last time the bishop asks: "Will you persevere in the holy virginity that you have professed?" Upon their "We will" the ceremonies of conferring the veil, the ring and the bridal wreath seal and confirm this vow. Having received the veil the virgins chant: "He has placed a sign on my brow so that I may admit no lover but him." After a prayer by the bishop he takes the ring and again calls to them: "Come to the nuptials, beloved . . ." Putting on the ring he says solemnly: "I betroth thee to Jesus Christ, Son of the all highest Father; may he safeguard thee unhurt. Therefore receive the ring of fidelity, the sign of the Holy Ghost, so that thou mayest henceforth be called spouse of God and faithfully serve him and be crowned eternally." Lifting up her right hand the virgin sings: "With his ring hath my Lord Jesus Christ betrothed me and adorned me with a wreath as a bride." A third time the bishop calls the bride of Christ and now places the bridal wreath on her head: ". . . As thou art crowned on earth by my hand so mayest thou deserve to be crowned with glory and honor by Christ in heaven." After some prayers by the bishop the nuptial action ends with the joyful declaration of the virgin: "Behold, what I have desired I see accomplished; what I hoped for I now have; I am joined to him in heaven whom I have loved with full devotion while on earth." The wedded spouse already lives in the anticipation of her eternal union with Christ in heaven. Some longer prayers of blessing by the bishop close this impressive part of the ceremony.

The Mass, which had been interrupted at the gradual, is now continued to the offertory, when the virgins joining intimately in the action of the Mass each offer up a burning candle at the altar. In the secret the bishop prays to God: "By means of the gifts offered grant to thy servants here present perseverance in perpetual virginity, so that at the coming of the highest King, they may enter with great joy through the open doors into the celestial kingdom." Having received their Lord in communion they all chant the following antiphon together before the altar: "Honey and milk have I received out of his mouth and his blood has adorned my cheeks."

In the last step of the ceremony at the end of the Mass the duty of singing God's praises is enjoined. After a short prayer the bishop extends a breviary to them which they all touch: "Receive the book so that you may begin to sing the canonical hours and read the office of the Church, in the name of the Father, and of the Son, and of the Holy Ghost. Amen." With a solemn Te Deum the beautiful ceremony ends, which apart from the sacraments is in the solemnity of its action and the progressive development of its theme one of the most striking liturgical functions of the Church.

III. From Church to Home

A sacramental used in every blessing is holy water. The natural symbolism of water for purification is thereby given a supernatural meaning and efficacy. As it is placed at our disposal when entering the church so we should have it ever ready for pious use in our homes. Salt is used in the blessing of holy water, and both the salt and the water receive a double blessing, the one of purgation and the other of positive energizing. "I exorcise thee, creature of salt," the blessing begins, "by the living God, by the true God, by the holy God . . . that thou mayest be for the healing of soul and body to all those receiving thee." The second prayer asks God "to bless and sanctify this creature of salt . . . that it may make for health of mind and body unto all who partake of it." The water is likewise exorcised in the name of the blessed Trinity and then a second prayer asks God to "pour into it the virtue of thy blessing." The salt is then mixed with the water in the form of a triple cross: "May the commixture of salt and water equally take place in the name of the Father, and of the Son, and of the Holy Ghost. Amen." A last prayer is said over the mixture: "We humbly pray and beseech thee, O Lord, to look with kindness upon this creature of salt and water, to bless it in thy mercy and hallow it with the dew of thy loving kindness: that wherever it will be sprinkled and thy holy name will be invoked in prayer, every assault of the unclean spirit may be baffled, all fear of the venomous serpent cast out and the presence of the Holy Spirit everywhere vouchsafed to us who entreat thy mercy. Through our Lord, Jesus Christ, etc."

A mixture of salt and water is made in the blessing of the church bells, which are washed with it while psalms are chanted. The prayers ask that we may experience an increase of devotion when we hear the bells ringing and that then "the snares of the devil be repelled, hail and tempests be averted." The bell is anointed with holy oil in the ceremony. The gospel that is read in the ceremony contains the significant message of Jesus to Martha of Bethany: "Only one thing is necessary. Mary has chosen the better part, which shall not be taken from her." This is the message the church bells constantly ring out even to our modern world of forgotten religion and of forgetful Catholics. In the ringing of the bells the voice of Christ calls to us, and whether we are in a position to answer its summons in person or no, Christ's message to Martha should come to our minds and thus revive in us the consciousness of the high calling we have as members of Christ.

Holy water is used in the blessing of the church organ, the music of which has for us no other purpose, not even aesthetic, than the better living of the life of Christ in divine worship. The prayer asks God to "bless the organ instrument, dedicated to thy worship, in order that the faithful, singing joyfully in spiritual canticles here on earth, may deserve to attain eternal joys in heaven."

Holy water should be used in every Christian home. The very gesture and word with which it is used is a concentrated confession of all our faith, of the Redemption and the Trinity, and the gesture traces the seal of Christ over mind and heart. The daily use of holy water with the deliberate and thoughtful making of the sign of the cross adds spiritual meaning to every action of the day and night, giving them increased value in the eyes of God. The home itself should be endowed with a special blessing. The ceremony begins with the now familiar greeting: "Peace be to this house. And to all dwelling therein." The prayer said after sprinkling the principal rooms with holy water asks God: "Hear us, holy Lord, almighty Father, eternal God, and deign to send down thy holy angel from heaven to guard, cherish, protect, assist and defend all dwelling in this house." The crucifix, which should hang in a prominent place in every house as a sign that Christ reigns there, is blessed with the following prayer: "We ask thee, holy Lord, almighty Father, eternal God, deign to bless this sign of the cross so that it may be a salutary remedy to the human race, bring solidity of faith, progress in good works, redemption of souls. May it be a solace and protection, a safeguard against the raging missiles of the enemies."

The life of union with Christ in his Church is thus enhanced by sanctification of the home through its blessing, and by the use of holy water and a crucifix. It is also fostered by our prayers, notably by some recitation of breviary prayers if possible, the morning Prime and evening Compline for instance, of which the next chapters will treat. There are also official prayers of the Church for meal time, the praying of which unites us intimately with members of the mystical body throughout the world and thus more intimately with Christ himself. The prayer before the noon meal begins: "The eyes of all, O Lord, hope in thee and thou givest them to eat in due time. Thou dost open thy hand and fill every living being with thy blessing. Glory be to the Father, etc." The Our Father is recited and then follows the request for the special blessing: "Bless us, O Lord, and these thy gifts, which we are about to receive from thy bounty; through Christ our Lord. Amen." A younger member addresses the elder of the family: "Pray, sir, a blessing," and the older member responds with the words: "May the King of eternal glory bring us to a share in the heavenly table." The Church's table prayers are instinct with the thought of material things as means of God's service and of time as the symbol for us of eternity. The evening blessing reads: "May the King of eternal glory lead us to the table of eternal life," to which all respond "Amen."

There are special blessings for use in the home when a person is sick, apart entirely from the sacramental administration of Extreme Unction. One of these is for sick children not old enough to receive the sacrament of the sick. Another is for adult persons who are ailing. The last prayer of this ritual blessing reads: "The Lord Jesus Christ be with thee to defend thee, in thee to preserve thee, before thee to lead thee, behind thee to guard thee, above thee to bless thee: Who liveth and reigneth with the Father and the Holy Ghost forever and ever. Amen."

The blessing for sick-bed linens makes a charming allusion to an incident in the life of Christ, who by "the touch of the hem of thy garment didst deign to heal the woman suffering from a flow of blood," and it asks that "those who are clad or covered with these vestments, cloths and linens, which we bless in thy name, may merit health of mind and body."

The ambulance brings the sick person from home to hospital for better medical care. Its blessing again alludes charmingly to the life of Christ on earth: "O Lord Jesus Christ, Son of the living God, who whilst wandering on earth, didst go about doing good and healing every ailment and infirmity of the people, and who didst restore to health of mind and body the paralytic lying on his bed, look thou, we beseech thee, upon the faith and the commiseration of thy servants, who being animated with the spirit of the true charity which thou didst foreshadow by thine example and teach by thy precept, wished to construct this vehicle after the manner of a bed for transporting the sick to a place of healing. . . . Grant that, under company of thy angels, they may arrive undisturbedly at the place of cure, etc."

IV. Blessing of Field and Shop

The Church extends her blessing hand to the objects of agriculture about the home with lavish abundance. Throughout most of her long existence, agriculture was the predominant occupation of men, and so there is no product or domestic animal of importance that has not its own ritual blessing. Besides the ordinary blessings of the ritual there are also the Rogation days and the Ember days, and the special blessings of food on Easter day, on the feast of the Assumption, and the like, all of which belong to this general group.

The ritual blessing of fields has an unusual character of solemnity. After the Lord's help is invoked and an initial prayer is recited, the priest, in allusion to his liturgical powers, asks of God: "Almighty, eternal God, who hast deigned among other things to give to thy priests the grace, that whatever is worthily and properly done by them in thy name is held in faith to be done by thee: we beseech thy clemency that whatever we are about to visit thou also mayest visit, whatever we are about to bless thou also mayest bless, and mayest extend the power of thy right hand to those things we are about to do. . . ." The Litany of All Saints is said on bended knee and the following petitions are added:

"That thou mayest deign to bless these fields (or acres, or hills, or pastures, or meadows)." "We beseech thee, hear us."

"That thou mayest deign to bless, preserve and guard these fields from all infesting of the devils." "We beseech thee, hear us."

"That thou mayest in thy clemency keep off from this place and put to flight lightning, hail, injurious tempests and harmful floods." "We beseech thee hear us."

A final prayer begs for nourishing rains and serene skies, so that the people may ever thank God for his gifts, fill the hungry with plenty, and cause the needy and the poor to praise the name of his glory.

The seed for the fields is blessed "so that it may not be exterminated by hail or flood, but remain ever unhurt, for the use of soul and body, and be brought to abundant and fullest maturity." All the farm products have their special blessings, *e.g.*, bread, beer, cheese and butter, lard, eggs, etc. Similarly there are blessings for cattle, fowl, bees, silkworms, and the like. Everywhere allusions are made to the final purpose of all life, health of body and soul, to the role material goods should play in God's world, and, where relevant, also to the specific use of things for divine worship.

Thus the prayer for the blessing of bees, whose chastity was considered emblematic by the Church Fathers in connection with the wax candle as the symbol of Christ: "O Lord, almighty God, who hast created heaven and earth and all the animals existing above and upon them so that men may use them, and who hast commanded that the ministers of holy Church light candles made by the labor of the bees in thy temple during the divine service in which the most holy body and blood of Jesus Christ thy Son is consecrated and consumed: may thy blessing descend upon these bees and this apiary . . . so that its products be dispensed unto thy glory, and that of thy Son and of the Holy Ghost, and the blessed virgin Mary."

Since silk stockings are so much the vogue today, the blessing of silkworms may be of special interest. Whether the silk of today is natural or artificial, it has the same relation to God. "O God, the Creator and Ruler of all, who in the creation of the animals hast given them the power of propagating their species, we beseech thee, to bless these silkworms, to foster and multiply them by thy kindness, so that thy altars adorned with their products, and thy faithful shining in the same, may glorify thee with their whole hearts as the giver of all goods."

All the spheres of human labor have their blessings of God through the loving ministrations of the Church. That of the limekiln asks that "by the fire's exerting the force of its strength may the workers receive by thy bounty a good quality of lime, and grant to them also that at the same time an increase of thy salutary grace may grow in them." The prayer for libraries asks God to bless them and avert destructive fire, and to increase their stock, "so that all who work there as officials or as students may progress"—how?—not in the modern fashion, but "in the knowledge of both human and divine things and equally in thy love."

Nor has the Church of all times ceased to extend her blessing hand in this our own day. The latest inventions of man receive their benediction even as they have their God-given destiny from all eternity. It would not be too far-fetched, one might claim with some plausibility, to say that these modern blessings in some way reflect also the greater modern spiritual need of man. In the older blessing of the bridge, for instance, there is a very simple petition for God's protection among the fortunes of this world. Bridges existed of old when the professed outlook of our civilization was acknowledgedly Christian. This is no longer true in our modern day. And in the newer blessings the tender care of the Church seems to have stressed more the message of the eternal things symbolized by the temporal and to take greater care to direct the minds of her faithful children to the higher meanings of life here below. It is not that the modern inventions are as such less tractable for the purpose of God, her blessings make that clear, but rather, one may venture to guess, that these inventions are used in a day and time when the world has greatly forgotten the things of God and of eternity. The Church is ever alert in the promotion of the mission of Christ.

The blessing for a fire engine is comparatively elaborate, containing a lengthy psalm, many dialog verses and answers, and three prayers, of which the last and longest is a compact sermon specially fitting for our day of irreligion. God is here addressed as the "just and merciful ruler of men, whom as its Maker every creature serves more promptly in such wise that this same fire burns unto the torment of the wicked and is mild unto the benefit of the good: graciously incline, we beseech thee, thine ear to our prayers, and pour thine abundant blessing upon this machine for the extinguishing of fires, so that as often as this machine is applied in living faith and holy desire against the forces of fire, the water thrown out by it may extinguish the burning flames, and snatch from the fire all its power, lest the fire bring damage to thy faithful hoping in thee and cause them injury in their goods: for the purpose that all, who have been freed from every fear and danger, may wholeheartedly come to their senses in regard to their vices, and being mindful of thy benefits, recognize with sincere heart, that such scourges come to them by reason of their iniquity and cease by thy mercy."

The blessings for an electric dynamo and a telegraph instrument are much alike. Both begin with the inspiring canticle of the Benedictus, the last verse of which is particularly relevant, in the one case literally and the other figuratively: "Enlighten them that sit in darkness and in the shadow of death, and direct our feet into the way of peace." Then follow psalms in each case. The antiphon for the dynamo blessing is "Light is risen to the just, and joy to the right of heart," and for the telegraph: "Blessed art thou, O Lord, who makest the clouds thy chariot, who walkest upon the wings of the winds, who makest thy angels spirits, and thy ministers a burning fire." Then follow a prayer for the intercession of the blessed Virgin and a final collect. For the dynamo the concluding prayer says beautifully: "Lord God almighty, who art the founder of all lights, bless this machine for making light, recently set up; and grant that after the obscurity of this world we may come to thee who art the Light unfailing." The last prayer for the telegraph instrument ends very pointedly: "O God, who walkest upon the wings of the winds, and alone dost wonderful things, grant that when, by the power given to this metal, in the flash of an eye thou dost transmit most swiftly what is far away to this place, and what is present to another place, we being instructed by the new inventions may by the help of thy grace more promptly and readily come to thee."

The blessing for the seismograph, another recent formulary, is unusual in its structure and especially its ending: "Almighty eternal God, who regardest the earth and makest it to tremble, flood this seismograph with thy blessing; and grant that the signs of the earth's tremors be properly registered and be correctly understood for the benefit of thy people and the greater glory of thy name. Through Christ our Lord. Amen. Virgin Mary, most sorrowful, be propitious to us and intercede for us. Saint Emidgus, pray for us, and in the name of Jesus Christ of Nazareth defend us and this seismograph from the attacks of the earthquake."

The blessing for airplanes begins with a series of appropriate verses and answers: "Our help is in the name of the Lord: Who made heaven and earth. Bless the Lord, O my soul: O Lord, my God, exceedingly art thou made wonderful. Who makest the cloud thy chariot: Who walkest upon the wings of the winds." There follow three prayers in collect form, the second of which asks that the travellers have a safe journey by the aid of the blessed Mother, while the third asks for the companionship of an angel. The first of these prayers is a succinct summary of the general message contained in the sacramental blessings we have been examining. "O God, who hast wrought all for thine own sake, and hast destined all the elements of this world for the use of man, bless, we beseech thee, this machine destined for aerial journeys; that, all injury and danger being removed, it may serve to propagate the praise and the glory of thy name more widely and to dispatch the affairs of men more promptly, and may nourish in the hearts of all the faithful using this machine desires for heavenly things."

CHAPTER XIV

THE DIVINE OFFICE

I. PRAISE OF GOD

THE term *divine office* means in general a duty or a function to be performed for God, a service that is rendered him. It is used in particular to designate the circle of daily prayers which the Church officially offers up to God through her ordained ministers and through others deputed to act for her in that regard. Since these prayers range over the various hours of the day they are sometimes called the Hour Prayers of the Church.

Sometimes the divine office is called simply the breviary. The latter term now refers more strictly to the book or set of books in which the Hour Prayers, both text and regulations, are officially set forth. It comes from the Latin *breviarium*, that is, an abridgment or compendium. In early days the Latin term was used for various kinds of abridgments as, for instance, a breviary of the Mass, of the gospels, and the like, but a very common use at all times seems to have been the breviary or abridgment of the psalter. When an official re-arrangement of the Church's Hour Prayers was made under Pope Gregory VII, who herein but followed in the footsteps of some of his predecessors, the term *breviary* established itself more

definitely to designate the collection of prayers constituting the divine office.

Insofar as we have been suffering from an extensive
loss of the liturgical sense, or of a proper sense for the
true nature and meaning of the liturgy, we should not
be surprised to note the great extent to which the breviary
has been a sealed book for many Catholics, in fact for the
great majority of them. This is quite in contrast with earlier
days of flourishing faith when even members of the laity
recited parts of the psalter regularly of their own accord,
and when practically all intelligent faithful knew something of the content of the breviary.

Judged in terms of the conditions that led for centuries to our present unliturgical attitude, the contrast with
our own day should not be surprising. But insofar as
there have always been some layfolk who continued to
appreciate the divine office, and insofar as the latter was
always recited by thousands who were delegated to do so
in the name of the Church, it is surprising indeed to note
the extent today of the great ignorance of the breviary
among Catholics, even among such as recite it officially.
Perhaps the phenomenon is accounted for in part by the
fact that the regular recitation of something so foreign
as the breviary to the prevalent atmosphere, to which we
all succumb in greater or less degree, readily took on
the nature of a mechanical and routine duty that just
had to be performed. Only too often its performance
was really motivated much more by a desire to escape
the sanctions imposed for its neglect, which are severe in
the case of persons in major orders, than by an appreciation of its inner spiritual nature.

At all events, the breviary has suffered its full share

of the general loss and oblivion and neglect of the liturgical spirit that has characterized Catholics as a whole in the past centuries. It is only in our own day that a change is taking place as a result of the general liturgical revival, and that the liturgical movement has begun to include the conscious organization of layfolk into a "League of the Divine Office." [1]

Certainly, the neglect which the study and appreciation of the divine office has suffered, is as undeserving as the wider neglect of the liturgy as a whole. Under all circumstances, the very obligation of many to recite it daily and the strong approval the Church has always put upon it, should suffice to urge on every Christian an earnest study of it, an attempt to see what it really contains. Two explanations of our present situation are possible. One of these is that the breviary is out of date in our day and age. But that will be true only if the Church of Christ is likewise out of date, instead of being destined to continue to the end of time. The other explanation is that many of us have been out of tune with the spiritual outlook that the breviary presupposes. Analogy with the other aspects of the liturgy would point to this as the true explanation. It certainly was the opinion of the saintly Pius X when he expressed his ardent desire that the true Christian spirit, not the present one, be made to flourish again among the faithful, and told us that the primary and indispensable source of this true spirit of Christ is active participation in the liturgy of the Church.

The entire divine office, its daily recitation, rests upon the principle of the duty of the creature to give praise

---

[1] See *Orate Fratres*, Vol. X (1935–36), pp. 177 and 230. In connection with this project a new booklet has been published: Hoornaert, *The Breviary and the Laity*, The Liturgical Press, Collegeville, Minnesota, 1936.

to its Creator. It is this principle that gives us the correct basis for the very existence of the divine office. All of us owe homage and glory to God. No other aim could have been consonant with the dignity and the infinite being of God than that of his own self, than that of attaining his own glory and of communicating his own goodness to creatures as both the source and the goal of all there is. In consequence no action of the creature can put the latter more in harmony with the Creator than a full and wholehearted acknowledgment of this divine goodness, a joyous confession of it, made with all the faculties with which that creature has been endowed by its Maker.

Such was the lesson of divine guidance given by God to his Chosen People in the Old Testament and put into practice in such a sublime manner in many of the books of the Old Law. "Praise with canticles, and bless the Lord in his works," exhorts the Book of Ecclesiasticus. "Magnify his name and give glory to him with the voice of your lips, and with the canticles of your mouths." [2] And the Apostle of the Gentiles exhorts us in these terms: "For we have not here a lasting city, but we seek one that is to come. By him therefore let us offer the sacrifice of praise always to God, that is to say, the fruit of lips confessing to his name." [3] "Offer to God the sacrifice of praise," says the psalmist [4] in the same inspired poem in which God himself declares: "The sacrifice of praise shall glorify me." [5]

The prayer of praise is therefore in a special sense a sacrifice which the members of Christ, as possessing a gen-

[2] 39:19–20
[3] Hebr. 13:14–15
[4] 49:14
[5] 49:23

eral priestly character, must offer up to God. *A fortiori*
it becomes a duty of the official priesthood of the Church.
There is no surprise then in the fact that Christ himself
gives us the example also in this regard. "In the New
Law our Savior is the model of prayer, the true adorer
of his Father. He alone can worthily adore and praise because he alone has the necessary perfection. Night and day
he set the example to his followers. He warned them to
watch and pray: he taught them how to pray; he gave them
a form of prayer; he prayed in life and at death." [6] Not
only did Christ pray thus alone, but he also had the apostles
join with him in prayer: "And a hymn being said, they
went out unto Mount Olivet." [7] Especially the whole last
prayer of Jesus before his passion is a sublime prayer for
the great glorification of the Father. [8]

II. Praise in the Trinity

The prayer of song of divine praise, which the creature
owes to God, finds its basic model in the divine life of
the Trinity itself. There is an active eternal relation between the divine persons; and in this relation the eternal
praise of infinite goodness sung by this infinite Goodness
itself must have an essential place. So much follows necessarily from the absolute perfection of the triune God.
"The perfect knowledge of the divine goodness in each of
the persons of God cannot but be identical with the sublime being of God. Hence there is so perfect a union
between the three persons in God. It is a union of love
that is most intimate; for the three persons are identically

[6] Quigley, *The Divine Office*, p. 7
[7] Matt. 26: 30
[8] John, chapter 17

one and the same divine substance. . . . In this intimate love, each of the divine persons gives himself over completely to the others in a sublime hymn of love, in a song of praise of the goodness of God. This song of praise to the divine goodness, sung from all eternity in the bosom of the Trinity, must be an infinitely perfect song; for it is sung with divine knowledge and love by the three persons of the Trinity." [9]

The purpose of creation by God, in turn, cannot but be an imitation and extension, feeble because finite, of this aspect of the infinite life of praise in the Trinity, therefore a finite echo by men of the infinite hymn of glory which God must necessarily render unto himself. Dom Grea could well say: "In order to understand this properly, let us consider that in the secret of his life God chants unto himself an eternal hymn which is nothing else than the expression of his perfections in his Word and in the Breath of his love. When he created the universe in his wisdom and goodness, he gave, as it were, an echo of this eternal canticle." [10]

From childhood on we have been familiar with the idea of seeing the greatness of God in nature. As a reaction to a materialistic bias, scientists themselves are now in greater numbers protesting that their wonderful discoveries have filled them with awe at the marvels of creation and its Creator. It was left to rational man, the acme of mundane creation, to disrupt the harmony of the canticle sung to God by nature. Through the fall in Paradise a discordant note was introduced into the eternal music of the spheres. Of the restoration of this broken relation with God, we have had frequent occasion to say something in

---

[9] Michel, *Life in Christ*, p. 4   [10] *La sainte liturgie*, p. 1

the course of the preceding chapters. Christ, in his redemption, restored man to the position which man could not of himself regain. Once restored, man was again capable of playing his part most abundantly in the concert of creation in a manner acceptable to God.

Because Christ, in reorganizing the divine symphony of nature and the supernatural, instituted a Church endowed with his divine powers and promised to remain with her to the end of days, man is now capable of a much higher type of divine service and praise than before. Through the Church and the liturgy he can now sing his song of praise to God with all the efficacy of the divine Life itself. In the union of the second person of the holy Trinity with human nature, man was introduced into the divine company of the Trinity itself. Through the Church, as continuer of the mediatory work of Christ, man partakes of the divine life of the Trinity and is given the supreme privilege and grace of playing a part in the very canticle of eternal praise sung without end in the eternal society of the divine persons.

Through the Church and her liturgy, the divine song of praise that man, and all creation with him, now renders to God has been endowed with a supernatural character that is as unique in the story of the world, as is the only begotten Son in the society of the triune God. Briefly but tellingly does Dom Sauter say: "The highest task of the creature is the glorification of God. In as far as the latter proceeds from the creature, it is but finite and natural—it becomes supernatural and infinite by means of the most holy mystery of the altar and the service of the altar, that is, the liturgy. A principal part in the liturgy is the liturgical word. The liturgical word is the revealed word of God and the word of his holy Church, as it is to be found in the liturgical books." [11]

From this standpoint we can better understand the high dignity of the divine office as the official prayer of praise which the Church renders to God through Christ. In it the members of Christ, united to him as their common head, present their songs of homage to the divine Trinity in the greatest variety of moods and sentiments. In it Christ himself is the chief spokesman, it is Christ himself who renders to his Father the homage of his adopted brethren, the same Christ who is our divine head living and praying intimately among us and at the same time living eternally in the bosom of the Trinity and sharing in its divine canticle interchangeably with the Father and the Holy Ghost.

But the liturgy of praise is at times also more than the address of Christ to the Father. It also addresses itself to Christ and is then the loving voice of the Bride speaking to the Bridegroom, or again it is the Bridegroom, divine teacher as he is also priest and king, dropping words of holy instruction and guidance into the heart of his beloved. "Generally speaking," says Dom Festugière, "the Church intimately united with Christ her head and sovereign priest, sends up her homage to the august Trinity in union with him and through him. But Christ is also her spouse, and a spouse who died on the cross for love of her. The Church never loses sight of the debt which such a love has created in her. Hence her tender love for the sacred humanity of Jesus is ever mingled with all the religious sentiments she utters in regard to the Father, the Word, and the Spirit; and she transforms a part of her latreutic chants or her

[11] *Der liturgische Choral*, p. 16

supplications into nuptial canticles and the sighings of the dove." [12]

In the divine office, then, the Church speaks to God, and Christ with her; the Church speaks to Christ; and Christ speaks to the Church. It is an intimate sharing the very life of God and a further realization of that divine intercourse established first of all through the incarnation and wrought by God into a real and continued human participation in the Divine, of which the liturgy of Christmastide sings as follows: "O admirable interchange! The Creator of mankind, assuming a living body, deigned to be born of a virgin; and becoming man without man's aid, bestowed on us his Divinity" (antiphon of Lauds, feast of the Circumcision).

III. The Office and the Mass

We have seen how the members of Christ draw most intimately upon his very being in the holy sacrifice, and how the sacraments are so many official channels by which they receive and renew their life in him and his life in them. All of these are so many sublime means, invented and instituted by God's infinite love for man, of establishing and confirming the "divine interchange" between God and man. These same means are all, especially the sacrifice, also acts of homage and praise to God, even while they are holy and divine actions of the official Church in which God enters and reaches down to our level to implant the seed of his grace in us. In the liturgy of praise enacted in the divine office man answers to the finer promptings of this divine inspiration, and turns his mind and actions freely

[12] *Qu'est-ce que la liturgie?* p. 77

to God in further homage of the creature to its Creator. In this divine song of praise, which includes also due petition and thanksgiving, we have the finer budding forth of the life implanted in men by the seed of grace, the rich blossoming of this seed into many-colored bouquets of holy praises, which the whole of creation through man joyously offers to God for all the wonderful things God has done to his children on earth. "My soul doth magnify the Lord; . . . For he that is mighty hath done great things unto me; and holy is his name" (*Magnificat*).

The divine office and the sacrifice of the Mass are thus elements of the same integral liturgy of the Church, of which the sacrifice is ever the core and center. But the elements of the liturgy other than the Mass and the sacraments are not for that reason of little or no importance; they achieve a high dignity and position just because they are reflections of the rich beauties and spiritual functions that belong to the liturgy as a whole. If the liturgy in general is the life of the mystical body lived in union with the head Christ and is Christ living in his mystical body, then this is true also of the divine office. It must be so since the latter is the complement of the sacrifice and sacraments. "The incorporation in Christ," says Dom Panfoeder, "which the liturgy commences in the sacraments and completes in the sacrifice, finds its echo in the liturgy of prayer. . . . In the liturgy of the sacraments Christ engrafts men upon himself as his members; in the sacrifice he offers them to the heavenly Father as an oblation together with himself; in the liturgical prayer he completes this act of oblation by a grand cry of Hosannah, which is at the same time his and that of the entire Church. Christ wrought an infinitely sublime masterpiece in his

Church. But within the Church the greatest thing he has wrought is the sacred liturgy, in which he himself presides as the liturge." [18] The divine office is thus the resultant expression, the outcome of the sacrifice. The Church, the union of the members living in Christ their head, who receive of the abundance of his life in the sacrifice and the sacraments, cannot but live out this life throughout the day, cannot but vibrate with the loving pulse of Christ himself, singing ever an eternal hymn of glory to the Godhead in the Trinity.

The divine office, then, derives its fuller meaning from its relation to the focal center of the Church's worship, the holy sacrifice, even as it originally derived its being from the same. A contemporary writer says in this respect: "The canonical hours [i.e., the divine office] are the extended Mass of the Catechumens spread over the entire day. They have the same elements as the Foremass which draws upon them; and through it they lead into the Eucharist. Whereas the Foremass prepares us immediately for the celebration of the sacrifice, the canonical hours lay a wider and deeper foundation for it, and at the same time extend the blessings of the sacrifice into the labors of the entire day." [14] The different parts of the divine office are therefore a remoter preparation for the daily sacrifice, or else an extension into all the day of the hymn of praise and thanksgiving that moves so rapidly to its close in the dramatic action of the Mass.

From this close relation we can the better understand why so many sentiments occur in common in both the Mass and the office of any day or feast. Particularly on

---

[18] *Christus unser Liturge*, pp. 47 and 55
[14] *Die Betende Kirche*, p. 215

the days of the great mysteries and the great saints we find the same passages in the epistle of the Mass and the lessons of the breviary, or in the chapter readings of Vespers and Lauds in particular. The same gospel occurs in both, and in the office we have an extension of it in the homily by some Church Father, just as in the Mass we have it in the sermon. Antiphons and versicles in the office have phrases and aspirations identical with some of the proper parts of the Mass, while in both Mass and office the principal prayer, or collect, asks for the same grace in the very same words. The Mass of the day or feast in fact determines the particular office that is to be said for the same occasion.

Again the divine office, like the Mass, follows the spiritual path of the liturgical year, and does so with much greater elaboration and variety of development. All, in fact, that has been said about the liturgy in general, its mission and its symbolism, its closeness to nature and to Christ, finds its realization eminently in the divine office as the latter follows the path of the liturgical year or the cycle of day and night. It takes its cue in both day and year from the earthly sun as the symbol of the divine Sun of Justice, and prays to God under the inspiration of the different mysteries of the life of Christ, of our redemption, stressing now one and now another as a link binding God to earth and earth to God.

IV. School of Divine Service

The divine office is for the member of Christ truly a school of growth in the mind and spirit of the divine Head. Throughout her official prayer the Church is nec-

essarily animated by the spirit of Christ; and we find reflected in it the rich variety of Christ, at once God and
man, Son of the Father and Bridegroom of the Church,
Head of the mystical body of the faithful. In the office
we have songs of praise in all the great variety of sentiments of which the human heart is capable, expressed in
the inspired language of the psalms; we have the greatest variety of instructions, prophecies, and inspired teachings of the apostles, the lessons of the Church Fathers,
and narratives of the lives of the saints of God; and again
the rich prayers of petition and supplication so expressive
of the tenderness of the Church for her children, and so
full of understanding of the true spirit of Christ. And
all of these, praise, readings, and prayers, are frequently
intensified by the inspiring chant of the Church, which
so well expresses the unity of mind and heart in the one
service, and again the deliberate nature of the homage
rendered, in which sentiment never runs to excess but always remains under control of reason, in which simple
faith is blended so harmoniously with love and confidence.

Especially is the life of Christ and his mind presented
to us in all its many-sided richness in the texts of the divine
office. We read from almost all the books of the sacred
Scriptures in the pages of the breviary. All of its pages are
filled with the idea of the Redemption, ever the central
theme of the liturgy. In them we meet, from various
angles, with the central idea of our salvation through
Christ. The life and teaching of Christ as depicted in the
gospels is there set before us in all its variety—both in its
actual fulfillment in the New Testament books, and in its
prophetic anticipations in the Old Testament. Every page

of the breviary calls us to a greater realization of the life
of Christ. There Christ is the source of inspiration, the
members live the life of his example and word, or again,
Christ himself speaks and prays in his members. Thus
with the aim of the glorification of God the breviary also
pursues that of the salvation of man. The two great aims
are in fact inseparable here as elsewhere in the liturgy, even
as they were inseparable in the creation of the world and in
the incarnation and the redemption. The individual who
recites the official prayer of the Church first of all pursues
these two aims rather objectively than subjectively. He
there strips himself of that which characterizes so much of
private prayer, the thought of self, and enters into the
broader sympathy and idea of the Church and of Christ,
whose care is that of the whole kingdom of God here on
earth.

But while this is true, the participation of the individual
in the liturgy must be an intelligent one; and it will needs
benefit the individual soul more to the extent to which he
consciously enters into all the sentiments of the Church.
It is indeed true that "the Church prays through my mouth:
I lend her my tongue so that she may pray for the great
concerns of the Redemption, but also that she may praise
God. There we weep, or rather the Church weeps with the
sorrowing in our tears, rejoices with the joyful through
our joys, repents with the repentant. All the sentiments
of our mother the Church find an echo in our widened
hearts." [15] Hence in the very prayer of the Church the
subjective needs of the individual soul also find their utmost fill. The breviary, if intelligently recited, is also a
guide of soul for the individual participant. While a few

[15] Parsch, in *Bericht der liturgischen Priester-Tagung in Wien 1924*, p. 122

passages of the psalms are difficult to understand, these psalms teem with passages of the sublimest sentiments and aspirations, ranging through all the moods that the human heart is capable of. "There is no mood of soul of the religious man, to which they have not given expression, from the deepest sense of sorrow and abandonment to the jubilant bliss of union with God, from the feeling of union with the great fellowship of the Lord to the most personal and solitary experience of God, from the knowledge of the terrible majesty of God to that of the sweetness of his love, from adoration, praise and thanksgiving to childlike supplication." [16]

Likewise there is no need of the soul that is overlooked in the prayers, no sentiment binding us to God that is not given expression to. In the readings the inspired words of the Old and New Testaments are put into mind of the participating Christian, or the exhortatory instruction of the Church Fathers. Everywhere in the breviary, the individual that makes the prayer of the Church his own finds his soul imbued with the inspired word of God, or with the best thoughts and sentiments that the great religious minds of the best periods of Catholic life have left to us. We need but recall some of the parts that recur time and again: the Our Father, the Creed, the Hail Mary, the Salva Regina or other hymns of the blessed virgin, the Gloria Patri, the Magnificat, the Benedictus, the Nunc Dimittis, the Benedicite and psalms of Sunday Lauds, the Te Deum. All through the breviary the soul finds itself heir to all the best that the Church, through the rich experience of the ages of living faith, has garnered and preserved for her children. Most appropriately has the breviary been called the

[16] *Die Betende Kirche,* pp. 192–193

Raphael of the soul, guiding it from the day of profession or subdeaconship to the last breath of life.

All of this receives added force for the individual and for his sanctification from the fact that he is not praying alone. "In the liturgical prayer, and hence in the breviary, it is not myself primarily, but the Church who prays; the spouse of Christ prays for the great needs of God's kingdom on earth. I feel myself a member of the great fellowship, a leaflet on the great tree of life, the Church, and I participate in her life and labor. . . . Now the Church is praising God through my lips, now she is wrestling through my hands for the souls of men." [17] The prayer of the individual reciting the divine office has an efficacy that goes beyond his own limited powers, it partakes of the force and efficacy of the prayer of the Church. In it the individual is uniting his own feeble efforts with those of the whole Church. Those in particular who pray the divine office primarily in the name of the Church, are praying with the full force of the perfect intention of the Bride of Christ and of the great acceptability of her prayer before God. But even where a person is reciting the breviary privately, *i.e.*, without an official commission from the Church, he is joining his efforts to the intention and the efficacy of the entire Church; and if not in space and time, he is at least spiritually united with his brethren in one and the same holy action.

V. Divisions of the Office

The origin of the divine office in early Christian centuries is not well known. However, scholars agree in general in

[17] Parsch, *op. cit.*, pp. 121-22

tracing its origin back to the Mass, and more specifically to the Mass of the Catechumens. "The synaxis, for which the early Christians assembled by night, consisted of the 'breaking of bread,' preceded by the singing of psalms and hymns, litanies and collects, readings, homilies, invocations, and canticles. This was one time the whole of the official liturgical prayer. From this somewhat crowded celebration . . . the Night Office (Matins, Lauds, and perhaps Vespers) came into existence, and afterwards threw out, like stars of second magnitude, Prime, Compline, and the Little Hours of the day." [18]

It is well known that the Jews were accustomed to assemble in their synagogues at stated hours. The first converts to Christianity, who were of course Jews, kept up this practice; they even joined in with their non-converted Jewish brethren, since they did not consider the New Law as in every way a breakoff but rather as a completion of the Old. Thus we read, for instance: "And continuing daily with one accord in the temple, and breaking bread from house to house." [19] The Acts of the Apostles also give us various instances of how the apostles observed the practice of assembling for prayer at different hours of the day. It was in the "third hour" of the morning when the apostles were gathered "all together in one place" that the Holy Ghost came down upon them. [20] Again we read that "Peter went up to the higher parts of the house to pray, about the sixth hour" or the hour of noon. [21] The healing of the lame man by Peter occurred in the afternoon as "Peter and

[18] Cabrol, in the introduction to *The Day Hours of the Church*, p. xvi
[19] Acts 2:46
[20] Acts 2:1-15
[21] Acts 10:9

John went up into the temple at the ninth hour of prayer.[22] These divisions of time follow the ancient custom of separating the day and the night into two groups of twelve hours, each group dividing again into quarters of three hours. This was evidently the customary way of reckoning for the Jews as we see also from the parable of the Lord of the vineyard, who after having hired laborers went out again at the third, sixth, and ninth hours to hire some more, and finally again at the eleventh, or just before night.[23]

In the primitive Christian assemblies great feasts were celebrated by a vigil which consisted of prayers, chanting and readings that lasted all night, and these were followed by the celebration of the Eucharist or the "breaking of the bread," e.g., Acts 20: 7–11. Various reasons are given for the celebration of such vigils at night: "Because people were then free from the duties and distractions of daytime; because there was need for much preaching and instruction; because the first Christians loved to pray and remembered the example of the nightly prayer of the Lord; [24] because the vigil of Easter, the principal one of the year and the model for all others, was held during the night preceding the morning of the resurrection." [25] At first the vigil celebration was nothing but a drawn-out Mass of the Catechumens or preparation for the Mass of the Faithful. But various divisions began to take form and gradually differentiated themselves into Vespers, Matins, and Lauds. Matins itself was for greater feasts divided into three parts or nocturns, while the prayers at stated times during the

[22] Acts 3:1
[23] Matt. 20:2–6
[24] Luke 6:12
[25] Rev. William Busch, in *Orate Fratres*, Vol. I (1926–27), p. 328

day gave rise to Terce, Sext, and None. The addition of Prime and Compline completed the cycle.

"Each day of twenty-four hours has its complete cycle of prayer," summarizes the same writer quoted above. "The night and the day are both divided into four parts of three hours each. For the night we have the First, Second, and Third Nocturns of Matins, and Lauds. For the day we have Terce, Sext, None and Vespers. Prime is added as a morning prayer, and Compline as a prayer before retiring at night. Observe that these eight divisions (not counting Prime and Compline) are all three hours apart, *i.e.*, each represents three hours. Observe also that each of the three Nocturns of Matins has three psalms, that Terce, Sext and None have each three psalms, while Lauds and Vespers, which end the night-group and the day-group, have the three augmented to five. This arrangement of threes gives us one psalm for every hour of the night and day. Their groupment into triads is symbolic of the blessed Trinity whose praise recurs in the last stanza of all the breviary hymns. And the triads, augmented once for the climax of the night-group and once for that of the day-group, give distinct rhythm and balance to the whole structure." [26]

The daily cycle of the divine office is then made up successively of Matins, Lauds, Prime, Terce, Sext, None, Vespers, and Compline. All of these hours, except Compline, are begun with the Our Father, which strikes the keynote of the entire office in its first part, the hallowing of the name of God, but adds likewise the petitions for divine help. The Our Father is followed by the Hail Mary (and by the Creed in Matins and Prime), whereupon the versicle "O

[26] Rev. William Busch, in *Orate Fratres*, Vol. II (1927–1928), p. 332

God, come to my assistance. O Lord, make haste to help me," is sung. This is followed in turn by the Glory be to the Father, and thus the entire office sends its praises to God and mingles with them the entire gamut of religious sentiments that give its rich and varied expression to the total relation that exists between the members of Christ and the Father in heaven.

The succession of the canonical hours forms a cyclic rhythm within the day. As the liturgical year turns about the center of our solar system and about Christ, so the canonical hours of the day turn about the Mass as the central enactment of the life of Christ in his mystical body, and take their cue also from the ever-recurring relation of the sun to the various periods of the day. As the rotation of the earth about its axis gives an ever varying aspect of her relation to the sun, and her day of twenty-four hours is ordered and divided accordingly, so does the day's cycle of divine praises give us constantly moving aspects, an ordered and progressive absorption and reflection, of the divine light of Christ. As the solar day may be called a miniature of the solar year, so the canonical hours may likewise be called a miniature of the liturgical year, a daily cyclic celebration of the great truths of the redemption. In examining this aspect of the divine office in the following chapter, we shall pass rapidly from one hour prayer to the other, stressing the fundamental ideas as they make of the whole a rounded-out pathway of the daily life of the soul.

CHAPTER XV

THE DAILY CYCLE OF PRAISE

I. Matins

THE vigil office of early Christian times developed into the different offices of Vespers, Matins, and Lauds in the course of time. We see an echo of this in the fact that even today the celebration of all the greater feasts of the church year begins with the Vespers of the evening before. But for ordinary circumstances Matins begins the office of the day, so that it is rightly called the first of the canonical hours. The word itself comes from the Latin *matutinae laudes,* or the early morning praises. The word was first used for the office of Lauds, but was later applied exclusively to the prayers and readings preceding this office of dawn. The canonical time for Matins is midnight, but in full accordance with the spirit and the old practice of the Church, it may be recited earlier, even in the afternoon before. This spirit of anticipation is universal in the liturgy. And especially with the coming of the major feasts the member of Christ tends to anticipate the exact hour of the respective day and mingle the joy of anticipation with thoughts and sentiments of spiritual preparation for its better celebration.

The office of Matins is properly regarded as a general wider preparation for the day and the feast to come. It is meditation and prayer mingled with spiritual readings focussing on the feast or mystery of the day and fitting the mind of the member of Christ for a more intimate participation in the latter. It consists chiefly of an alternate chanting of psalms and of holy readings, nine such on all important feasts. These are divided into three nocturns of three psalms and lessons respectively. The psalms, as usual, express the various sentiments of the Church of Christ as well as of the faithful soul. They are less closely related to the feast than the other parts of Matins, sometimes showing no connection whatever but serving as a general elevation of mind and heart to God. As has been stated before, they run through the entire gamut of Christian sentiments and are alternately Christ speaking to us, or we speaking with him to the Father, but always do they fill the soul with holy aspirations as sublime in their nature as they are rich in their variety. The lessons or readings are instructions on the mystery of the season being celebrated, or on the saint, and on the gospel of the day, or else a more unrelated infusion of holy thoughts or of illustrations of the way of God with his children on earth.

"This office," says Dom Cabrol, "the longest of the Canonical Hours, is also in some respects the most important. It is the midnight prayer, and reminds us of the earliest Christian meetings, not only by the hour at which it is said, but also by its structure. At this hour Christ was betrayed and sold, and at the same hour he endured the anguish of his agony in the garden on that night when the sufferings of his passion began. The soul at that hour of the night seems less under the dominion of the senses."[1]

[1] *Liturgical Prayer*, p. 143

After the Our Father, Hail Mary, and Creed are recited in silence, the following verses and answers are said aloud: "O Lord, open thou my lips. And my mouth shall show forth thy praise. Incline unto mine aid, O Lord. O Lord, make haste to help me. Glory be to the Father, etc." [2] The general tenor and sentiments of these words speak for themselves; they could by themselves serve very profitably as points for meditation, as could also the compendium of praise to the Trinity, the "Glory be," which recurs almost incessantly after every psalm and every set of lessons.

The keynote of the office is then struck by the invitatory verse, which is, for better meditation and spiritual absorption, repeated after each verse of psalm 94. It always offers a holy thought followed by the exhortation to offer homage to God in or through Christ. On ordinary Sundays the verse reads, "The Lord who made us, come let us adore." A similar thought occurs in practically all the invitatories, with a variation suitable to the occasion. Thus on Christmas we have, "Christ is born unto us, come let us adore," and on the feast of All Saints, "The Lord King of Kings, come let us adore, for he is the crown of all the saints." Psalm 94, after the verses of which the invitatory recurs in whole or in part, bids us "sing unto the Lord . . . the God of our salvation . . . for the Lord will not cast off his people; for in his hand are all the ends of the earth. . . . Today if ye will hear his voice, harden not your heart . . . as in the day of 'temptation' in the wilderness."

The hymn follows, which on different days stresses the

[2] The passages of Matins are at times taken from Bute, *The Roman Breviary*, and those of the other hours generally from *The Day Hours of the Church*.

rising from sleep, the analogy between night and sin, and looks for solace from God the Light of lights. The Sunday hymn of summer sings: "Arising at night let us all keep watch meditating ever in psalms . . . so that singing to our loving King, we may merit to enter the celestial court of heaven with his saints, etc." In the Monday hymn "we beseech the Father to be present with us in our chant, who have left our beds refreshed with sleep. . . . Let the darkness yield to light . . . so that whatever guilt has entered by night may be dispersed by the light." Others ask that "the Light of light, the Day, may help our petitions, who break in on the night with song; that God free us, steeped in sleep, from harmful quiet . . . and forgive us in what we may have sinned" (Tuesday and Wednesday).

After the inspiring hymn follow the psalms of the first nocturn. The psalms are introduced and followed by antiphons in varying order according to different seasons of the year. The antiphons invariably give a point for meditation during the chanting of a psalm. At times they contain a key thought of the psalms themselves and at other times a thought of the feast. Thus on summer Sundays the first antiphon reads, "Happy the man who meditates on the law of the Lord" and is compiled from parts of the first psalm of the psalter which is recited here. In Advent the first Sunday antiphon reads, "Behold the King cometh, the Most High, with great power, to save the nations. Alleluia." The psalms and antiphons are followed by a verse with answer and a silent Our Father to form a gradual transition to the reading of the lessons. The verse and answer for the summer Sunday is: "I have remembered thy name, O Lord, in the night. And have kept thy law."

For Advent: "Out of Sion, the perfection of beauty. Our God shall manifestly come." And for Eastertide: "The Lord is risen from the grave, alleluia. Who hung for us upon the tree, alleluia."

The lessons are each preceded by a blessing and followed by a responsory. The general absolution of the first nocturn asks "Graciously hear, O Lord Jesus Christ, the prayers of thy servants, and have mercy on us: who livest and reignest . . ." and of the second nocturn "May his loving kindness and mercy help us, who liveth and reigneth. . . ." Besides the general absolution for each set of lessons there is the individual blessing for each of the three lessons. In the first two nocturns the blessings are addressed consecutively to the different persons of the blessed Trinity. Thus for the first nocturn we have, "May the eternal Father bless us with an eternal blessing. Amen," and, "May the Son, the only begotten, mercifully bless and keep us. Amen," and, "May the grace of God the Spirit enlighten all our hearts and minds. Amen." The responsory after each lesson is again an ejaculatory prayer or a holy thought containing also a verse, and repeated answer. Two examples must suffice. The first responsory on the ordinary Sundays after Pentecost reads: "Prepare your hearts unto the Lord and serve him alone: and he will deliver you out of the hands of your enemies. *Verse:* Return unto him with all your hearts, and put away the strange gods from among you. *Answer:* And he will deliver you out of the hand of your enemies." The first responsory of the second nocturn, second Advent Sunday, is: "Behold there cometh the Lord, our defender, the holy one of Israel, wearing a royal crown upon his head. *Verse:* And his dominion shall be from sea even to sea, and from the river even to the ends of the earth. *Answer:* Wearing a royal crown upon his head."

The whole structure of Matins shows an admirable psychological wisdom. The alternation of psalms and lessons is well calculated to promote a meditative prayer. The periods of spiritual excitation of heart and will in the psalms are followed by readings which appeal more to the intellect. The versicle and Our Father and blessing between psalms and lessons take away the abruptness of the transition, while the responsory after each lesson prevents the official instruction from becoming purely intellectual or else too monotonous. On all the larger feasts of three nocturns, there follows the Te Deum in place of the ninth responsory. This inspiring hymn of praise, which glorifies God and Jesus Christ in such sublime ejaculations, is a fitting close to the night office and at the same time forms a suitable transition to the office of Lauds which follows thereupon.

II. Lauds

Lauds is properly the prayer of the dawn of day. It is the official morning hymn of praise which the Church offers up to God at the first break of a new day in the Lord. Every new day is for the member of Christ a new day of salvatior and redemption, and the renewed advent of the protective and blessing hand of the Savior is fittingly seen in the scattering of the shades of night and sin by the rising sun in the glowing east. It is in full harmony with the old Christian visualization of the east or the orient as the source of divine light and life. "O Orient!" says one of the Major Antiphons of Advent. "Splendor of eternal light, and Sun of Justice! Come and enlighten them that sit in darkness and in the shadow of death."

The theme is dominant in the hymn of Lauds which is said towards the end of the hour and not in the beginning as at Matins. As the hymn of Matins stresses the surrounding darkness and prays for the coming light, so Lauds greets the arriving dawn of day and addresses convertibly the natural sun as the symbol of Christ or Christ of whom the sun is symbol. The summer Sunday hymn for Lauds sings as follows:

> *"Lo, fainter now lie spread the shades of night*
> *And upwards shoot the trembling gleams of morn;*
> *Suppliant we bend before the Lord of Light,*
> *And pray at early dawn. . . . ."*
>
> (THE DAY HOURS)

The Monday hymn begins:

> *"Of the Father effluence bright*
> *Out of light evolving light,*
> *Light from light, unfailing ray,*
> *Day creative of the day."* [3]

On Tuesday the hymn says beautifully: "The winged messenger of day proclaims the coming light; us does Christ, the Inspirer of Minds, calls to life"; and on Wednesday: "Night and darkness and clouds and the confusion and dirt of the world, depart! The light enters, the sky brightens, Christ comes!" Since the central idea of Lauds is that of the salvation Christ has wrought and brings before us again, the text of this hour is full of praise and rejoicing.

[3] *Op. cit.*

After the usual beginning of the hour prayer, with Pater, Ave, and the versicle asking for the Lord's help, four psalms and a canticle are chanted. These are preceded and followed by antiphons. The customary five antiphons, for all larger feasts, are also used in the Vespers and the Little Hours, that is, Prime, Terce, Sext and None. They are particularly expressive of the mystery of the feast or season or else of the general tenor of Lauds. Thus some of the antiphons for the ordinary Sunday office are: "Sing joyfully unto God, all the earth, alleluia"; "I will bless thee all my life long, O Lord: and in thy name I will lift up my hands, alleluia"; "Alleluia, praise ye the Lord from the heavens, alleluia, alleluia." For the seasonal liturgy we shall quote from the antiphons for Passion Sunday: "Behold, O Lord my affliction, for the enemy hath magnified himself"; "My people, what have I done unto thee, or wherein have I grieved thee? Answer thou me"; "Shall evil be rendered for good? for they have dug a pit for my soul."

Outside of the season of sorrow the antiphons of Lauds resound with the joyous cry of alleluia, and the psalms themselves develop increasingly the note of praise, ending regularly with a canticle from the Old Testament which is then followed by a specific "Laudate" psalm of praise. The Sunday and feast-day canticle, the famous Benedicite, is a sublime appeal to all the creatures and the forces of nature to join in the Church's official morning praise of their common Creator and Lord. "All ye works of the Lord, bless the Lord. . . . All ye angels of the Lord . . . Sun and moon, . . . light and darkness, lightning and clouds, all the earth, bless the Lord, praise and exalt him forever."

The exultant song of the psalms is followed by a brief, more sober reading or little chapter. On the ordinary Sundays the text is: "Benediction, and glory, and wisdom, and thanksgiving, honor, power, and strength, to our God for ever and ever." To which the answer of "Thanks be to God" is given. The little chapter for Passion Sunday reads: "Brethren: Christ being come a Highpriest of the good things to come, by a greater and more perfect tabernacle not made with hands, that is, not of this creation, neither by the blood of goats or of calves, but by his own blood, entered once in the holies, having obtained eternal redemption." In the one instance we have the characteristic note of Lauds and in the other of the liturgical mystery of the season.

With the little chapter as a sort of breathing spell, the exultant note of song is resumed in the hymn of which we have already made mention. It reaches its climax in the wonderful canticle of the Redemption, the Benedictus of the aged Zachary. The antiphon for this canticle is proper for every Sunday of the year. During the week the antiphons are taken from the canticle itself. On Passion Sunday we have the following verse and answer: "Deliver me from mine enemies, O my God. And defend me from them that rise up against me"; and the antiphon: "Jesus said unto the multitude of the Jews and unto the chief priests: He that is of God heareth the words of God: ye therefore hear them not because ye are not of God." In chanting the canticle of the aged Zachary, we may well be imbued with something of his own joy. Like him we have seen, and today again see, the sign of salvation. Hence we sing out in his words: "Blessed be the Lord God of Israel: because he hath visited and wrought the redemption of his people." Today Christ has again come "to enlighten them that sit in darkness and in the shadow of death; to direct our feet into the way of peace. Glory be to the Father, etc."

After the Benedictus the collect of the day's feast, the same that is said at Mass and in other parts of the office, is said. Thus the official prayer of the day sets the tone for the union of the soul with God that is to be cemented step by step through the sacrifice of the altar and through the entire offering of the day's praise in the rest of the office. An anthem of praise to the blessed virgin Mary, mother of the mystical body of Christ, is a fitting conclusion to this ideal morning song of praise sent up to God on High by the Bride of Christ in the name of the divine Bridegroom himself.

III. PRIME

Prime is said to be more distinctly of monastic origin. Since Lauds ended rather early in the day, especially in summertime, there was a long period lapsing between it and the hour of Terce. And so some of the monks, it has been said, would sleep through from after Lauds to Terce instead of rising at the first hour of the day. Prime was instituted to stop this abuse and it was recited at the first hour or about six in the morning. It was thus the prayer that looked immediately to the beginning of the day's work upon which it asked God's special blessing. In contrast with Lauds it is the ideal subjective morning prayer, that of conscious sinful human nature always aware of its need of divine help. In consequence the main theme of Prime is the dependence of man on God and the loving desire of the member of Christ to preserve intact his union with the divine source of all life. The recurrent theme of this hour is therefore a humble request for the guidance and the blessing of God in all the day's labor and activities. Since most of the prayers of Prime are the same for all days and feasts, it is an admirable morning prayer for the busy layman to use also privately even if no time is available for his reciting other hours of the breviary during day or night.

The monastic origin of Prime has been made accountable for something of its structure, especially of the last part. "At first Prime followed the pattern of the other Minor Hours (Terce, Sext, None); that is, it consisted of a beginning hymn, some psalms, a short chapter and a concluding prayer. Monastic practice soon added the remaining elements of our Prime of today, which were at first called 'Office of the Chapter' because they were sung or recited in the chapter room or general assembly room of the monastery. Thus were added the reading of the martyrology, further prayers for protection and blessing, and later on also prayers for the dead. From the monasteries this form of Prime was then adopted into the official breviary or divine office of the Church." [4]

After the usual beginnings the hymn is at once said, the famous *Jam lucis ordo sidere*. This hymn may be considered a résumé of the entire office of Prime. The star of morn being risen "may God, in all our words and deeds, keep us from harm this day. May he restrain our tongues from strife and quarrels and close our eyes to vanities. May the intimate thoughts of our heart remain pure, and temperance in food and drink tame the pride of the flesh, so that at the end of the day, purged by abstinence, we

[4] From the "Introduction" (p. 6) of *The Hour of Prime*

may sing to the glory of God." Then follow the psalms which vary for every day.

On Trinity Sunday and on the ordinary Sundays after Pentecost and Epiphany, the psalms are followed by the Athanasian Creed, a remarkable profession of faith in the full dogma of the trinity of persons in the one God. There follows a little chapter. "To the King of ages, immortal and invisible, the only God, be honor and glory forever, Amen," it reads on Sundays and feasts; and on ordinary week days: "Love peace and truth, says the Lord almighty." The short responsory that follows is a cry for mercy: "Christ, Son of the living God, have mercy on us," after the repetition of which with the Glory be to the Father, the appeal is made more urgent: "Arise, Christ, help us. And free us for thy name's sake." These cries imitate those of the blind man on the road to Jericho, whose appeal was not in vain. A short series of prayers in verse and answer form is now said whenever no feast of double rank occurs, after which the collect repeats the above appeal in the more formal style: "O Lord, God almighty, who hast brought us to the beginning of this day, defend us in the same by thy power, that we may not fall this day into any sin, but that all our thoughts, words, and works may be directed to the fulfillment of thy will."

The second part of Prime begins with the reading of the Martyrology (only when Prime is said in choir). In good liturgical form the petition of the collect is to be furthered by that of the blessed Virgin and the saints who should "intercede for us with the Lord, that we may receive help and salvation from him who liveth and reigneth for ever and ever." The cry, "O God, come to my assistance," with its response is repeated three times. After the Our Father we ask again that God may "direct the work of our hands" and "vouchsafe this day to direct and sanctify, to rule and govern our hearts and bodies, our thoughts, words, and deeds"—which request is tersely summed up in the official blessing: "May the almighty Lord order our days and actions in his peace. Amen."

Another short reading follows, which varies according to seasons and feasts. On the ordinary Sundays it reads: "May the Lord direct our hearts and bodies in the charity of God and the patience of Christ." Prime ends with a second blessing still more summary in form and inclusive of eternity as well as time: "May the Lord bless us, and defend us from all evil, and bring us to eternal life: and may the souls of the faithful departed through the mercy of God rest in peace. Amen."

The complete sacrifice of mind and body to God that repetition makes so emphatic in Prime has not yet been made to the full. The entire day is consecrated to God, through whose guidance and protection the work of the day that is beginning will be doubly blessed. The offering of self to the glory of God will continue in the other Hour Prayers of the day.

IV. Terce, Sext, None

Terce, Sext, and None are an expression of the truth that we should pray often and constantly turn the mind to God. Our work should never be so engrossing in a secular way as to cause us to forget entirely our dignity and privilege as members of the mystical body of Christ; in fact, all our work should be a continued service of God throughout the day. The little hours of Terce, Sext and None are so many short breathing spells from the daily routine of work, during which the mind turns from earthly occupations to sing a special hymn of praise to God. It might be better to say, the very conditions of earthly time and life are reminders to the living member of Christ of the things of God and eternity and lead naturally to these Hour Prayers. For they, like all the others of the office, are not to be looked upon as examples of flight from earthly existence. They are rather an elevation of the things of daily life to the plane of the eternal existence of God, a continued living out of the consecration of all creation to the glory and honor of its Creator. In accordance with the ancient form of reckoning time Terce would be recited about nine in the morning, Sext at noon, and None about three in the afternoon.

Terce receives its name from the third hour of the morning according to the old reckoning. It is the hour in which the Holy Ghost descended upon the infant Church at Jerusalem. The Christian cannot pass up the moment without a special commemoration. In the hymn we ask the Holy Spirit "now" to descend into our hearts "together with Father and Son" so that our "love may burn with a holy fire, and our ardor enkindle our neighbors," and that our "flesh, tongue, mind, senses, vigor may sound forth a confession" of our faith and love to all the world. Three psalms follow which differ day by day, as do those of Sext and None. Then comes the little chapter, also varying for different feasts and seasons. On the ordinary Sunday and weekday it is charming in its simple expression of the operation of the Holy Spirit, the Spirit of divine love. "God is charity: and he that abideth in charity abideth in God, and God in him," we pray on Sundays, and then the short responsory: "Incline my heart, O God, unto thy testimonies. . . . Quicken thou me in thy way. . . ." On weekdays: "Heal me, O Lord, and I shall be healed: save me, and I shall be saved: for thou art my praise," with its short responsory, "Heal thou my soul, because I have sinned against thee. . . . I said: O Lord, have mercy on me. . . ." The official collect of the day concludes the hour.

Sext is said at the heat of noon and its note is that of the burden of the day, both corporally and spiritually. God alone is our help and consolation under these circumstances, and so the hymn begs him, "to extinguish the flames of strife, to take away injurious heat, to give health of body, and true peace of heart." The little chapter exhorts us to mutual charity, which lightens all burdens and without which we are not acceptable to God: "Bear ye one another's burdens, and so you shall fulfil the law of Christ" (Sundays), to which we answer beautifully: "For ever, O Lord, thy word endureth . . ." Or again: "Owe no man anything, but to love one another; for he that loveth his neighbor hath fulfilled the law" (weekdays). Thus even the little hours increase the life of Christ in us, reminding us of the essence of his life and of our mutual fellowship in him very opportunely at a time when we are most troubled by the contacts of earth.

None, the hour of Christ's death, brings us toward the evening of the day. We are reminded of the last things, of the reward awaiting us after the toils of this life. It is ever the double life of the Christian that the liturgy emphasizes, his life in time and his life in all eternity, and above all his sharing in that eternal life here and now. The hymn prays that God, "determining the successive phases of the daily light, bestow the evening light in which life shall never go out, but shall have eternal glory as the reward of a holy death." Most tellingly does the little chapter likewise bring before us the keynote of the hour: "For you are bought with a great price. Glorify and bear God in your body" (Sundays); and "Converse in fear during the time of your sojourning here: knowing that you were not redeemed with corruptible things as gold or silver, but with the precious blood of Christ, as of a lamb unspotted" (weekdays). None thus emphasizes the reward for the laborer who has hired out for the day, and fittingly leads us to and prepares us for the evening prayer of Vespers. Most successfully have our thoughts been held to our true end, the eternal life in Christ, and with the toil of the earthly day ended, we can the more heartily join in the official hymn of thanks of the Church at the close of day. It is ever ours to throb with the life divine of Christ and his Church.

V. VESPERS

Vespers is the official evening song of praise rendered to God by the Bride of Christ in union with her divine Spouse. It is in some ways the evening counterpart of the morning Lauds, being not only parallel in spirit and purpose but also in external structure. Vespers is said as soon as the labor of the day is over. "The daily task is done; before taking his night's rest the Christian spends some time in prayer. From its very origin this office was full of intense poetic feeling. The sun is sinking below the horizon, shadows are creeping over the earth, the time for rest has come. For worldlings this is the time for pleasure, and even the servants of God, who have separated themselves from the world, are not exempt from temptations; a throng of evil spirits has spread over the world with the darkness; night is the season of terrible trials and dangerous isolation; a subtle languor takes possession of man as sleep draws near; it is not the body only which becomes inert, the will itself feels its strength waning, the conscience wavers . . . a greater grace is needed to resist the wicked spirit; therefore prayer must be more fervent. It is the hour, too, of the *Sacrificium vespertinum*, the *evening sacrifice*, the hour of incense and lights." [5]

The psalms of Vespers vary considerably with different feasts and days, but are generally of a messianic import, especially those chanted on the principal feasts and on Sundays. They begin with the *Dixit Dominus* (ps. 109) which speaks of the power and reign of the Messias who "shall judge among the nations" and who is "a priest forever according to the order of Melchisedech." Of the psalms of Vespers Dom Baudot writes: "As we reflect that the declining day is like the end of our life, and the night like death, we raise our minds to another more radiant and more lasting day for which our days here on earth are a preparation. If we bear these thoughts in mind as we recite the vesper psalms, they will seem to echo the song of our risen Lord in which all the blessed in heaven unite: they will also remind us of the mystery of the Last Supper, of the night when Jesus sat at table with his disciples and instituted the Eucharist, and gave to his apostles, together with the priesthood, the power of perpetuating both these wonders." [6]

[5] Cabrol, *Liturgical Prayer*, p. 146
[6] *The Breviary*, p. 137

The little chapter following the psalms, which is the same for the ordinary Sundays and the weekdays, gives the following thought for the close of the day: "Blessed be the God and Father of our Lord Jesus Christ, the Father of mercies, and the God of all comfort, who comforteth us in all our tribulations." The hymn follows which it will no longer surprise us to learn mingles with the thought of the sinking sun, thoughts of God's protection, and of our eternal rest: "The fiery sun recedes. Do Thou, Light, eternal Unity, blessed Trinity, pour light into our hearts . . . The chaos of darkness draws nigh, hear our tearful prayers. . . . Shed upon us the gift of eternal grace. . . . Expel the night of our hearts, cleanse our minds of stain, break the chains of sin. . . . By the strength of grace lave the wounds of our scorched minds, that tears may wash away our wicked deeds, no evils may draw near, and we may not know the sting of death" (various days of the week).

The climax of the vesper song of praise is reached in the beautiful Magnificat. This is indeed "the canticle of the Virgin of Virgins, which is contrasted with the vigorous, masculine Benedictus, has more of the tender mood of the feminine soul. In it the faithful, personally conscious of their great good fortune, thank God for all that he in fidelity to his promise has done unto them. The union with God, the supreme aim of all prayer and all worship, finds its most eloquent expression in the Magnificat at the end of the office of the day." [7] The trials of the day have indeed mellowed us, and at eventide we are more susceptible to the tender emotions of the beautiful hymn. With full hearts should we "magnify the Lord" in this vesper song

[7] *Die Betende Kirche*, p. 205

in the very words of our protecting Mother, for this day again God "hath regarded the humility of his servant" and "hath done great things" to him. For the believing soul ever living of the life of Christ, every day is full of the marvels of God.

VI. COMPLINE

If Lauds is followed by the more subjective morning prayer of Prime, then Vespers has its corresponding Compline. Compline is a subjective night prayer arising like Prime out of the life of the ancient monasteries. The monks did not retire with the vesper song, and so said a final prayer later just before retiring. Thus arose the Compline of the breviary. It breathes the monastic spirit, which, after all, is but in concentrated form the spirit of the universal Christian life. All members of the living Christ are called to an imitation of his asceticism, the essence of which, a dying to self in order to live to God, is the keynote of the liturgy as of the whole Redemption. In Compline this spirit is uppermost. Hence, like Prime, it is a most appropriate prayer also for the laity, and for private recitation.[8]

A threefold idea runs through this night prayer. In night or darkness, the liturgy has ever seen the symbol of evil or sin, whence we have the phrase of "the powers of darkness." Darkness and night, setting in after the life of the day has ended, also symbolize death. The parallel between the temporal sleep which ends the day and the eternal sleep which ends life here below is but one aspect

---

[8] A handy manual for the private recitation of Compline is Attwater, *Into Thy Hands*, which gives the text in English and Latin for the week. Quotations here are from this booklet.

of the ever recurring parallel in the liturgy intermingling the temporal life and the eternal. In Compline, the soul prays for protection or help in all these kinds of sleep, the natural sleep of night, the sleep of the soul in sin, the sleep of death at the end of life. After the recitation of this official prayer of the Church according to the mind of Christ, the soul may go to rest in full confidence, no matter whether the next awakening will be in this world or in the next.

Compline, unlike the other hour prayers, begins abruptly with a request for a blessing: "Pray, Sir, a blessing." The presiding person at group recitation, or else the person reciting in private, expresses the blessing in these significant words: "The Lord almighty grant us a peaceful night and a happy end. Amen." To this double thought-content of sleep and death, the short reading that follows adds a third, that of temptation and sin: "Brethren, be sober and watch because your adversary the devil, as a roaring lion, goeth about seeking whom he may devour; whom resist ye strong in faith. But do thou, O Lord, have mercy on us." Thereupon we are again reminded that "Our help is in the name of the Lord, who made heaven and earth." A silent Our Father is said and the confession of faults is begun.

The Confiteor may be looked upon as an answer to the exhortation of the short reading. All the saints are called upon to ask God for his forgiveness of the faults of the day. The customary prayers for forgiveness follow upon the Confiteor as at Mass. When several recite Compline together, these prayers are said in the usual liturgical form of a dialog of mutual confession and mutual prayer for forgiveness. In true Christian charity those praying together then call upon the Lord to aid them: "Convert us, O Lord, our Savior. And turn away thine anger from us. O God, come to mine assistance. O Lord, make haste to help me. Glory be to the Father, etc." The psalms follow, three in number as usual.

In the hymn we have the characteristic note of the departing light of day and of petition for the needed protection of God during the night: "Now with the fast departing light, Maker of all, we ask of thee, of thy great mercy, through the night our guardian and defence to be. Far off let idle visions fly, no phantom of the night molest, curb thou our raging enemy, that we in chaste repose may rest." In full confidence we turn to the Lord in the words of the little chapter: "But thou, O Lord, art amongst us, and thy holy name is called upon; forsake us not, O Lord our God." In the answering responsory with its beautiful refrain, we apply the words of the dying Savior, so appropriate both before our temporal and before our eternal repose: "Into thy hands, O Lord, I commend my spirit. Thou hast redeemed us, O Lord, God of truth." With increasing consciousness of our position we again ask of God: "Keep us, O Lord, as the apple of thine eye. Protect us under the shadow of thy wings."

Another reference to death is applied to the condition of approaching night in the Canticle of Simeon. We have seen another day of salvation and gratefully ask the Lord to dismiss us in peace: "Now thou dost dismiss thy servant, O Lord, according to thy word in peace: because mine eyes have seen thy salvation." The antiphon of the canticle reads most beautifully: "Save us, O Lord, when we are awake, and keep us while we sleep, that we may watch with Christ and rest in peace." The collect sums up all our petitions for divine protection. It asks that God "visit this dwelling," *i.e.*, those who live in it, and "drive far from it all snares of the enemy," let his "holy angels dwell herein, who may keep us in peace," and may his "blessing be always upon us." It is the last prayer recited in common and is followed by the official blessing: "May the almighty and merciful Lord, Father, Son and Holy Ghost, bless and keep us. Amen."

The *Salve Regina,* or other anthem to the blessed Virgin according to the season, finally puts us also under her protection. Then the versicle "May the divine help remain always with us" leads over to the Our Father, Hail Mary, and Creed. The latter are no longer said aloud. With them we slip into the silence of the night under the protection of God and his saints, of which the official prayer of the Church has made us doubly certain. The true member of Christ has professed his faith in all his actions of the day, and now, as it were, he falls into the peaceful sleep of the Lord in the very confession of the faith whose formula has just died on his lips.

CHAPTER XVI

THE LITURGICAL CHANT

I. ART AND THE LITURGY

WE have seen in preceding chapters how the Church makes use of all the means at the disposal of mankind for the better performance of her service of divine worship unto God. In this service of God nothing can be deemed too good. While everything created necessarily remains infinitely below the true dignity and nature of God, man, acting in accordance with his own nature, gives expression to the supereminence of God by employing all the best achievements of all the arts, the highest creations of the human mind and the highest developments of material creation, in the expression of his homage to his Maker. Hence Pius X could declare so definitely that "the Church has always recognized and favoured the progress of the arts, admitting to the service of religion everything good and beautiful discovered by genius in the course of ages— always, however, with due regard to the liturgical laws." [1] The liturgy taken at its best, when viewed from this stand-point, is not only the depositary of the best religious sentiments of the entire span of the world's existence, but also the depositary of some of the best accomplishments of the artistic powers of man or else the inspiration of them.

[1] Motu proprio, November 22, 1904

Around the traditional worship of the Church have been gathered some of the best products of artistic genius in painting and sculpture, architecture, poetry and music.

Nor can we be greatly surprised at this. For the spirit of the liturgy is a supreme expression of the spirit of art. In the liturgy we find embodied in the highest degree some of the characteristics that are common to all art. The liturgy is essentially the external embodiment of an interior soul and spirit. In fact, in its sacramental mysteries it is above all else the incarnation of the truly Divine, the making present of the supernatural in its own mystical but real actuality, and not only an expression of the reflected divine as naturally but very imperfectly embodied in created minds. There is likewise something mysterious and mystical about all art. By means of the external all true art brings us into contact with the unseen, with the spiritual. It, too, is the embodiment of something that is essentially more than the merely external or corporal. From this standpoint the liturgy is the most precious, the richest art, since its inner reality at its best is the Divine itself as shared in by man through Christ.

Again all art is organic and social in character. It is organized around a focal center or ideal; and its purpose is fundamentally expression for social communication. Likewise is the liturgy, in its larger aspects as well as in its minutest examples, a progressive organic action. In the liturgy there is nothing of the haphazard. If in single instances we can not fully account for the presence of a detail here or there, this is due to the fact that the liturgy is in no way the product of mathematical precalculation; it is too human for that, too living and in its growth too spontaneous.

Art, again, almost alone among the purely natural higher achievements of man is capable of fully bridging the gaps that divide nations and peoples. True art is ever international in its appeal. The liturgy is more than international; it is most truly supra-national because supernatural. It aims ever to unite all men in the charity of Christ. All its actions are collective in nature, are actions of that mystical body of which all men alike are destined to be living members through their union with the one common head Christ.

Art is eminently the product of love, of devotion to an ideal, to a cause that reckons neither its failures nor its sacrifices. The mainspring of liturgical participation likewise is love. In it, too, the divine ideal is reached by sacrifice and self-denial, through a persevering courage inspired by the love that never falters.[2] Art and liturgy are truly kin, as are nature and supernature. And their meeting place is in the performance of the liturgical worship, where art is elevated to the highest dignity, just as all nature there reaches its true destiny of being wedded to the supernatural. "Art in the hallowed precincts of the liturgy is the expression of reverence and love. . . . When love moves the heart, the word becomes a poem, prayer a psalm, and speech a melodious song. This is also true when that love speaks of which Christ prayed to the Father in a most solemn moment: May the love, wherewith thou hast loved me, be in them (John 17: 26)."[3]

As the liturgy is supreme in life by reason of the holiness of its action and the holiness of its aim, there is only one condition under which we can properly speak of a liturgical

---

[2] *Cf. Mysterium,* pp. 198ff.
[3] *Benediktinische Monatschrift,* 1924, p. 2

art. By no means does all art harmonize with the great aims of the liturgy. In the wedding of the two it is not liturgy that must adjust itself to the different inspirations of any kind of art; it is the art that must enter into the service of the liturgy. Not even all sacred or religious art is also liturgical art. For the latter, the union of art and liturgy must be organic and not accidental, and that can ever be truly so only when the smaller merges in the greater, when the lesser in dignity is properly aligned with that which is more sublime in its being and end.

True liturgical art must therefore subserve the same end as the liturgy, the glorification of God and the sanctification of man; and it must do so not only in some way after the manner of the liturgy but as an organic element that loses itself in the greater liturgical action in order to find its own highest life. Evidently this can be realized only when the inspiration—both the ideals and the ideas—has come from the liturgy. Art in general is wider in scope than liturgical art and includes the latter; but when the liturgy gives its name to art, the latter must live of the life of the liturgy. It is a true instinct, therefore, that prompts contemporaries to write of the possible influence of the liturgical movement on church architecture. If any art in connection with the liturgy is to undergo changes, this must happen only under the inspiration of and in connection with the liturgy. Art in the service of the liturgy is only a tool, a means, but a means in which the liturgical action reaches the highest perfection of expression that created mind can give it.

Among the arts music plays a special role in the liturgy of the Church. To indicate the peculiar appropriateness of music in the liturgy, it has been pointed out by some that music is the art of the interior man, it is the special language of the inner soul. Like the soul music is said to be mysterious, striving to rise above the earthly unto God. Music, we are again told, is divine. God himself is music. God is the infinite perfection of all being and of all possibilities in a most perfect harmony; while music is a wonderful order and harmony in the unlimited realms of sound. The being of God inspires the soul to sing, even as the birds of the meadows are made to open their throats in a wonderful symphony at the splendors of his own infinite glory. Music is therefore the image of God. Among arts, it is the most spiritual, truly celestial, a bit of resplendent reality transplanted from the realm of the spirit world. And as it comes from God, so it ever leads back to him. Hence there is none that has a better right to music than the Church, the depositary of the divine here on earth. In the Church, music enters into the very fibre and action of the liturgy, while in comparison with it other art only enhances the liturgical environment. In the Church, music unites the members of the family of God, and unites the family to God. By means of music the spirit is better lifted from this earth and carried up to the throne of God himself. Music is indeed almost a necessity in the Church, especially in her more elaborate and more solemn services, in her more public worship. And particularly is this true of the Church as the body of the militant, suffering, and triumphant souls united in the glory of Christ and living intimately the life of God.[4]

II. Liturgical Music

Music in the divine service of the Church, like the liturgy itself, finds additional justification, if such is needed, in the

[4] *Cf.* Kling, *Katholische Kirchenmusik*, II, pp. 80ff., 100

very nature of man. Like the birds of dell and vale man, when most natural, sings out in the joy of his heart. He has the word of his mouth wherewith to communicate his thought, but the word does not suffice as the adequate expression of emotional thought, of the more intense sentiments of joy and exaltation, of the deeper feelings of sorrow. The man of nature quite freely sings out the intenser moods of his heart; and the liturgy, as we have seen, does not suppress nature but elevates and perfects it. The chanted word and phrase is the most perfect mode of expression, the most noble mode of acting out his inner sentiments that man is capable of. If ordinary expression is sufficient for the affairs of ordinary life, the nobler expression of melody is most appropriate for the sublimer sentiments that establish a bond of living union between the creature and the Creator. Music is eminently adapted to further the spirit of the liturgy.

With that qualification of music we have also given the first requisites of any liturgical music. Liturgical music, like all liturgical art, must subserve as perfectly as possible the object and aim of the liturgy. No one has expressed this better than the great liturgical pope, who was also the restorer of the ancient, traditional church music. "Sacred music, being a complementary part of the solemn liturgy, participates in the general scope of the liturgy, which is the glory of God and the sanctification and edification of the faithful. It contributes to the decorum and splendor of the ecclesiastical ceremonies, and since its principal office is to clothe with suitable melody the liturgical text proposed for the understanding of the faithful, its proper aim is to add greater efficacy to the text in order that through it the faithful may be the more easily moved to devotion and better disposed for the reception of the fruits of grace belonging to the celebration of the most holy mysteries." [5]

Several purposes are indicated by the pontiff. First of all the purpose of church music must be that of honoring God. This is the primary end of the liturgy, without which the liturgy would no longer be itself and the church music would no longer be liturgical. Now the liturgical music can attain this aim in a way not attained by the words and actions of the liturgy alone, only if it adds something to the words and actions. The music does this when it lends emphasis to the meaning of the liturgical action; it must give fuller expression to the holy prayers of praise and homage contained in the liturgy. Furthermore this emphasis cannot be merely an abstract or theoretical one. It must be concrete and as practical as the liturgy itself. This means that the music fulfils its aim only if it brings home the meaning and inspiration of these prayers more forcibly to the people participating in the divine worship. It must tend to intensify this participation, to elevate it; therefore to edify the faithful, to lift their hearts and minds more completely, more perfectly to God. The liturgical music must draw the souls nearer to the center of the liturgy, nearer to the divine contained in it. Anything else is contrary to the purpose of the liturgy and may not be tolerated. "I am the Lord thy God, a jealous God," we are told; [6] and it is a warning that has a most appropriate application in the matter here under consideration.

"In general it must be considered a very grave abuse," says Pius X, "when the liturgy in ecclesiastical functions is made to appear secondary to and in a manner at the service of the music, for the music is merely a part of the

---

[5] Motu proprio   [6] Deut. 5:9

liturgy and its humble handmaid." [7] Elsewhere he frankly depicts some of the abuses: "For the devout psalmody of the clergy, in which the people also used to join, there have been substituted interminable musical compositions on the words of the psalms, all of them modelled on old theatrical works, and most of them of such meagre artistic value that they would not be tolerated for a moment even in our second-rate concerts." [8] Above all, the vengeance of a jealous God is rightly to be feared whenever the music of the church services in reality subserves some private end.

This is the case whenever the church service is advertised or attended by reason of the fact that a special mass of some noted composer is to be rendered, a new mass by a budding musician, or any mass sung by some noted organization of singers. Such events are then made the features of the liturgical worship, and it is these events for which the people come and not the church service as such. This may even be true of the Gregorian chant, if the chant is announced as the drawing card that makes it worth while to attend, say, Mass service in a particular place. *A fortiori*, no special orchestra or soloist should draw the attention to the performers as such and away from the central action of the holy liturgy. In this matter, too, the offenses became historically more frequent with the loss of the liturgical sense at the end of the Middle Ages. It may, however, be doubted whether at that time "the liturgical interest had to give way to the artistic pleasure of non-clerical singers quite automatically," just because the singers were no longer exclusively men, as a writer affirms. [9]

[7] Motu proprio
[8] Letter to the Cardinal Vicar of Rome, December 8, 1903
[9] Wagner, *Einfuehrung in die katholische kirchenmusik*, p. 171

Even where the individual solo may be ever so musical and ever so prayerful, and be moreover a splendid example of sacred art, it will not be liturgical as long as it remains an individual prayer. Every melody sung at liturgical services must in its nature and inspiration be the outcome of the greater liturgical action that is being officially performed. All its thoughts, sentiments must be those of the liturgy, and it must not call attention to itself as something apart from the holy action. The point is worth repeating, since with music in particular the danger is greater. Pius X says in the Motu proprio already quoted several times: Whether it be owing "to the pleasure that music directly produces and that is not always easily contained within the right limits, or finally to the many prejudices on the matter, so lightly introduced and so tenaciously maintained even among responsible and pious persons, the fact remains that there is a general tendency to deviate from the right rule prescribed by the end for which art is admitted to the service of the public worship and which is set forth very clearly in the ecclesiastical canons."

To sum up, liturgical music must be more than art. It is both art and liturgy, and therefore also religion in practice. From all these standpoints it must be true to itself, to its entire nature. The demand of truth is made upon church music in the name of art. Aesthetics demands truth, not a false sentimentalism that is chaotic in its joys and sorrows. In all high art there is dignity, serious elevation and nobility of spirit; and in church music these must be apparent in the harmony, in the melody, in the accompaniment of the liturgical word and action. In it there must be nothing small, ridiculous, exaggerated, whimsical, theatrical. Truth is likewise demanded in the name of the liturgy. The church music must be an integral part of the liturgical worship. It must enhance the solemnity of the sacrifice, emphasize the particular mood of the season. It must, like all the liturgy, be obedient to the demands of the Church, be pious, noble, holy, sanctifying. Finally truth is demanded of church music in the name of religion. Church music must be prayer, must point to God, be beautiful, not ugly, must further the actions of religious symbolism.[10]

III. Gregorian Chant

What we have said so far about liturgical music should find full application in the relation of the Gregorian chant or plainsong to the liturgy. Pius X put this whole matter succinctly in his Motu proprio. After saying that sacred music should possess in the highest degree the qualities proper to the liturgy, especially sanctity, beauty of form and universality, he adds that these qualities are found in an eminent degree in Gregorian chant. The latter is preeminently the sacred music, and all other music, he says, is good insofar as it approaches the Gregorian.

We are not here concerned with the legal aspects of the question of Gregorian chant. The Canon Law says simply that "the liturgical laws concerning sacred music shall be observed." [11] The Roman Missal has always given the Gregorian chant as the official chant of its services. And Pius X in his Motu proprio, as a decree of the Congregation of Holy Rites says, "happily restored the venerable Gregorian chant to its primitive ecclesiastical use," and he

[10] *Cf.* Kling, *Katholische Kirchenmusik,* II, pp. 96–99
[11] Can. 1264

desired the authentic body of collected chant to "have the force of law for the universal Church." [12] As the Motu proprio itself indicates, not all polyphonic music is prohibited in the church services, but plainsong is recognized as the official liturgical chant of the Church. Hence we should have no difficulty to find in it the various characteristics of all true liturgical music. And nothing else should be better calculated to give us a proper appreciation both of the chant itself, and of the movement of its restoration inaugurated by Pius X.

That the Gregorian chant, when intelligently rendered, fulfills the primary liturgical demand of being prayer cannot be doubted. In fact, there is no meaning to the chant apart from its recognition as a high form of prayer. The purely aesthetic rendering of it, as well as the mechanical running off of its melodies, not infrequently met with, does not do it justice. Only the soul that is attuned to the religious sense with which the liturgy is imbued, can produce an effective rendition of the chant, or can, in turn, fully appreciate the richness of meaning that great men of all times have attributed to it. And still, the chant is so often judged from the effect produced in practice hours by persons who have never been instructed in its musical peculiarities or its religious message and nature!

As with the liturgy in general, or with the breviary for instance, the approval and the laws of the Church make it the duty of all whom these laws strike, not only to perform the liturgical requirements but also to try to enter into the spirit of the liturgy or its chant, before being so ready to pass a condemnatory judgment. Here the same question arises that was mentioned in the first chapter regard-

---

[12] Wapelhorst, *Compendium Sacrae liturgiae*, p. 178

ing the entire liturgy, not so much the question of whether the chant of the Church is outmoded or out of date, but whether we are not out of tune with the Church, the official spokesman of Christ and guide of souls, and with the true Christian spirit. It might be worth our while to reflect on this question and to try to enter somewhat into the spirit so well portrayed in the following enthusiastic words:

The basic theocentric idea of all the liturgy is also the principal motif of the Gregorian music. The latter does not aim at the human heart, it does not appeal to the human intellect, but with the whole man it stands before the throne of God. It does not strive after a deep impression on sensitive hearts, but above all it desires nothing more than to be the expression of a deep-felt adoration and humble homage rendered by the creature to the Creator, by the child of God to its heavenly Father. Gregorian chant, like the liturgy in general, is glorification of God, praise of God, not a matter of human entertainment, nor even a bait for souls. Its beauties and its somberness, its riches and poverty, its overflow of feeling and its self-constraint—all these flow from the same source: a deep reverence for the majesty of God as experienced by the fellowship of the saints.[18]

The Gregorian chant is eminently adapted to unite the hearts of all in a common fellowship of prayer and worship. The unity of faith, of heart, of worship, is paralleled by unity of song. In the Gregorian chant there is only one voice. In its musical expression of the liturgical sentiments there is always unison of melody. The congregation chanting is never divided against itself; as all

[18] *Cf.* Kling, *op. cit.*, II, pp. 70–71

hearts are united in the same service so all voices are united in the same melodious expression of the common worship. This is true of all the faithful among themselves assisting at the service, and it is likewise true of priest and people. The chant therefore emphasizes the common action of priest and people, their harmonious co-operation. By means of the chant the people participate more intimately in the action of the liturgy as prescribed by the Church, they align themselves more intimately with the official source whence flows the divine life.

The greater possibility of uniting the minds and hearts of the faithful by means of the choral music lies in the very nature of the chant. It is fundamentally simple, so that the unlearned, the uncultured, may catch something of it and enter into its spirit. But its simplicity is that of greatness, and so it offers food also for the most cultured minds. It is one and the same chant for the lowly and the great.

In spite of its simplicity, however, it can like the psalms give expression to a great variety of moods and sentiments, and therefore it so readily interprets all the sentiments of the liturgy throughout the varying seasons. "Every one of the eight ecclesiastical modes, according to which the antiphons are composed and the psalms are sung, has its own character. Through her choice of mode the Church always gives a new, distinctive color to the song. What longing there is, for example, in the second mode, how mystic the fourth sounds, how solemn the seventh; how moved the fifth is with emotion, and how virile and strong the eighth!" [14] Throughout the church year with its varying moods one and the same chant forms the basis for

[14] *Die Betende Kirche*, p. 195

more intensely living the unified life of the members of Christ in the official worship of the one Church.

In its unifying embrace, the chant recognizes no boundaries of country or nationality. Other music has its national composers, its national stamp and character. Not so the chant. It is in essence truly international. As the liturgy itself is the same for different countries, so that Catholics of one land may in another find the same worship as at home, so the chant is the common chant of all and helps to emphasize the sense of familiarity felt in all Catholic churches. The chant has been called "the song of peace and reconciliation. In it the voices of men, divided by land and sea, unite into a supernatural harmony. Wherever it is sounded everyone feels at home, however far from his native hearth; there separated brothers and hostile peoples clasp their hands in peace. There the fire of hate and the torch of dissension are extinguished. The Gregorian chant is the great canticle of Christian love, the wedding hymn of the liturgical league of nations." [15]

In every way, then, the chant helps to fulfill the prayer of Christ that all may be one in him: "The ecclesiastical chant is indeed of the greatest importance for our Catholic people. It reconciles and amalgamates, educates and elevates, consoles and renders happy, promotes religious edification and sanctification." [16]

IV. Chant and the Mass

The harmony of spirit between liturgy and chant is intelligible from the close historical connection between the two. There are certain parts of the present Mass

[15] Kling, *op. cit.*, I, pp. 72–3   [16] *Op. cit.*, II, p. 26

which were formerly not recited by the priest at all, being chanted by the people or the choir. With the texts thus sung the priest had nothing to do. The singers in those days had a more real part to play in the liturgy than at present, when the priest at the altar prays also those parts that are chanted by others. The chanted texts and the parts prayed by the priest personally, then, together made up the liturgical text of the sacrifice and the common sacrificial action of priest and people. The change to the present arrangement, in which the priest prays all the parts, came only in time, when the customs of our present low Mass set in. Chant and Mass therefore originally developed together, as did the chant and many other parts of the liturgy.

Hence the liturgy and the chant belong together both in origin and development. "The ecclesiastical music was developed with and in the liturgy," says a modern authority on the chant; "both were regulated and fixed at the same time, so that every important liturgical function had a corresponding musical action accompanying it. Many liturgical changes reacted on the chant of the Church. Musical and liturgical elements interpenetrate to such an extent that they cannot be properly separated. The liturgy as a whole seems to call for the complement of chant, and without the co-operation of the two many things in the Mass and the office would have developed differently." [17] From this it is evident how eminently active a participation in the Mass the chanting of the proper parts according to the direction of the Church must be even today. There is consequently no surprise in the fact that the call of Pope Pius X for active participation in the public worship

[17] Wagner, *Einfuehrung in die katholische Kirchenmusik*, p. 7

of the Church was made in the very same Motu proprio that restored the Gregorian chant to its former place in the liturgy. Singing the chanted parts of the Mass is not merely adding external ornament to the liturgical worship, but is rather most active entering into the worship, a fully approved and most active participation in it.

From the mutual development of chant and liturgy we can better understand the delicacy with which the chant fulfills its office in the liturgy of the Mass. The purpose of the chant in the Mass is more closely identical with that of the earlier parts, especially the Mass of the Catechumens. It must help the faithful to arrive at an elevated, holy state of mind, at a common unity of mind in God. These are the indispensable conditions for more fruitful participation in the holy action of the Mass at its highest, *i.e.*, the Canon, and in the following action of the banquet.

The holy action of the Canon itself is a mystical communion of the faithful with their Head, in which the Head himself descends upon the altar for the better attainment of their union with him. The action it too sublime, in the eyes of the Church, even for the loud recitation of words, whence there is no surprise in the fact that the chant plays no part in the Canon. The silence of the chant is here, if the expression may be used, most eloquent of the ineffable sanctity of the liturgical action in the mind of the Church. By permission of the Church, indeed, a phrase is sung after the Consecration, but it is no part of the text of the Canon. Only at the end of the Canon, when the mind is to be immediately prepared for the communion, the chant again enters properly into the action of the Mass.

The chant is most effective in the service it renders in

the earlier parts leading up to the Canon. Musically it is at its height of elaboration in the gradual. Here it is meant to emphasize the spirit of the readings; and it pours out its inspiration with the greatest feeling when it prepares the soul for the divine word of Christ in the gospel. In the gospel Christ himself speaks, and thereafter, as the holy action of the Mass increases in intensity, the chant recedes more and more into the background. With the singing of the preface, the priest seems to take over any partial leadership that may have been extant in the chant. Following the preface, the chant is but an answering conclusion to his prayer, and thereafter it lapses into silence during the climax of the sacred action, as we have seen.[18]

The mutual development of liturgy and chant also furnishes a ready explanation of the fact that the melodies of the chant are so generally a reflection of the words they accompany. In the different seasons of the year the chant for the proper parts of the Mass and office is in the truest sense a musical interpretation of the sentiments expressed in these texts. Not only chronologically are the two related, but also spiritually. "The fundamental aspect of the plain chant," says an expert on the matter, "the aspect we have completely neglected up to now, and the one which the Christian souls are called to taste and comprehend, is the intimate compenetration existing between the ideas of the liturgy and the melodies of the Gregorian repertory. Although the ideas gave birth to the melodies, the latter in their turn have given its greatest force of expression to the liturgy." [19]

[18] Cf. an excellent article on "Christozentrische Kirchenmusik" by Dom Boeser in Benediktinische Monatschrift, Vol. 6 (1934), pp. 1–16
[19] La Vie Liturgique, Supplement, 1909, p. 21

The words and melodies belong intimately together; there is a harmonious interrelation and variation throughout the different liturgical seasons. That alone explains why the Gregorian chant has none of the faults that we described above as belonging to false liturgical music, and for that reason alone we can speak so properly of the inner spirituality of the chant, of "its praying with Christ to the Father, its freedom from mere sensory appeal, from all egoistic vanities, from all playing to the applause of the masses, its pure unselfish following of the lead of the liturgy." [20] There naturally follows also the need of absorbing the general spirit of the liturgy and of its seasons, for all those especially who wish to conduct and render the chant in church services. As Dom Johner says: "It is the indispensable duty of the choirmaster thoroughly to familiarize himself with the essentials of the liturgy, its structure, and the predominating thoughts for the seasons and feasts, in order that he may be able to instruct his singers in a satisfactory manner." This alone will awaken a proper interest in singers and non-singers alike, and prevent a mechanical rendition of the Gregorian church prayer. [21]

V. CHANT AND THE LITURGICAL YEAR

The mere mention of this intimate correlation between text and melody and the corresponding seasonal variations in the musical sentiments will open up new vistas even to the amateur follower of the Church's liturgy, such as every Christian should be at the very least. Not only will

[20] *Benediktinische Monatsschrift, loc. cit.,* p. 6
[21] *A New School of Gregorian Chant,* p. 227

he note more readily the great differences in the melodies, say, between Advent and Easter or Christmas, but he will also understand the appropriateness of these differences. The Advent melodies are in part sober, at times sad, and again hopeful and joyous—well expressive of the mixed feelings of sorrow and joy in the liturgy preparatory to Christmas. The Christmastide melodies are at times expressive of a childlike joy, and again of a simple quiet grandeur that indicates most successfully the awe and wonder of the Christmas liturgy in the face of the divine mystery being revealed to men and being re-enacted in the liturgy of the time.

The introit of the first Sunday of Advent begins with the words, "To thee have I lifted up my soul. In thee, O my God, I put my trust." The melody accompanying them in its turn emphasizes the combined sentiments of confidence in God and our own lowliness before him, all instinct with a wistfulness and longing that seems to be fully conscious of the fact that man deserves nothing of the great goodness and mercy of God. Compare this with the introit melodies of Christmas and the difference is striking, just as is the graded progress in the successive Masses. The first Mass with its messianic psalm verse "The Lord said to me: thou art my Son, this day have I begotten thee," sings out in a melody that is full of awe at the mystery before which our comprehension fails. The second Mass, "A light shall shine upon us this day: for our Lord is born to us," contains a note of growing realization and joy with its tone sustained on a higher level. Then the third Mass on a still higher tone bursts out in the fullness of joy at man's realization of good tidings of the day's mystery: "A child is born to us, and a Son is given to us. . . . Sing ye to the Lord a new canticle."

With Septuagesima we naturally expect a change to come. The joyous note of Christmastide is replaced by the austere melancholy of song that is so well in harmony with the messages of the liturgy, and prepares for the spirit of penance and self-denial of Lent. "The groans of death surrounded me," sings the introit of Septuagesima Sunday in a melody that rises at times only to emphasize all the more the predominant descending movement of the somber sentiments of this time. The alleluia, the official shout of joy, is now suppressed and a less flexible tract supplants the melody of the graduals. Now, too, the richness of the melodies of Christmas has disappeared. The business of the Christian life has begun in earnest.

The music of Lent but serves to emphasize the mood of Septuagesima. Compare, for instance, the somberness, the narrow range, of the introit of the second Sunday, even in the "Deliver us, O God of Israel, from all our tribulations," where the melody is least unvaried. Sometimes the melodies of Lent become almost depressing. They are full of the sense of our abasement and suffering, of the sentiment of penitence, not unmixed, however, with occasional indications of the hope that should naturally spring from it.

Our deliverance from the Lenten sense of sin and its merit comes with Easter, and gloriously does the general chant sing out the victory of Christ. "I arose, and am still with thee, alleluia," the introit says, but the music of it is still full of the mystery, of the wonder of it, not yet fully understood, or perhaps too great at first for expression. But the gradual, "This is the day which the Lord hath made: let us be glad and rejoice," seems to have recaught its breath, and the joy of it is unbounded. The text of Easter teems with alleluias, and the melody gives them their due emphasis. Only an understanding of the spirit of the Easter liturgy reveals all the holy joy hidden, say, in the alleluia song of the *Ite, missa est* of the octave. The joy continues, but Ascension, bringing on the triumphal entry of Christ into heaven, is not without a touch of sadness at his departure from the earth, and the double strain is felt in its music. Both notes, those of joy and of sorrow, are through a better understanding now of the true nature of the work of Christ properly sobered in the music of the Ascension, in whose character there is "joy without exuberance, melancholy without depression." [22]

Even in the use of the same Gregorian mode for different texts, we cannot but note how the text, if understood, helps to interpret the music. The Magnificat, for instance, breathes inspiration into every one of the modes in which it is sung, just as the exultation of the Laudate psalm after benediction services is unmistakable. Again, the music of the Sanctus ever breathes of joy and happiness in the Lord, while the Agnus Dei is full of reverential beseeching, in which there is a holy confidence in the Lord. The music of the *In paradisum*, sung when a corpse is led out of church after the burial Mass, is a delicately sparkling gem, whose joyous note cannot be understood, and therefore not interpreted, except on the basis of the sublime words of the text: "May the angels lead thee into paradise. May the martyrs receive thee at thy arrival and lead thee

[22] A masterful musical interpretation of the moods of the liturgical year is contained in a series of articles by Dom Ermin Vitry that appeared in *La Vie Liturgique, Supplement*, 1909–10, unfortunately out of print, to which the present author is glad to acknowledge his indebtedness.

into the holy city of Jerusalem. May the choir of angels come to meet thee and with Lazarus, who was once poor, mayest thou share an eternal rest."

Splendid examples of harmony between liturgy and Gregorian musical text are furnished by some of the hymns and sequences of the official service. The *Dies irae* may be somewhat post-liturgical in its extremer sense of fear, but of the wonderful adaptation of melody to ideas there can be no doubt. Could other music give the same perfect interpretations as the accepted melody of the chant? Even some of the mystery of the liturgy's messages is admirably reproduced. Take the *Vexilla regis* of the Passion Sunday Vespers and of Good Friday. The note is somber but not tragic, and the indication of buoyancy in it but interprets the sense of the text. Striking is the *Pueri Haebraeorum* of Palm Sunday, sung at the distribution of the palms. The words describe the joyful acclamation at the entry into Jerusalem, but the melody is full of the sense of the events to come and has its eye riveted also on the cross that is to lead the procession, to which is attached the palm of coming martyrdom.

The *Victimae paschali* of Easter is full of the wonder experienced at the open tomb and at the words of the angel—a holy and great wonder that finds its expression in the simplicity of dialog and melody but suddenly bursts forth in a phrase of full realization with the words, "we know that Christ indeed has risen." Richer in variety is the *Lauda Sion* of Corpus Christi. It is indeed a paean to the eucharistic Life, full of its richness, its inexhaustible joy, and not without a sense of its sublime mystery. Over against this type of chant, we may contrast that of a Credo. How well the alternating phrases blend into a whole.

And withal, how self-possessed is this confession of faith. In measured words and melody the different truths of the faith are brought forth and professed, not with the forced conviction of emotion, but in the calmness of a faith that is unshakable.

"The liturgical chant," says Dom Sauter, "occupies the important and honorable position of the dramatic word, now in historical narrative, now in the form of instruction, now sighing and in tears. It rises to the high heavens with its clear song of victory, then again pays a grateful homage to the Savior on the altar in accents of tender sweetness, and again represents the Lord himself in his conversations with the beloved soul. Now it is steeped in solitary meditation on the mysterious depths of the mystical action, and again it raises its voice aloud inviting all creatures to a common jubilation. Such is the task and the position of the liturgical chant. The chant is, to put it in brief, the enlivening word in the celebration of the offering, the enlightening word in the application of the offering, the word of mutual understanding between God and his people, between the people and their God." [28]

Sublime as the heights are to which the chant attains, it never loses the essential characteristics that it possesses in common with all the liturgy, since it is an integral element of this liturgy. It is ever fundamentally simple, concentrating on a few motives, but using these with telling impressiveness. Its motives are developed with a constant onward stride. The chant never pauses nor hesitates, its action is the progressive development of the liturgy itself. But even in its strongest emotional elaborations it never goes astray by overshooting its mark. The

[28] *Der liturgische Choral*, pp. 7–8

chant is ever conscious of the position of man as a creature of God. Avoiding the excess of extremes, it ever preserves the dignity of the liturgy of God, the unwordly purity of its heart, the simple intelligibility of its appeal, rendering ever the deliberate homage, praise, and sacrifice, that is God's due from rational human nature.

AUTHORS AND EDITIONS QUOTED

Adam, Karl: *The Spirit of Catholicism.* The Macmillan Co., 1930.

Anger, Abbé: *The Doctrine of the Mystical Body of Christ.* Benziger Brothers, 1931.

Attwater, Donald: *Into Thy Hands.* The Liturgical Press. 2nd ed., 1935.

Baudot, Dom Jules: *The Breviary.* B. Herder Book Co. St. Louis, 1929.

Beauduin, Dom Lambert: *Liturgy the Life of the Church.* The Liturgical Press, Collegeville, Minn. 2nd ed., 1929.

Benedictine Nuns of the Abbey of Our Lady: *The Day Hours of the Church.* Burns Oates and Washbourne. London, 1921.

Bericht der Priester-Tagung in Wien, 1924. Druck und Verlag St. Gabriel. Moedling, Austria, 1925.

Bichlmair, Georg, S.J.: *Urchristentum und katholische Kirche.* Verlagsanstalt Tyrolia. Innsbruck, 1924.

Boeser, Dom Fidelis: *The Mass-Liturgy.* The Bruce Publishing Co. Milwaukee, 1932.

Busch, William: *The Mass-Drama.* The Liturgical Press, 2nd ed., 1933.

Bute, John, Marquess of: *The Roman Breviary.* 4 vols. William Blackwood and Sons. London, 1908.

Cabrol, Dom Fernand: *Liturgical Prayer.* Burns Oates and Washbourne. London, 1922.

Cabrol, Dom Fernand: "Liturgie" in the *Dictionnaire de Théologie catholique.*

Caronti, Abbot Emmanuele: *The Spirit of the Liturgy.* The Liturgical Press. 2nd ed., 1932.

Cours et Conference de la Semaine Liturgique de Maredsous, 1912. Abbaye de Maredsous. Belgique, 1913.

Croegaert, Auguste: *La femme chrétienne et la restauration liturgique.* Vromant & Co. Bruxelles, 1922.

Ellard, Gerald, S.J.: *Christian Life and Worship.* The Bruce Publishing Co. Milwaukee, 1933.

Festugière, Dom M.: *Qu'est-ce que la liturgie?* Abbaye de Maredsous, Belgique, 1914.

Goeb, Abbot Cuthbert: *Offeramus.* The Liturgical Press. 13th ed., 1935.

Grabmann, Martin: *Das Seelenleben Des heiligen Thomas von Aquin.* Theatiner-verlag. Muenchen, 1924.

Grea, Dom A.: *De l'Eglise et de sa divine constitution.* Vols. I and II. Maison de la Bonne Presse. Paris. New ed., 1907.

Grea, Dom A.: *La sainte liturgie.* Maison de la Bonne Presse. Paris, 1909.

Guardini, Romano: *Vom Geist der Liturgie.* Vol. I of *Ecclesia Orans.* Herder & Co. Freiburg i.B. 8–12 ed., 1922.

Guèranger, Dom Prosper: *The Liturgical Year.* 15 vols. Benziger Brothers, 1910.

Haering, Dom Otto: *Living with the Church.* Benziger Brothers, 1930.

Hammenstede, Dom Albert: *Die Liturgie als Erlebnis.* Vol. III of *Ecclesia Orans.* Herder & Co. Freiburg i.B., 1921.

Hellriegel, M. B. and Jasper, A. A.: *The True Basis of Christian Solidarity.* Central Bureau of the Central Verein. St. Louis, 2nd ed., 1934.

Herwegen, Abbot Ildefons: *Lumen Christi.* Theatiner-verlag. Muenchen 1924.

Hoornaert, Rodolphe: *The Breviary and the Laity.* The Liturgical Press, 1936.

Johner, Dom Dominic: *A New School of Gregorian Chant.* Fr. Pustet & Co. N.Y. 3rd English ed., 1925.

Kling, Wilhelm: *Katholische Kirchenmusik.* 2 vols. Verlag von Ferdinan Schoeningh. Paderborn.

Kramp, Joseph, S.J.: *Eucharistia.* The E. M. Lohmann Co. St. Paul, 1926.

Kramp, Joseph, S.J.: *The Liturgical Sacrifice of the New Law.* B. Herder Book Co. St. Louis, 1926.

Lefebvre, Dom Gaspar: *Catholic Liturgy.* Sands & Co. London, 1924.

Lynch, J. S. M.: *The Rite of Ordination.* The Cathedral Library Association. N.Y. 4th ed., 1907.

Maria-Laach, Monks of: *Die Betende Kirche.* Sankt Augustinerverlag. Berlin. 1st ed., 1924.

Maria-Laach, Monks of: *Mysterium.* Verlag der Aschendorffschen Verlagsbuchhandlung. Muenster i.W., 1926.

Michel, Dom Virgil: *Life in Christ.* (In mimeoprint.) Burgess Publishing Co., Minneapolis, Minn. 2nd ed., 1935.

Michel, Dom Virgil: *My Sacrifice and Yours.* The Liturgical Press. 2nd ed., 1928.

Michel, Stegmann, and Sisters of St. Dominic: *The Christ-Life Series in Religion.* 8 bks. and 2 teachers' manuals. Macmillan Co. 1934–35.

Motu Proprio of Pius X and Other Papal Documents on Liturgical Music. The Catholic Education Press. Washington, 1928.

Parsch, Pius: *Messerklaerung.* Verlag Volksliturgisches Apostolat, Klosterneuburg bei Wien. 2nd ed., 1935.

Panfoeder, Dom Chrysostom: *Christus unser Liturge.* Mathias Gruenewald Verlag. Mainz, 1924.

Panfoeder, Dom Chrysostom: *Das Persoenliche in der Liturgie.* Mathias Gruenewald Verlag. Mainz, 1925.

Panfoeder, Dom Chrysostom: *Die Kirche als liturgische Gemeinschaft.* Mathias Gruenewald Verlag. Mainz.

Power, Richard E: *God's Healing.* The Liturgical Press, 1929.

Power, Richard E: *Marriage in Christ.* The Liturgical Press, 2nd ed., 1929.

Power, Richard E: *The Gift of Life.* The Liturgical Press. 3rd ed., 1935.

Power, Richard E: *The Seal of the Spirit.* The Liturgical Press. 3rd ed., 1930.

Quigley, E. J.: *The Divine Office.* B. Herder Book Co. St. Louis. 2nd ed., 1930.

Ryelandt, Dom I.: *Pour mieux communier.* Abbaye de Maredsous, Belgique. 12th thousand, 1925.

Sauter, Dom Benedikt: *Der liturgische Choral.* Herdersche Verlagshandlung. Freiburg i.B., 1903.

St. John's Abbey, Monks of: *The Hour of Prime.* The Liturgical Press. 1935.

Vismara, E. M.: *Liturgia cristiana é la partezipazione del populo.* Vicenza, 1919.

Wagner, Peter: *Einfuehrung in die katholische Kirchenmusik.* Druck und Verlag von L. Schwann. Duesseldorf, 1919.

Wapelhorst, Innocentius, O.F.M.: *Compendium Sacrae Liturgiae.* Benziger Brothers, N.Y. Ed. nona, 1915.

INDEX

345

CPSIA information can be obtained
at www.ICGtesting.com
Printed in the USA
LVHW010042200723
752769LV00008B/372/J

9 781990 685347